For Bruce Mickleburgh

Beyond Silence

Chinese Canadian Literature in English

Lien Chao

TSAR
Toronto
1997

We acknowledge the support of the Canada Council for the Arts for our publishing program. We also acknowledge support from the Ontario Arts Council.

Chapter 3, "Anthologizing the Collective: The Epic Struggles to Establish Chinese Canadian Literature in English," was first published in *Essays on Canadian Writing* 57 (1995); the publishers are grateful for permission to reproduce it in this volume.

Cover art: *Night Alert* (1994) 27" x 27" Chinese ink and water colour, by Peng Ma.

Canadian Cataloguing in Publication Data

Chao, Lien, 1950-
Beyond silence: Chinese Canadian literature in English

Includes bibliographical references.
ISBN 0-920661-69-6

1. Canadian literature (English)–Chinese-Canadian authors–History and criticism.*
2. Canadian literature (English)–20th century–History and criticism.* I. Title.

PS8089.5.C48C48 1997 C810.9'.8951 C97-932524-2
PR9188.2.C48C48 1997

Printed in Canada by Coach House Printing.

TSAR Publications
P. O. Box 6996, Station A
Toronto, Ontario M5W 1X7
Canada

Acknowledgements

I would like to thank Bruce Mickleburgh, Virginia Rock, and Ann Saddlemyer, who helped me obtain the opportunity to come to Canada in 1984 to study Canadian literature. I am also grateful to Northrop Frye, Margaret Laurence, W O Mitchell, the Ontario Women Teachers' Federation, and many other warm-hearted Canadians for their generosity.

My special thanks go to Arun Mukherjee, Frank Davey, Virginia Rock, and Jim Wong-Chu whose encouragement and constructive criticism have been most appreciated.

I am very grateful to TSAR Publications, to Nurjehan Aziz and M G Vassanji whose support of racial minority writers help many of us become published writers in Canada. I also want to thank the Writers' Union of Canada for its Professional Training Program which provided me an opportunity to work with my editor.

My special gratitude goes to Stanley Jeffers who for many years was the first reader of my manuscript. My appreciation also goes to Leslie Sanders, Terry Goldie, and Margo Gewurtz for their support.

Finally, I want to thank my partner Peng Ma for permission to use his painting; my daughter Avianna for her assistance with the design of the cover; and my parents for their understanding and support.

Lien Chao

Contents

Introduction

In Canadian writing the two major (but by no means only) new forms to appear have been those that embody ethnicity and the female.
LINDA HUTCHEON

Criminal like man with no culture / very difficult to find true identity.
SEAN GUNN

The Chinese have a mythological origin in North America which is difficult to retrieve. The alleged discovery of this continent by a Chinese Buddhist monk named Hoei-shin in the fifth century remains today a controversial hypothesis. It is a historical fact, however, that Chinese have settled in Canada for one hundred and thirty-seven years.[1] Like other immigrants, Chinese sought dreams and hopes; but unlike European immigrants, for about one hundred years Chinese in Canada were treated as an undesirable race and convenient scapegoats for social woes. While the contributions made by Chinese immigrants were not recognized in Canadian history, racial discrimination against Asians in Canada, especially the Chinese, was recorded in three Royal Commission documents (in 1885, 1902 and 1908).[2] With head taxes and an exclusion act imposed on them, Chinese were branded as the unwanted race in Canada.

In order to minimize their contact with the dominant groups, for many decades Chinese in Canada were confined in Chinatowns and had absolutely no access to the mainstream media. They were collectively silenced. In the 1970s, however, community activists started to break through the wall of alienation and isolation. In 1976, a group of native-born Chinese in Vancouver organized a Writers' Workshop together with Japanese Canadians, the result of which was a joint and ground-breaking anthology published in 1979. This was not just an isolated literary event but part of a political campaign to challenge racial discrimination in Canadian society and the powers endorsing it. Like a spark igniting a wild fire, the first generation of Chinese Canadian writers emerged from the Writers' Workshop.

Their collective voice brings out a largely unrecorded Canadian experience and heritage that have been excluded or misrepresented by the dominant media. In various literary forms, writers from the community started to redress this historical injustice, to deal with issues of Chinese Canadian history and confront racism past and present. Twenty years later, a body of Chinese Canadian literature has been created in English in all genres and forms. Though recent, the growing corpus of this minority literature demonstrates the potential of becoming a significant component of Canadian literature.

The topic of Chinese Canadian literature suggested itself to me in 1988 upon reading a review of Paul Yee's photographic essay *Salt Water City: An Illustrated History of the Chinese in Vancouver* (Lacey C11). Reading the book itself, later, was an emotional experience; it aroused anger and sadness at the way the Chinese were treated. But I was also intellectually stimulated into pursuing a research project to which I felt strongly connected.

There were few literary publications by Chinese Canadians at that time, so I dug out every piece of material in the library concerning Chinese immigrants, Chinese in Canada, and Chinese Canadians, these being the stages that Chinese Canadians have gone through in their long journey toward Canadian citizenship. I was overjoyed to find a copy of *Inalienable Rice: A Chinese & Japanese Anthology* published by the Chinese Canadian Writers' Workshop in Vancouver in 1979. After reading this first anthology, I sensed that a community-based Chinese Canadian literature had been born, and I wished to be part of its growth.

Chinese Canadian literature did not exist in the literary canon at that time. The work had to be sought one at a time. I found an only copy of Jim Wong-Chu's poetry collection *Chinatown Ghosts* (1986) in a book store; I learned that Winston Christopher Kam's play *Bachelor-Man* was staged by Theatre Passe Muraille in November 1987; after meeting Kam I got hold of his manuscript and a video tape made during a performance; I also read that Fred Wah's *Waiting for Saskatchewan* won the 1985 Governor General's Literary Award for poetry. Meanwhile many new Chinese Canadian writers were publishing. The first chapter of Denise Chong's family memoir,

The Concubine's Children, was published in the October issue of *Saturday Night* in 1988; Paul Yee's *Tales from Gold Mountain* came out in 1989; Sky Lee's novel, *Disappearing Moon Cafe*, was published in 1990 and aroused immediate public attention, laying down a cornerstone for Chinese Canadian literature; Evelyn Lau's *Runaway: Diary of a Street Kid* released in 1989 became an instant market success and the author, a media focus; it was followed by Lau's poetry and short story collections; and then, in 1991 came the long awaited second anthology, *Many-Mouthed Birds: Contemporary Writing by Chinese Canadians*. There had never been a time in which so many Chinese Canadian writers were publishing for the first time and being reviewed and recognized! As well, there had never been a time when there was such a need for critical interpretations of Chinese Canadian literature.

Contemporary Chinese Canadian literature is community based. Its interior landscapes are emotionally connected with the historical Chinatowns in which the stories and characters are situated. Here, generations of Chinese immigrants first arrived and worked; here, for many decades they were confined and built their community; also here in the Chinatowns, new generations were born and raised, including writers, and traditional Chinese culture was regenerated and circulated with a Canadian consciousness. Chinese Canadian literature is characterized by the historical experience of the community; consistent literary tropes and expressions have been developed to reclaim the collective community history and to redefine a collectively shared Chinese Canadian identity.

I wish to dedicate my work to the Chinese Canadian community, from which I have long since derived my personal identity. This project has been a double journey for me, academically and personally. The process of researching the community history; reading the texts and attempting to synthesize shared paradigms from across the genres; introducing the topic of Chinese Canadian literature at various academic conferences in Canada and the United States; anticipating and participating in the "Writing Thru' Race" conference in July 1994 in Vancouver; meeting Westcoast Chinese Canadian writers, and becoming a member of the Asian Canadian Writers' Workshop myself—these have been the indispensable stages of my journey.

My personal identity has developed along with this study. I came to Toronto in 1984 from mainland China as an independent student; I only became a landed immigrant after the events in Tien An Men Square in 1989. I remember that every September before I was "landed," in order to renew my visa and work permit I had to line up for half a day in front of the Immigration Canada office in Forest Hill in Toronto. Among other applicants in the line, many were foreign housekeepers and babysitters from Asian countries, especially from the Philippines. While listening to their chat, I knew I was one of the few lucky Asian women who, instead of being a housekeeper, had the opportunity to pursue graduate work in English.

As a graduate student studying Canadian literature and European drama, I became familiar with the existing literary canon, in which European values were taught through literary texts as a universal experience. Students like myself who did not belong to the dominant groups in society found our subjectivity either rendered irrelevant, thus nonexistent in the canonical texts, or stereotyped into caricatures which offended us collectively. Unless we adopted white values and tried to sound white, we would find ourselves constantly being denied a legitimate voice either in the texts or in analyzing them as readers. It was my experience with the mainstream canon that prompted me to challenge its composition by introducing Chinese Canadian literature.

In search of critical models for Chinese Canadian literature, I found similar quests made earlier by South Asian Canadian and Asian American writers and critics. As early as 1985, *A Meeting of Streams: South Asian Canadian Literature,* edited by M G Vassanji, was published by TSAR Publications. In 1988, Williams-Wallace published Arun Mukherjee's first essay collection, *Towards An Aesthetic of Opposition: Essays on Literature, Criticism, and Cultural Imperialism* (reissued by TSAR as *Oppositional Aesthetics: Readings from a Hyphenated Space*). From south of the border, Asian American literature started to enter almost all the state universities; critical books have been published: *Aiiieeeee! An Anthology of Asian-American Writers* was published in 1974; later in 1991, *The Big Aiiieeeee! An Anthology of Chinese American and Japanese American Literature* was published; Amy Ling published *Between Worlds: Women Writers of Chinese Ancestry* in 1990; Cynthia Wong's *Reading Asian American Literature* was published in 1993; and the list keeps growing in both countries.

I hope this book will help bridge the gap between Chinese Canadian literature and mainstream Canadian literature. By now the bridge is being built, though back in 1988 that was still a wish cherished by emerging Chinese Canadian writers. The only way a minority literature can be treated as equal to mainstream literature is if serious critical attention is paid to its development. The development of Asian Canadian literature has definitely caught mainstream attention, with the ground-breaking special issue of *Canadian Literature: East Asian Canadian Connections,* which, however, as its editor W H New pointed out, could "scarcely do more than provide another set of 'mentions' " (6–7).

The scope of this study covers contemporary Chinese Canadian works written in English only, with Denise Chong's *The Concubine's Children* (1994) as the publication cut-off line. This selection does not preclude writings in Chinese or in French by Chinese Canadians from being read also as branches of Chinese Canadian literature. In fact there exist a huge quantity of journalism and literary texts published in Chinese by the communities across Canada. But the difficulty of translating texts from Chinese into English is an enormous task which cannot be attempted here. Writings in Chinese obviously deserve a separate and detailed study in their own right. Leaving out writings in the Chinese language from this study might suggest that the heritage language still remains silent and invisible in contemporary Canadian society; however, the functional existence of Chinese across all Chinatowns in North America indicates its parallel power to English somewhere in this culture.

This book consists of eight chapters, starting with a rereading of Chinese Canadian history (Chapter 1). This is followed by a theoretical attempt to summarize the discursive strategies that have repeatedly occurred in Chinese Canadian writings (Chapter 2). Next are five individual chapters analyzing selected literary works by genre, namely, anthology (Chapter 3), folklore (Chapter 4), drama (Chapter 5), prose (Chapter 6), and poetry (Chapter 7). A separate chapter deals with Evelyn Lau's *Runaway: Diary of a Street Kid* (1989), the CBC movie of Lau's diary, and her latest short- story collection, *Fresh Girls and Other Stories* (1993). This structure treats the works considered here as part of a collective literature, at the same time reflecting its diversity. The generic division also looks forward to future development of this growing literature with its new writers already producing in all the genres

Chinese Canadians have a history of one hundred and thirty-seven years; their lived experience needs to be recorded in Canadian history and literature. Whereas their images have been invented and reinvented as negations of the dominant groups, it is time that they invent their own images and tell their stories in English, one of the official languages of Canada. It is time that Chinese Canadians reclaim their community history and individual identities. A full-fledged, contemporary Chinese Canadian literature has entered the Canadian literary landscape with its own heroes and heroines, ghosts and devils, tragedies and comedies. This literature celebrates the survival and the development of the community and its individuals. As a minority literature, Chinese Canadian literature—like other such literatures—raises a resistant voice against European cultural hegemony in Canadian literature. From within Chinatown, contemporary Chinese Canadian writers set off in the 1970s to establish a community literature; encouraged by their works, my work joins the "epic struggles" (Garrick Chu viii) to help establish Chinese Canadian literature critically.

1. Rereading Chinese Canadian History and the Need to Access Mainstream Discourse

One curious fact about the existing literature in Canada on racial discrimination is that a relatively large proportion of it was produced either by the governments or by government-affiliated, government-funded organizations, often in the form of in-house research, special task forces or commissions, or through special research activities contracted with university -based academics . . .
KWOK B CHAN

. . . to historicize any structure, to write its history, is to mythologize it.
CLAUDE LÉVI-STRAUSS

In 1761 French Sinologist M Deguignes published his research on a Buddhist monk named Hoei-shin, who had returned in the year 499 AD from a forty years' voyage of discovery to Fushang, which lay 30,000 *li* to the east of China. (1 *li* = 500 meters, i.e. half a kilometre.) The original document was an entry in the Year Book of the Chinese Empire, *Liang Shu*, collected in the *Encyclopedia of Mantuanlin*, the court archives. *Fushang*, from which Hoei-shin returned after his forty years' journey, was later identified by scholars as a geographical area in Western America, ranging from Mexico to British Columbia.[1]

The hypothesis that Chinese might have discovered America in the fifth century, 993 years earlier than Christopher Columbus, was investigated by several scholars. Among them, C F Neumann, professor of oriental languages and history at the University of Munich, published in 1841 Hoei-shin's original narrative in *Liang Shu* together with his own commentary. In 1875 American scholar C G Leland, supervised by Neumann, published Hoei-shin's entire narrative in English translation. According to both scholars, Hoei-shin's narrative captures convincing details of exotic landscapes presumably of an earlier and unrecorded America.

The genre to which Hoei-shin's narrative most likely belongs, according to the two Sinologists, is alien to the Buddhist monk's practice and specialty. Although they did not specify the genre, my guess is that they probably referred to the genre of travelogue or popular travel literature:

> Some of the peculiarities observed by Hoei-shin—as, for example, the manner of wooing, the exposure of the dead, and the possible origin of his Kingdom of Women—existed in a strongly-marked form among the Red Indians; others recall New Mexican or Aztec culture, as it may have been driven south; and there are, withal Siberian-Mongolian traces. But I cannot resist the feeling, which has grown on me through years of study on this subject, that in the fifth century the Buddhist monk visited a race combining characteristics and customs which afterwards spread to the south and the east. All that he observed is singularly American, and from the tone of the narrative, was evidently new to the missionary. (Leland 60)

The inspiration provided by this mythological voyage goes beyond the question of historical accuracy. Whether Hoei-shin was a historical voyager or a "lying priest," or whether Fushang was Mexico or Vancouver or Japan or an invention (Leland 185), are less likely today to make an ideological impact on world history. Leland might disagree with my fictionalization of what he considered to be a historical fact. He chided novelists and poets who confused history with "absurd inventions and marvellous tales, [so] that even at the present day discredit is thrown by a certain class of critics on the entire narrative" (vi).

As a nineteenth-century historian, Leland failed to see that Hoei-shin's discovery of Fushang could not replace Christopher Columbus's discovery of "India," which was too deeply entrenched in the dominant (Western) world's mythology and construction of itself. As an academic, Leland was probably too naive to see that history means not only historical data but also the constitution of history as politics. Lévi-Strauss points out that history is never only history *of* but history *for* (emphasis mine); history is constituted from selected data for a specific manifestation or latent purpose (257).

In the nineteenth century, China was defeated by joint Western imperial military powers. Starting with the First Opium War with Britain from 1840 to 1842, China was forced to open her five port cities (Guangzhou, Xiamen, Fuzhou, Ningbo and Shanghai) to foreign traders with tax exemptions, as well as to cede the island of Hong Kong. China also had to pay indemnities of forty million silver dollars to Western nations. After the Opium Wars, the Western powers arrived to carve out residential enclaves in Chinese cities and spheres of influence in the whole country.

Under the historical circumstances, it was politically impossible for Leland or any other scholar to argue that a Chinese Buddhist monk was actually the first discoverer of America. Had China been a strong imperialist power in the nineteenth century, this mythological voyage might have been reconstructed by institutional historians, using selected data and maybe even archaeological artifacts. It might then have become the earliest documented historical discovery of America, a history-*for* an imperialist nation with relevant ideological manifestation.

Whereas versions of origin(s) and of history are continuously invented and reinvented by historians, genealogists, and epic writers, the voyage of the Chinese Buddhist monk to America in the fifth century has never been publicized beyond the interests of a few academic scholars. In his contemptuous comments on the "absurd inventions and marvellous tales" developed by poets and writers of romances, Leland was too limited by his time and his discipline to see that imaginative and metaphorical language was shared by historical narrative and fictional accounts. Again, Lévi-Strauss's observation is pertinent: "to *historicize* any structure, to write its history, is to mythologize it" (104). Furthermore, Leland did not recognize that to mythologize any historical experience is to legitimize it, and to make it part of the existing cultural reference systems. Hence by positioning the Buddhist monk's voyage at the beginning of Chinese Canadian immigration history, I seek an engendering, mythological origin for my imagination. With this mythical beginning as a prelude to the journey undertaken by the Chinese Canadians in the last one hundred and thirty some years, I search for the "marvellous tales" written by poets and storytellers of Chinese descent in Canada.

If Hoei-shin's journey to the West can be read as a mythological origin of the Chinese on the American continent, the tale of the fifty Chinese artisans' being assimilated into the Native tribes in British Columbia is a story of the origin of Chinese settlement in Canada. In 1788, fifty Chinese artisans disembarked at Nootka Sound on Vancouver Island to help Captain Meares develop a fur-trading post. It is said that with the assistance of the Native people, Chinese carpenters built a two-storey house and a forty-ton schooner, *North West America*. Later, the Spanish drove out Captain Meares, fearing threat of future competition; however, most of the Chinese crew members decided to settle down on the island. They raised families with Native women and eventually grew old and died in the New World.

Various archaeological artifacts from that time remain today. They include objects used by the artisans, paintings by later artists to depict this event, reports written by American sailors five years later in 1793, and by Fort Nisquallie of the Hudson's Bay Company fifty years later in 1838.[2] These pieces of evidence tell many stories from which a conclusion can be drawn: Chinese immigrants made a settlement in Canada in the eighteenth century. Furthermore, the Chinese settlement is very different from that of the Europeans. During the same historical period, European missionaries, traders and settlers, both French and English, came to colonize North America and its Native peoples.

By tracing the mythological journey of the Chinese Buddhist monk in the fifth century and the settlement of the fifty Chinese artisans in the eighteenth century, I am not applying, but rather challenging, a well accepted Canadian sociological paradigm, "who got here first has the most say," theorized by John Porter in *The Vertical Mosaic* (1965):

> In any society which has to seek members from outside there will be varying judgements about the extensive reservoirs of recruits that exist in the world. In this process of evaluation the first ethnic group to come into previously unpopulated territory, as the effective possessor, has the most say. This group becomes the charter group of the society, and among the many privileges and prerogatives which it retains are decisions about what other groups are to be let in and what they will be permitted to do. (60)

This problematic Canadian social law, "who got here *first* has the most say" became "who got here *second* has the most say" in the 1990s, as acknowledgement of the aboriginal people's right to the land achieved some recognition (Lupul 3). However, both versions derived from Anglo-French colonialism and nativism. Without legislative settlement of Native peoples' rights to their land, without admission of Native peoples and visible minority groups into the power structure, the rhetorical difference between "who got here first" and "who got here second" does not alter the fact that the two charter groups still have the most say in contemporary Canadian society. Since history is not history *of* but history *for*, Canadian history written by the two charter groups in the two official languages speaks to the interest and value of the dominant groups. In Canadian history, the contributions made by the Chinese immigrants to this nation, and to British Columbia in particular, are largely untold and therefore unrecognized.

Chinese immigration shares common ground with European, African, and other Asian immigration to Canada in terms of the cause of immigration, motivation, and the class status of the immigrants. Observing international migrations, sociologist Peter Li notes, "It was a combination of factors in the home country and the receiving state, which served as 'pushing' and 'pulling' forces, that propelled the wave of human movement from one country to another" (12-13). The pushing force in Chinese migration to North America consisted primarily of natural and human disasters. In the nineteenth century, the majority of Chinese immigrants to Canada came from the Pearl River Delta, southern China; Taishan is one of four counties that sent most of the immigrants because of floods, typhoons, earthquakes, famines, and a local war.[3]

While the pushing force was strong, the pulling force more strongly propelled southern Chinese peasants to seek opportunities in North America. The term "Gold Mountain" (*gun shan*), a synonym for the California gold rush, which was extended later to include Canada, suggests hope, prosperity, and stability.[4] The gold rush was never fair play for everybody, nor were the frontiers a free world. The term, "a Chinaman's chance," originating from the gold rush, has a racist overtone. Chinese were allowed to work only in the mines abandoned by white miners, and some were even murdered for the bit of gold they eventually accumulated. While the chance for Chinese gold miners to make a fortune was very slim, many of them took up other frontier jobs. During the period of the 1860s and 70s, Chinese were also employed in various public construction jobs in British Columbia: building the Cariboo Wagon Road in 1863, driving horse teams through the dangerous canyons, stringing telephone wires for Western Union in 1866, digging canals, reclaiming wasteland, and establishing the fish canneries and lumber industry (Lee Wai-man 17-18; Paul Yee 12).

In addition to the large number of Chinese contract labourers, many Chinese came as independent immigrants. They were miners, merchants, domestic servants, restaurant owners and other service workers. They started various service businesses, out of which grew the large service industries later needed in a modern industrial society. The most significant contribution made by the Chinese immigrants to Canada's Confederation and its future as a nation was their collective participation in building the British Columbia section of the Canadian Pacific Railway (CPR).

The CPR British Columbia section was Canada's reward to the British colony for its commitment to join the Confederation. It was built between May 14, 1880 and July 29, 1885 (Chan 63). Approximately 17,000 Chinese labourers (Paul Yee 17) were recruited from Hong Kong and southern China by Chinese contractors who worked for Andrew Onderdonk, the contractor for this part of the railway. Chinese labourers were underpaid and worked in the most dangerous areas without safety devices (Li Dong Hai 131; Wickberg 23) or medical attendance (Paul Yee 80); there was also lack of fresh food supply (Chan 63). As a result, numerous deaths were caused by accidents and diseases. According to the conservative estimate of Onderdonk's testimony to the 1885 Royal Commission, 600 Chinese died in the construction. This was a ratio of more than 4 Chinese deaths to every mile of railway. According to an estimate made by a community resource, 4,000 Chinese workers died, more than 26 Chinese deaths to every mile of this section of the railway(Lo 60). In 1891 the Chinese Consolidated Benevolent Association of Victoria alone arranged for a collection of more than 300 unidentified corpses from the Fraser and Thompson canyons to be returned to China for a proper burial (Wickberg 24).

The contributions made by the Chinese labourers were denied recognition. By July 29, 1885, approaching the last spike, Onderdonk had saved three to five million dollars by recruiting cheap Chinese labourers (Chan 63). But no Chinese workers were invited to the ceremony, nor were they mentioned in the history of the CPR. Not only were the Chinese railway workers refused the pledged return tickets to China, having helped realize the first Canadian national dream of coast-to-coast unification, they were also immediately abandoned and targeted by racism.

The contributions made by Chinese immigrants to the development of British Columbia and Canada were, in fact, widely known on the frontiers. Dr J S Helmcken, who had lived in Vancouver for thirty-five years by 1885, testified positively for the Royal Commission on Chinese Immigration:

> The Chinese have cultivated the soil, raised vegetables, are employed in tanneries and at the canneries, in boot and shoe making, some in coal and gold mining and other labours. Having done these things, they have benefited the country. They have been producers—the one thing the country stands in need of. (56)

The CPR contractor Onderdonk also testified before the 1885 Royal Commission: "Ninety-nine per cent of the Chinese here are industrious and steady"; "any radical or sudden restriction will close down many industries and seriously injure the prosperity of British Columbia" (150). Both Onderdonk and Sir Matthew Begbie, Chief Justice of British Columbia, praised the four personal qualities of the Chinese as: "industry, economy, sobriety and law-abidingness" (148, 71). Begbie further summarized "the six undoubted facts" of Chinese immigration to British Columbia:

> 1st. That Chinamen are very largely, and till within a year, mainly, employed in all the labourious parts of our coal mines; 2nd. They constitute three-fourths of the working hands about every salmon cannery; 3rd. They are a very large majority of the labourers employed in gold mines; 4th. They are the model

> market gardeners of the province, and produce the greater part of the vegetables grown here; 5th. They have been found to be absolutely indispensable in the construction of the railway; 6th. They are largely, sometimes, exclusively, employed in nearly every manufactory or undertaking of any description, not being under the authority of a board of council elected exclusively by white votes. (75)

If the contributions made by Chinese immigrants to British Columbia and to Canada have been legitimately attested to, why has there never been any social acknowledgement of them as a group of pioneering Canadians or nation builders? Instead of recognition, Chinese immigrants and their descendants have been discriminated against and segregated from the rest of society.

Had the Chinese immigrants any access to mainstream politics, media, religion, and literature in the nineteenth century, their contributions would probably have been incorporated into Canadian history. However, because of their high concentration in the labour force and their almost universal bachelor status, they were stereotyped as "Chinamen" with a capital letter C. Sir Begbie explained the meaning of this widespread racist term "Chinamen," which was invented to categorize the Chinese as a human machine: "They do, and they do well, what white women cannot do, and do what white men will not do"; "they are generally abused, and yet everybody employs them" (Royal Commission 1885, 77).

A reciprocal relationship between social class and ethnicity has always existed in Canadian society. When physical and cultural features of racial groups—skin colour, food habits, hairstyles or fashions—are encoded with social attributes, such as intelligence, morality, behaviour, and personality, society is stratified along racial lines. In this social stratification, the economic and political elites are usually paired, exhibiting a racial homogeneity. Typically people of colour are usually paired with low-paying jobs, manual labour, and service industry. Furthermore, social stratification helps ensure a cheap labour pool for the periodic expansion and recession cycles of capitalism. In the Canadian job market, Chinese immigrants were historically kept at the entrance level (Peter Li 7; Porter 63).

While Puritan virtues had been generally promoted in the social dream of upward mobility by the European immigrants in North America, Chinese labourers' simple lifestyle and hard work were ironically viewed as threats to white stability. The 1885 Royal Commission publicly enforced the discriminatory attitude against pioneering Chinese, whose endurance of physical hardships was termed as an inadequate lifestyle for Canadian living:

> ... that the Chinese immigration is a bachelor immigration; that the Chinaman can live in a space and on food wholly inadequate for a white labourer; that they are independent of and indifferent to all the comforts of life as they are understood in white communities; these, which are admitted facts, may be serious not merely for the labourer but for the nation, and it is our duty to probe the facts to the bottom. (xiv)

In addition to characterizing lifestyles, racial difference was used as rationale by European immigrants to judge Chinese as nonassimilable. The first prime minister of Canada, Sir John A Macdonald, remarked that the original racial difference between white and nonwhite peoples would always cause antagonism and set them apart in any social disputes:

> These groups stand rightly apart. No such [illegible] can [illegible] between them as takes place between the Irish, German, French, etc. The yellow and white or black and white will not mix, and the antagonism of race is always intensified if one of two peoples has oppressed the other, or regarded it with social scorn. (Royal Commission 1885, xcviii-xcix)

Further, Macdonald told Parliament that the Chinese were "not a wholesome element," that they constituted "an alien race in every sense that would not and could not be expected to assimilate with our Aryan population." He specified that the problem was to discover how many Chinese labourers could be admitted, "without introducing a permanent evil to the country by allowing to come into it ... an inferior ... foreign and alien race."[5]

Anti-Chinese and anti-Oriental racism continued in mainstream Canadian politics from the 1860s to the 1920s. During the 1921 federal election, in order to win the vote of unionized labour with a national membership of 225,000, William L Mackenzie King made a promise of "more effective restriction of Chinese immigration"; speaking agitatedly of white racial and cultural hegemony, he said: "that Canada should remain a white man's country is believed to be not only desirable for economic and social reasons, but necessary on political and national grounds" (Lee Wai-man 131-32). In 1947 when thousands of European immigrants landed in Canada, Mackenzie King announced the national immigration strategy of excluding Oriental immigrants: "The people of Canada do not wish, as a result of mass immigration, to make a fundamental alteration in the character of our population. Large scale immigration from the Orient would change that fundamental composition of the Canadian population."[6]

Chinese were the only racial group that had to pay increasing head taxes upon landing in Canada. British Columbia made Chinese immigrants pay a $10 head tax in 1884. Upon the recommendation of the 1885 Royal Commission, after the completion of the CPR, upon landing a $50 head tax was imposed on every Chinese immigrant, except diplomats, students, and tourists. In 1900, this head tax increased to $100. Upon the recommendation of the 1902 Royal Commission, the head tax increased to $500 in 1903. A total revenue of $23 million from 1886 to 1943 (Peter Li 38) was collected from head taxes and registration fees from Chinese Canadians leaving and reentering the country. This money was later spent on overseas advertisement to recruit and help white European immigrants to come to Canada (Lee Wai-man 126). After 1903, it was financially impossible for the Chinese labourers and average shopkeepers to bring their wives and children to Canada. On June 30, 1923 Bill 45, known as the Chinese Exclusion Act, was passed, allowing only diplomats, children born in Canada, students, and merchants to enter Canada. This bill virtually crushed the dreams of Chinese labourers to have their families reunited in Canada. It came into effect on July 1, 1923, just twenty-four hours after it was sanctioned. During the next twenty-four years, only forty-four Chinese entered Canada (Paul Yee 53). Returning Chinese Canadians were jailed in the Immigration Detention Building until their previous residence status could be verified (Wickberg 157; Lee Wai-man 160). The Chinese Exclusion Act also required every Chinese in Canada to register with the Immigration Department, even if born in Canada. The Exclusion Act also deprived Chinese in Canada of an equal opportunity for naturalization and citizenship rights.

The Chinese Exclusion Act helped reinforce the sex imbalance in the Chinese Canadian communities. In 1911 the sex imbalance among the Chinese in Canada was already twenty-five times higher than the national ratio (Peter Li 60). The Act prolonged the married-bachelor characteristics of the community for several more decades. The sex ratio among the Chinese in Canada did not reach an equilibrium until as recently as 1981. July 1, 1923, Canada Day, the day the Chinese Exclusion Act came into effect, was historically regarded as the Humiliation Day by the Chinese Canadian community for many decades.

Chinese Canadians were also denied their rights to vote in elections. Vancouver's Charter of 1886 barred Chinese (as well as "Hindus," Japanese, and Natives) from voting in the municipal elections. The Dominion Election Act of 1920 (Statutes of Canada, 1920, c.40) determined all voters in federal elections to be British subjects. Chinese were also barred from voting in provincial elections.

However, anti-Chinese racism was not isolated to Canada. From 1882 to 1902, the US Congress passed thirteen discriminatory laws against the Chinese. The 1882 Exclusion Law banned Chinese labourers from immigration and deprived the Chinese in America of citizenship rights. It marked the beginning of a national policy of racial discrimination against a minority that hardly made up one per cent of the American population. Since then, persecutions of the Chinese in various ways became as notorious as that of the Blacks in American society (Wu 5). The Canadian government simply followed suit, passing similar laws to limit Chinese immigration in 1885 and 1902, which eventually led to excluding Chinese immigration altogether in 1923. Moreover, the historical development of cheap Chinese labour should also be associated with the decline of the black slave trade and the abolition of the slave system in the United States.

Some Chinese labourers were actually captured from their native land in southern China, confined in "pig-pens," sold and shipped to South America and the West Indies plantations around the 1850s (Chan 40).

The 1923 Chinese Exclusion Act was revoked in 1947. The change was not a result of the acceptance of the principle of human rights in Canada, a principle not acknowledged until the 1960s. Domestic changes in Canada for Chinese Canadians resulted, ironically, as one of the repurcussions of World War Two. During the War, China was a Western ally against Japan in the Far East. As well, several hundred young Chinese Canadians fought in the Canadian military forces, even though they were not entitled to citizenship rights. 1945 was probably the first time the term "Chinese Canadian" was used by the media, when the discharged soldiers asked to be allowed to vote (Lee Wai-man 124). In British Columbia, Chinese could not vote until as late as the spring of 1949.

In 1967, a universal point system for Canadian immigration was established. For the first time, immigrants of different races, skin colours, and religious backgrounds were judged by the same standard. After several decades' separation, the wives (if they were still alive) and children of the aged Chinese labourers (if they were still alive) finally could apply to come to Canada to be reunited with their husbands and fathers.

In almost every Canadian city there grew a Chinatown. In the past one hundred years, the image of Chinatown has changed dramatically, reflecting the social changes in the broader Canadian society. As discussed above, underlining the earlier Canadian immigration policies was the assimilation model and the unassimilability of Chinese and other coloured peoples. For over one hundred years, the Canadian media promoted various negative stereotypes against the Chinese community. Chinatowns were presented as dirty and dangerous, full of opium dens, gambling houses, brothels, and dirty vegetable markets, where illegal immigrants, aliens, and criminals gathered. Reverend John Mackay, who subscribed to the idea of "the yellow peril," warned the public that before 1914 Chinese would submerge white civilization in a Canadian society which was not sufficiently strong to meet such a challenge (Baureiss 24). A lurid piece of fiction, *The Writing on the Wall*, written by H Glynn-Ward and published in 1923 by *The Vancouver Sun*, touched every nerve of white racism, catering to white superiority and fear of the other races. In the story, omniscient Chinese criminal lords used opium to enslave white girls as prostitutes, while planning the subjection of British Columbia to the Oriental will (Wickberg 121). Even as late as 1962, *Maclean's* magazine manipulated the public using the same racist thesis that the Chinese could not be assimilated due to their high illiteracy, quasi-self-government by the clan system, high criminal record, and illegal activities such as violating Canadian taxation and immigration laws (Phillips 11, 40-48). By presenting the Chinese as alien and Chinese culture as evil, the media inflamed white xenophobia and prolonged the structural sanctions against the Chinese in Canada. This in turn ensured the low political and economic status of the Chinese Canadians for several more decades in contemporary society.

The negative stereotypes of Chinatown and its inhabitants isolated Chinese from the rest of Canadian society. For many decades almost all Chinese immigrants, transient labourers, and married-bachelors were confined to Chinatowns. Here they could find a place to stay, find their food, and seek friendship and support in place of the families they lacked. Chinatown businesses employed mostly Chinese, and so they helped recent immigrants survive. Illegal activities such as gambling, opium-smoking, and prostitution in Chinatowns were historical and cultural byproducts of anti-Chinese racism. The 6% Chinese female to male ratio, a direct result of increasing head taxes and exclusion laws, led to prostitution. Segregation of the Chinese meant that they could not attend the cinema or any other places of normal recreation, except for church, where it was hoped they would be converted to Christianity. Some married-bachelors (married men with absent wives) found their own recreation in gambling or opium-smoking. However, the Chinatown syndrome started to change when the attitude of the dominant groups towards Chinese started to change, and when the political and economic status of the Chinese in Canada began to improve. After the Chinese Exclusion Act was repealed in 1947, especially after the sex ratio reached a balance in 1981 and conjugal and family life was restored, Chinatowns started to look more attractive.

At present Chinatowns are primarily commercial districts, where ethnic food, goods and services are marketed. In most of the Canadian cities Chinatowns are designated tourist zones by the municipal governments, enabling Chinese businesses to open seven days a week, catering to people from different racial and cultural backgrounds. Nevertheless, for Chinese Canadians Chinatowns still bear the stigma inherited fromhistorical anti-Chinese racism. They bear the mark of a segregation that is self-imposed in order to avoid competition or conflict with the dominant groups. Chinatowns, where the employees are almost homogeneously Chinese and the businesses are almost exclusively of the service variety, remain an entrance-job market for non-English-speaking Chinese. Whereas the occupational choices for Chinese Canadians and new Chinese immigrants have generally improved, statistics show that Chinese Canadians are under-represented in politics, government offices, social sciences, teaching, transportation, art, and literature, and over-represented in the service industry, natural science, and engineering.

The pioneering generations of Chinese immigrants, the contract labourers who were collectively called "sojourners," are dying out. Because their prime years were spent as bachelors or married-bachelors, the appearance of the Canadian-born generations has been delayed significantly in Chinese Canadian communities across the country. A hundred and thirty-seven years after the Chinese landed in Canada as a noticeable racial group, the Chinese population in Canada still shows a higher number of foreign-born than native-born people. New immigrants of Chinese origin come from all over the world, making the Chinese community multicultural itself. The homogeneous Taishan population and culture of the 1860s has long been replaced by a linguistically diversified Chinese community. Due to the large number of Chinese immigrants coming to Canada in the last ten years, the Chinese Canadian community remains largely an immigrant community. Its racial visibility at the entrance status makes structural assimilation for Chinese Canadians a continuing struggle.

Although this chapter has depicted Chinese immigrants and their descendants as persecuted and marginalized by anti-Chinese racism in Canada, it is important to note that their experience is not an autonomous, isolated historical case. Pointing out the problems in history studies in general, Michel Foucault calls upon historians to establish a "diverse series, intertwined and often divergent but not autonomous, which enables us to circumscribe the 'place' of the event, the margins of its chance variability, and the conditions of its appearance" (*The Archaeology of Knowledge* 68). When British Columbia disenfranchised the Chinese, it did likewise to Native peoples, "Hindu" (actually Indian, or South Asian) and Japanese immigrants and their descendants born in Canada. While Chinese labourers were regarded as an unacceptable competition by organized white labour, so were the Japanese immigrants; thus the 1902 Royal Commission was called to inquire into the conditions of both racial groups. The Chinese Canadian experience is part of the racial discrimination and segregation imposed on non-white minority groups and aboriginal peoples in Canada and the United States. In particular, the increasing use of cheap Chinese labour in the world labour market, and racial segregation and discrimination against it for over a century, could be regarded as a continuation of the abolished slave system. As well, Chinese Canadian experience should be related to the imperialist aggression against mainland China. Following the Opium Wars, China lost part of its sovereignty, as well as some of its national resources and riches. Chinese national pride was seriously undermined when foreigners treated Chinese as second-rate citizens in their own country. Chinese emigrating to Canada obviously could not escape this treatment.

The historical data and documents selected in this chapter help illustrate the practice of institutionalized racism in Canadian history. When Chinese in Canada were treated as a racial problem for investigation and victimization in mainstream discourse, the community became a convenient target for stereotyping and discrimination. Rereading Chinese Canadian history reveals the historic power configuration in Canadian culture. The function of this chapter is indicated by its position as a necessary context for the study of Chinese Canadian literature. Without examining the historical conditions under which the Chinese in Canada have survived as a community, the study of Chinese Canadian literature as a minority discourse becomes totally groundless. Edward Said remarks that "ideas, cultures, and histories cannot seriously be understood or studied without their force, or more precisely their configurations of power, also being studied" (*Orientalism* 5). Arun Mukherjee's remark on literary studies that leave out social and political contexts is also relevant: "Hegemony is thus achieved, on the one hand by a careful selection of artists and, on the other hand, it is achieved by neglecting the socio-political contexts and concentrating exclusively on technique" (5).

Chinese Canadian literature is a collectively based and context-oriented minority discourse. Many of the first generation Chinese Canadian writers were cultural activists who participated in the Chinese Canadian Writers' Workshop in Vancouver in the 1970s. Since then they have undertaken the historical task of transforming the community's collective silence into a resistant voice in English. This voice, in diverse literary genres and forms, expresses collective and individual experience and identity.

2. *The Transformation from Silence to Voice and Other Discursive Strategies*

The very choice of the language in which to compose is itself a political statement on the part of the writer . . . BARBARA HARLOW

In the task of reevaluating values, our marginality can be our chief asset.
ABDUL R JANMOHAMED & DAVID LLOYD

Rereading Chinese Canadian history highlights the need for social justice yet to be done. Although Chinese Canadians deserve the title of pioneers and nation-builders, systematic racism in Canadian history has denied them the recognition. Had the Chinese been given access to mainstream politics, media, religion, and literature, their contributions to Canada, their legends and mythologies would have been incorporated into Canadian culture long before the 1990s. However, century-long racial discrimination and segregation have deprived them of their history and their Canadian identity. Sociologist Peter Li summarizes the Chinese experience in Canada: "Aside from the indigenous people, no other racial or ethnic group had experienced such harsh treatment in Canada as the Chinese" (1). In fact, Chinese Canadians were reduced to being what West Indian Canadian writer Claire Harris calls "eternal immigrants," "forever poised on the verge of not belonging" (115).

This chapter adopts a power paradigm of silence vs voice to identify the historical transition experienced by Chinese Canadians from a collective silence to a voice in the official discourse. Silence imposed by the dominant groups, paradoxically engendered the Chinese community with a double life force. On the one hand it helped the community preserve its language as a functional tool, and on the other it gave birth to contemporary Chinese Canadian literature in

English. This chapter evaluates the power of the heritage Chinese language in the survival of the community; it reviews some of the historical efforts made by the community in order to communicate with mainstream Canadians during the last hundreds years. As well, it reviews the few mainstream literary works that depict the subject matter of Chinese immigrants. I will examine the consistent discursive strategies and recurrent literary tropes emerging from Chinese Canadian literature. As a community-based minority literature, Chinese Canadian literature employs the anthology as a founding form and all the existing mainstream literary genres as its vehicles. The writers adopt dialogue as an approach to Canadian history and launch a bone-hunting journey as a metonymy of research to recover the historical documents in the community.[1] A sociohistorical milieu, "Golden Mountain," is consistently validated in Chinese Canadian writings in which bachelor labourers and their generations are positioned as the speaking subjects. By celebrating the survival and the development of the community, Chinese Canadian literature displays "the collective self" as the sum of its common values[2] and honours individual men and women who have endured unusual physical and human hardships and whose lives constitute a resistant voice against racial discrimination.

During their one hundred years of silence Chinese immigrants and their descendants were confined within Chinatowns; they were left to communicate in their own (heritage) language. The heritage language played a pivotal role in the collective survival of the community. Jean-Michel Lacroix's research on Canadian ethnic minority newspapers locates twenty-three newspapers historically published by Chinese communities across the country (87-111). Some were established at the turn of the century, for example *The Chinese Times* founded in 1907 and *The New Republic / Son Mom Gwok* in 1911, both in Chinese. Lacroix's research also shows that at least ten of the newspapers published were in either English or a bilingual English-Chinese or French-Chinese format (87-111). In the bilingual format, Chinese was used as a bridging language to help the community gradually learn to grasp the official languages. The contents of these Chinese newspapers provided full reports on the social and cultural activities in the community.

The Chinese Times of December 1915 illustrates the role of the heritage language. The front-page headline was occupied daily by an essay written on a political topic involving world power politics, women's issues, or Chinese government politics. The news coverage extended to the diverse geographical locations of the Chinese immigrants. For instance, it was reported on December 18, 1915 that a Chinese community in Mexico was raided and robbed; its members were either killed by the raiding troops or they fled home (3). The newspaper also carried advertisements for all trades, including teaching; for example, throughout the month a visual artist advertised private lessons in water-colour and oil painting. The variety of businesses and cultural activities within the Chinatowns suggests a self-sufficient economy, while its rich content and wide context demonstrate the power of the heritage language when employed to voice resistance against hegemony. The fact that the Chinese language has been kept alive and fully functional within the community guarantees the preservation of a minority culture from being assimilated by the powerful English environment.

Evidence shows that collective efforts were made in the Chinese Canadian community to help members communicate with the rest of Canada in the official languages, especially in English. As early as 1894–95, a bilingual handbook entitled *Chinese and English Phrase Book and Dictionary* was published to help labourers from Taishan grasp basic English.[3] This phrase book covers a wide range of situations, such as daily greetings, vocabularies for employment, sample business letters, and various legal disputes with the whites concerning racial and cultural issues. It is also marked phonetically in the Taishan dialect in order to give the readers, who came almost exclusively from the same county, a sense of spoken English, even though Taishan phonetic signs might not be accurate for marking English pronunciation. The phrase book was widely marketed in North American Chinatowns for three to four decades and probably went through several reprints. Its wide circulation underscores the considerable efforts made historically by early Chinese immigrants to speak English and to communicate with mainstream society.

Individual writers of Chinese descent also ventured into mainstream literature. A recent discovery of literary works published in the late nineteenth and early twentieth centuries by two Eurasian sisters, daughters of a Chinese mother and an English father, Edith

Eaton, pen name Sui Sin Far, (1865-1914) and Winnifred Eaton Reeve, pen name Onoto Watanna, (1875-1954), reclaims two literary ancestors for the Chinese Canadian community. Born in Canada, the sisters have lived and published in both Canada and the United States. While American scholars have tried to claim the Eaton sisters, calling Edith Eaton the first Chinese-American woman writer, James Doyle attempts to enshrine them in Canadian literary history.[4] Although today's reader might find the characters in their writings sentimental or somewhat stereotypical (Doyle 56), nevertheless the characters may best illustrate the sociohistorical context in which the authors lived. This is why the nationality of the Eaton sisters is probably not as important as their Eurasian identity, which made a significant impact on their literary production. Through their writings, Chinese immigrants and the Eurasian experience were introduced into mainstream literature at least half a century before such voices could again come out from the communities in both countries.

The historical efforts made by Chinese Canadians, collectively and individually, to communicate with the dominant groups in English were less fruitful, because they were one-sided attempts. Nevertheless, the invisibility and silence of the Chinese in Canada did not go totally unremarked in mainstream society. A few mainstream Canadian writers did speak out about this silence. Published in 1955, a short poem "All the Spikes But the Last" by Montreal poet F R Scott challenges the 1952 Governor General's Literary Award winner E J Pratt's epic poem *Towards the Last Spike* for excluding the 17,000 Chinese men recruited for constructing the most dangerous section of the CPR in British Columbia. Scott's poem contains a chain of six questions, protesting against existing Canadian history and literature for denying Chinese Canadians the recognition they deserved as nation-builders. "All the Spikes But the Last" reads:

> Where are the coolies in your poem, Ned?
> Where are the thousands from China who swung their picks with
> bare hands at forty below?
>
> Between the first and the million other spikes they drove,
> and the dressed-up act of Donald Smith, who has sung their
> story?
>
> Did they fare so well in the land they helped to unite? Did they

get one of the 25,000,000 CPR acres?

Is all Canada has to say to them written in the Chinese
Immigration Act? (194)

Racial mistreatment is also the subject of French Canadian writer Gabrielle Roy's short story "Where Will You Go, Sam Lee Wong?" collected in *Garden in the Wind* (1975). Although Sam Lee Wong's café is a familiar site in a prairie town after twenty-five years' settlement, the Chinese bachelor is still greeted "Chinky, chinky Chinaman" in the street (89). Being "forever poised on the verge of not belonging," Sam Lee Wong personifies the image of the "eternal immigrant" observed by Claire Harris. Scott and Roy were among the very few mainstream Canadian writers who raised questions about the marginality of the Chinese immigrants and Chinese Canadians.[5]

In terms of research and writing, historically there had been a few examples of "sporadic production and scholarship" published by academics on Chinese immigrants and their history. However, like the few creative writings depicting Chinese Canadians, the sporadic research and its publication did not represent the development of the community, and so as Richard Fung notes:

> The effect . . . is a lack of momentum. We are unable to develop coherent strategies to learn from the past and from each other. The lack of a community-generated critical context, coupled with the relatively monocultural, monochromatic nature of the group of established critics and scholars, means that those producers attempting to recreate the media in our own terms, to centre the margins, often appear to be starting from scratch . . . (17)

Occasional scholarly works on Chinese Canadians may have raised the awareness of the community's collective marginality.

The silence of the Chinese Canadian community in mainstream Canadian society is not simply a negation of the mainstream. While silence is "indirectly, metaphysically, made present by its *pathos*—taking this word in its best sense" (Derrida 37), what silence can connote is infinite. However, if silence provokes through its pathos, it can only provoke speech. An imposed cultural silence can give birth to a resistant voice. Thus, in the cultural field, silence and voice are inseparable partners that contribute to the existing discourse. Since silence is not as noticeable as speech, in order to reach the otherwise inaccessible silence, speech has to be born in its space. Only then can the disadvantage of silence be transformed into a resource of words. In her novel *Disappearing Moon Cafe*, Sky Lee observes that not only is there a "secret code" between silence and speech, their related positions are also interchangeable:

> Maybe this is a Chinese-in-Canada trait, a part of the great wall of silence and invisibility we have built around us. I have a misgiving that the telling of our history is forbidden. I have violated a secret code. There is power in silence, as this is the way we have always maintained strict control against the more disturbing aspects in our human nature. But what about speaking out for a change, despite its unpredictable impact! (180)

"There is power in silence" as there is in speech. Silence vs speech is an interrelated power paradigm. The "unpredictable impact" resulting from transforming silence into voice can disturb the stability of the existing social structure. Therefore it is important for the marginalized to see that its silence *can* be transformed to a voice in the dominant discourse, and so lead to social changes. Dauenhauer searches for the interplay between silence and voice:

> Every performance, whether of discourse or of silence, belonging to the signitive domain is temporal, incomplete, and lacking in radical autonomy of meaning. . . There is no good reason for assigning ontological priority to discourse over silence. Each makes an irreducible contribution to the sense of the other and to that of the entire domain of signitive performances. (106)

Dauenhauer's observation that discourse and silence are ontologically equal establishes the possibility of their mutual transformation. Furthermore, because discourse is a heterogeneous field conceived by the participants of various social and linguistic forces, no partner can sustain absolute or permanent control of the field. Thus, domination vs marginalization, silence vs voice, are paradigms of a relative and temporal power relationship. Discourse is therefore a forum and a meeting place, where dialogue, dispute, conflict, and reconciliation occur though not without the administration of power and resistance. While discursive polarities inaugurate each other and conjoin in dialogues, their provisional positions become interchangeable.

Without assigning a superiority to speech, or to silence, the ontological equality between silence and speech makes discourse an active meeting place for dialogues. Politically and culturally, dialogue should be accepted as the indispensable social practice in society, especially in a diversified society such as Canada. It may also be implemented as a critical approach to cultural and literary output by various marginalized groups. Using dialogue as an approach prevents one from slipping into various essentialisms, or from taking the dominant discourse as the only valid version of social expression. Since dialogue introduces new voices into the existing discourse, it helps prevent the latter from becoming ossified. The media for dialogues in Canadian society ideally should include both the official and the minority languages. However, history has taught activists from minority communities that in order to have a voice, they have to speak the official languages.

As more and more recent immigrants and the second and third Canadian-born generations are educated in the public school system, they are likely to seek careers outside of Chinatown. The community grows more aware of its rights in society and of the need to challenge racial stereotypes. Adopting English as the language of writing then becomes a political task. As Barbara Harlow notes, "the very choice of the language in which to compose is itself a political statement on the part of the writer" (xviii). In choosing English as their working language contemporary Chinese Canadian writers, like the writer, the publisher, and the readers of the bilingual phrase book and the Eaton sisters before them, acknowledge the need to communicate with the rest of society. Although Chinese language still plays an important role in the community today, continuous enclosure in that language for contemporary Chinese Canadian writers would suggest a self-imposed and self-prolonged silence and isolation in Canadian culture.

Using English as the working language is, however, sometimes an inevitable choice for native-born Chinese Canadian writers, because English is the only written language they know. Sky Lee talks about the shift from Chinese to English for her generation, which makes it the first generation in the community to gain a voice in Canadian society. Lee observes the phenomenon:

> Our generation is the first generation to regain a voice. Our original cultural voice was lost in the process of being displaced from China to Canada. That move takes several generations. I'm often ashamed to say that my voice is in my colonizer's language, in English. I am not fluent or literate in my heritage language. (Andrews D17)

Here Lee sees an ambiguous relationship between the English language and herself as a contemporary Chinese Canadian writer. Since racist discrimination against Chinese Canadians was imposed historically through the dominant discourse, English has done the same cultural damage to them as it did to people in the British colonies. This is probably why Lee says that she is ashamed, or perhaps rather aware, of the fact that her voice has to go through the medium of English, her colonizer's language. However, one hundred and thirty-seven years after its settlement, the Chinese Canadian community has finally achieved a reterritorialization[6] when its first-generation writers started to publish in English. It is also the first time that Chinese Canadian writers can share their community history and personal experiences through literary forms with a wider audience.

The long silence of the Chinese Canadian community in mainstream Canadian discourse was, significantly, finally broken by a collective endeavour. In the process of developing Chinese Canadian literature, the anthology form has become an established discursive practice. The birth of Chinese Canadian literature was marked by the publication of its first anthology, *Inalienable Rice*, in 1979. Its continuous development as a community literature was marked by the publication of the second anthology, *Many-Mouthed Birds*, in 1991. Since the anthology form manifests a common interest, the publication of the two anthologies authenticated a collective signature for contemporary Chinese Canadian writers. Together they signified a discursive transition from silence to voice.

The development of Chinese Canadian literature demonstrates a process of dealing with historical damage inflicted on the community by institutionalized racism. Abdul R JanMohamed and David Lloyd observe the kind of damage done to minority peoples by dominant discourse: "Given such a historically sustained negation of minority voices, we must realize that minority discourse is, in the first instance, the product of damage—damage more or less systematically inflicted on cultures produced as minorities by the dominant culture" (4). Writing about the community's historical experience can prevent the silenced and the damaged from being further "subjected to 'institutional forgetting' "; this institutionally preferred forgetfulness, continuing the "form of control of one's memory and history, is one of the gravest forms of damage done to minority cultures" (JanMohamed and Lloyd 6).

Using the technique of dialogue in various forms, contemporary Chinese Canadian writers have striven to revive the lived experience of early Chinese immigrants. They have had to deal with the lack of written records about Chinese immigrants and their descendants in Canadian archives, except for racial stereotypes generated by mainstream media and the immigration documents, by instigating their own search for historical documents and recording fragments of memories from the community's oral tradition.

Dialogue with the community ancestors becomes an indispensable research process. This dialogue is usually initiated by a contemporary speaker to an addressee who is a family or community elder. Although the addressee has usually already passed away, through dialogue the contemporary speaker is reconnected with the ancestor's memory and with his or her lived experience. Jim Wong-Chu, Fred Wah, Sky Lee, Denise Chong, and others employ an autobiographical narrator or persona, who searches for his or her own identity through dialogues with deceased ancestors. In some cases, the addressee cannot answer directly, but it is in his or her persistent presence that a narrative is born. In other cases, the provocative silence urges the narrator to search through the collective memory or family genealogy. The form of dialogue positions contemporary Chinese Canadian writers in the historical space to redress the biases of Canadian history and to reclaim their community history. The connection between the community history and its contemporary literature demonstrates a distinctive feature of this minority discourse, which, in turn, constructs the concept of "the collective self," another quintessential feature of Chinese Canadian literature.

"The collective self" is a prominent identity construction model for Chinese Canadians. The formation of this model is directly related to how Chinese were historically treated in Canada. Instead of being received as individuals, they were always regarded as a racial group, either as a cheap labour force to be used or expelled, or as an alien race to be excluded from professional jobs, citizenship rights, and immigration altogether. Thus racist immigration policies and the public image of the community paradoxically helped Chinese Canadians develop a collective identity. Without a recognized community history, individual Chinese Canadians cannot hope to receive equality and respect from fellow Canadians. As a political paradigm then, the collective self emerges from many contemporary Chinese Canadian writings as an underlining concept. Using this paradigm, the new literature celebrates the struggle and survival of the community, offering an illuminating model of a double identity to other minority literatures in Canada.

In addition to the two widely employed discursive strategies discussed above, dialogue as an approach to history and "the collective self" as an identity construction model, Chinese Canadian writers developed other consistent literary tropes. The process of transforming the historical silence into a literary voice requires Chinese Canadian writers to abrogate the existing racial stereotypes and to appropriate them by constructing the heroes and heroines of the community.[7] Gold Mountain is depicted as a mythological setting and a milieu in which many of the stories are disclosed. The image contains the mythical power that a developing literature needs. Gold Mountain is also a historical term, originating from the colloquial Chinese phrase *Gum-shun*, which has been used in Chinatowns for over a century. This connection, which bespeaks a historical epistemology, illustrates a community-based Chinese Canadian literature whose expressions are developed from the community's lived experience. Furthermore, the image of Gold Mountain also connotes the dream, the fate, and the destination of the Chinese immigrants who sought equal opportunities in the New World, where thousands of others came from all over the world in search of the same dream. Among works that employed Gold Mountain as a historical background, Paul Yee's *Tales from the Gold Mountain* casts the milieu in a wide range of frontier settings (see Chapter Four). It is by reclaiming the presence of Chinese immigrants in the Gold Mountain milieu that Yee's tales glorify them as the nation-builders and pioneers of the country.

The need to rediscover the history of Gold Mountain urges contemporary Chinese Canadian writers to take a metonymic journey through their writings. The trope "searching for the bones" is widely adopted by novelist Sky Lee, folklorist Paul Yee, poet Jim Wong-Chu, dramatist Winston Christopher Kam, and others to recover the contributions made by the Chinese railway workers. As mentioned above, in Chapter One, in 1891 the Chinese Consolidated Benevolent Association of Victoria organized a historical journey to collect the unburied bones of the Chinese railway workers along the finished CPR in order to have them sent back to China for proper burial. Deriving from that historical event, "the bone-hunting journey" is not simply another version of the journey motif borrowed from the mainstream literary repertoire. As a historical trope, "the bone-hunting journey" calls on society to recognize Chinese Canadians as pioneers in Canadian discourse; at the same time, via this trope, contemporary Chinese Canadian writers start the reclamation campaign to establish the community archives. Various versions of this trope are developed around the central image of "the bones." They include "searching for the bones," "the unburied bones," "mending the bones," "burying the bones," and "visiting the bones." As an important metaphor and a powerful signifier deriving directly from Chinese Canadian history, the "bones" of the community ancestors live on to tell their untold stories in contemporary Chinese Canadian literature.

Underlining the motif of the bone-hunting journey is the task of recovering the family genealogy, Chinese Canadian women's herstory, and community history. As most of the Chinese Canadian writers are also community activists and archivists, the need to reclaim the community history preceded their literary endeavour. The photographic history books, such as *Saltwater City: An Illustrated History of the Chinese in Vancouver* compiled by Paul Yee and *Portraits of a Challenge: An Illustrated History of the Chinese Canadians* by Lee

Wai-man, which I have cited in Chapter One as part of the historical documents on the subject, were produced to help fellow Chinese Canadians review their collective history. The interviews collected in *Jin Guo: Voices of Chinese Canadian Women* (1992), which are fragments of lived experiences retrieved from personal memories, testifies to the Chinese women's collective experience in Canada. The illustrated book *Westcoast Chinese Boy* (1979) by visual artist Sing Lim captures Vancouver's Chinatown in the late nineteenth and early twentieth centuries. The community activists and archivists collected and published various testimonial materials, such as family photographs, letters, personal memories, and immigration documents in community history books. The preservation of these materials not only establishes the community's own archives, which provides its members with a history, but also supplies its creative writers with a valuable historical resource.

Adopting and adapting family saga or genealogy, Chinese Canadian writers are rewriting the community history in various literary forms. Edward Said emphasises the significance of constructing a minority history parallel to the dominant history: "while identity is crucial, just to assert a different identity is never enough. The main thing is to be able to see that Caliban has a history capable of development, as part of the process of work, growth, and maturity to which only Europeans had seemed entitled" (*Culture and Imperialism* 213). Family genealogy has become a popular format across the generic divisions of both prose and poetry in Chinese Canadian literature. Through this format, the writers present a growing community that has gone through a migration phase and a hundred-year marginalization before achieving a reterritorialization and seeing its descendants writing in English. These historical phases illustrate what Said calls "a history capable of development."

Having achieving reterritorialization, it was time the contemporary Chinese Canadian writers composed the community's experience in its literature. While Chinese Canadian literature establishes Chinese Canadians as speaking subjects, it rejects a simple appropriation of the existing racial stereotypes with merely positive images. Without idealizing its agents as super heroes or heroines, Chinese Canadian literature embraces different identity construction models and welcomes complicated emotional landscapes and multidimensional characters. Parallel to the reclamation of the collective history is a self-imposed reevaluation of the traditional Chinese cultural baggage. By presenting women's experience in traditional male-oriented Chinese culture, especially in the historical Chinatown that is made up of bachelors and married-bachelors, Winston Christopher Kam, Sky Lee, Paul Yee, Denise Chong, and others challenge sexism and other modes of internal inequality and injustice. Self-imposed reevaluation also includes examination of traditional self-images, identity construction models, generational conflicts between immigrant parents and Canadian-bred generations, homophobia, interracial marriages, and attitude toward Eurasian offsprings within the Chinese community.

While most of the first-generation writers chose to explore individual identities through collectively-based values, "the collective self" is neither a unifying subject nor an imposition regarding what Chinese Canadian writers are expected to write. In order to avoid suggesting that Chinese Canadian literature is homogeneous, the last chapter of this study examines Evelyn Lau's controversial model of rebellion and her immediate success in the mainstream with the publication of her first book, *Runaway: Diary of a Street Kid* (1989). Whereas Lau's alternative model of rebellion posts a challenge to contemporary Chinese Canadian literature, "the collective self" continues to illuminate the shared values and identity in many Chinese Canadian writings. Essayist Fung summarizes the change of subject position as significant in Chinese Canadian writings in *Yellow Peril Reconsidered* (1990):

> While many independent projects center around countering the hegemony of the dominant media, we must ensure that our agenda is not determined by a simple reaction to the stereotypes others have of us . . . we need to situate and question ourselves as *subjects*. Not how we are seen but how *we* see. We must center our work on our own problems, desires and foibles. (19)

With rounded characters and lived experiences contextualized in Canadian history, Chinese Canadian literature enters the mainstream with its distinctive voice as a community-based minority literature. As a minority discourse, it nurtures a dynamic vision deriving from its double linguistic and cultural heritage.

*

In this chapter I have analyzed the power structure of the silence vs voice dichotomy. As imposed silence is neither a sign of muteness nor an expression of passivity, Chinese Canadians' hundred-year silence in mainstream Canadian culture signifies a collective resistance against the latter's racial and cultural hegemony. For many decades, this resistance was voiced in the Chinese language, thereby creating an enclosed alternative subculture in Chinatown. At the same time, collective and individual efforts were made historically from within the community in order to communicate with the rest of Canada. However, these efforts were less fruitful because institutionalized racism not only denied Chinese Canadians an equal access, but also imposed on them various racial stereotypes. Breaking through the historical silence for contemporary Chinese Canadian writers means to construct the community's unrecorded history in English, in the language that originally ordered the silencing. Writing the historical experience into the dominant discourse is the first step undertaken by contemporary Chinese Canadians in order to stop "institutional forgetting" from further damaging the community.

As the dichotomy binds the partners in a temporary relationship, silence and speech are, arguably, ontologically equal. The interdependence between silence and speech makes a discursive field a meeting place rather than a territory that can be ruled by a single dominant voice. Although changes in the power structure do not happen progressively, writing the historically marginalized subjects into English is the initial step towards changing the epistemology and the agency in the dominant discourse. Consequently, dialogue becomes a preferable approach in Chinese Canadian literature in order to retrieve the community history from the existing archives and from the collective memories. Through dialogues, contemporary Chinese Canadians enter the dominant discourse to abrogate the existing racial stereotypes and to voice their unrecorded experience.

In its dialogues with Canadian history and literature, Chinese Canadian literature develops its distinctive political paradigm and recurrent literary tropes. These prevalent strategies include the paradigm of "the collective self," "Gold Mountain milieu," and the "bone-hunting journey." These devices help manifest the collective features of this minority discourse, especially its needs to reclaim the community history and to construct a double cultural identity. The following chapters will elaborate these strategies by analyzing various literary texts classified according to the conventional genre divisions.

The characteristics of Chinese Canadian literature establish a parallel relationship with other branches of Canadian literature. In order to be appreciated as equals, Chinese Canadian writers make great efforts to achieve what Said calls *"the voyage in,"* a collective advancement from the minority community to mainstream. Said notes:

> The conscious effort to enter into the discourse of Europe and the West, to mix with it, transform it, to make it acknowledge marginalized or suppressed or forgotten histories is of particular interest . . . in an earlier generation of resistance writing. This kind of work was carried out by dozens of scholars, critics, and intellectuals in the peripheral world; I call this effort *the voyage in*. (*Culture and Imperialism* 216)

Said refers specifically to the first generation postcolonial writers using the colonizers' languages to represent their experience. The process of *"the voyage in"* effectively illuminates the achievements made by the first-generation Chinese Canadian writers. *"Voyage in"* implies a passage similar to the "epic struggles" identified by the participants of the Chinese Canadian Writers' Workshop who later published *Inalienable Rice* (viii). Only by undertaking the epic voyage to enter mainstream discourse can Chinese Canadians share their experiences with Canadian readers in general.

"The voyage in" should not be only taken as a one-way route for minority Canadian writers to enter the mainstream. It ought to be accepted as a passage for mutual appropriation. Said's remark that human history is made from cultural borrowing, "appropriations, common experiences, and interdependencies of all kinds" (*Culture and Imperialism* 217), explains this mutual need. The birth of Chinese Canadian literature, one hundred and thirty-seven years after the community's settlement in Canada embodies a hybrid nature conceived from cultural borrowing, especially from the mainstream. At the same time, while English is made to bear witness to the otherwise "impermeable" Chinese Canadian experience, it is equally appropriated by the minority speaking subjects and their experiences.

Front covers of *Inalienable Rice* (1979) and *Many-Mouthed Birds* (1991).

3. Anthologizing the Collective: The Epic Struggles to Establish Chinese Canadian Literature in English

Given such a historically sustained negation of minority voices, we must realize that minority discourse is, in the first instance, the product of damage—damage more or less systematically inflicted on cultures produced as minorities by the dominant culture.

ABDUL R JANMOHAMED & DAVID LLOYD

By the development of our own Asian Canadian literature, both creative and analytical, we are setting out to bridge that separation from ourselves and other Asian Canadians. *Inalienable Rice*

Contemporary Chinese Canadian literature is community based. In its development, a literary form—the anthology—has been employed as a political and aesthetic manifesto to announce the collective cause and to reveal the sensitivity of Chinese Canadians. This chapter focuses on the two anthologies: *Inalienable Rice: A Chinese & Japanese Canadian Anthology*[1] (1979) and *Many-Mouthed Birds: Contemporary Writing By Chinese Canadians* (1991), and introduces another joint publication, *Yellow Peril: Reconsidered* (1990), which is based on a national touring exhibition of works by artists, writers, filmmakers and videographers from Asian Canadian communities. Although it was hardly noticed outside of the community, the publication of *Inalienable Rice* marks the birth of the community-based literature; *Many-Mouthed Birds* enters Canadian literature as a new landmark, signifying its continuous growth.

The anthology is one of the literary forms most capable of embracing writings in different genres and of introducing an emerging literature into the mainstream. Twelve years apart, the two anthologies embody and illustrate the "epic struggles" outlined in *Inalienable Rice* (viii), of trying to establish Chinese Canadian literature in English. The discursive configuration in the anthologies represents the collective endeavour of Chinese Canadian writers to transform the community's hundred-year silence into a resistant voice.This chapter examines some of the intrinsic and extrinsic elements that have contributed to the final making of both anthologies, using the critical model of the literary mode of production developed by Terry Eagleton (48).

As discussed in the previous chapter, several generations after the initial settlement the time came for Chinese Canadian writers to choose English as the working language. This inevitability should not obscure the fact that racial minority writers in Canada always have to choose between the official languages and their heritage language if they are fluent in both. The fact that there is little published criticism of writings in languages other than English or French bespeaks the marginality of minority Canadian literatures written in most heritage languages. Observing this problem, Jars Balan pointed out in 1982: "the most significant gap in our knowledge is Canadian literature in languages other than English or French, which has been excluded from most discussions and assessments of Canadian letters" (ix). So far this gap has not been bridged. Asian Canadian writers who have been acknowledged by the mainstream literary canon are those who have adopted English as their working language. Canadian writings in heritage languages other than English or French are, in fact, still ignored by the mainstream. For the first generation Chinese Canadian writers, breaking through silence and marginality clearly means writing in English.

Because breaking through silence was the political stance of the participants in the Chinese Canadian Writers' Workshop in the 1970s, *Inalienable Rice* did not discuss the bi-lingual option for its representation. However, the editors of *Many-Mouthed Birds* faced a difficult decision when submissions "in English or in Chinese by writers of Chinese descent living or who have lived in Canada" were invited as Bennett Lee notes (1). Their decision involved canonization. Lee argues that the technical difficulty of translating Chinese into English cannot be resolved easily:

> The gulf between Chinese and Western literary traditions is difficult to bridge in translation because Chinese is a high-context language that assumes a commonly shared cultural identity and world view which requires explanation to make the translated text accessible to the non-Chinese reader. This exercise can be self-defeating, like explaining the punchline to a joke. In the end we decided that compelling sociology did not necessarily make for engaging literature and included only writing in English. (3)

The result is that the submissions in Chinese were inevitably marginalized.

The anthology, as an established literary mode of collective production, carries a discursive power in at least two areas not possessed by single-author publications. First, most anthologies bear a larger-than-life title, which positions the anthologized texts in an established national literature[2] or grants recognition to an emerging literature. Second, the anthology usually inherits a larger-than-life role; it often begins with an introduction or preface written by an influential editor, who frequently emphasizes the significance of the anthology for its time. Endowed with the historic and symbolic signification, repeatedly anthologized texts are likely to become the canonical texts in a national literature. This larger-than-itself literary mode of production constitutes the most effective way, among the existing literary genres, to launch an emerging minority literature.

The anthology best advances the political cause embedded in the idea of a Chinese Canadian literature. Donald Yee, a contributor to *Inalienable Rice*, points out that Chinese Canadian writers have to write about racism, while celebrating the struggle, survival, and growth of the individuals and the community:

> Racism was part of our history. But there were also neglected heroes and stories, glazed-over events, and memories. Chinese Canadians had a history, and in this lay the sense of community and the context of our belonging here, in Canada. These we believed were important cultural components of our lives . . . (66)

Yee outlines two political tasks for future Chinese Canadian writing. The first is to rewrite existing Canadian history in order to right the wrongs. The second is to reclaim the community heroes and heroines from the existing racial stereotypes so that contemporary Chinese Canadians may expect to have more respectable personal identities.

Twelve years later, the same political tasks are foregrounded in *Many-Mouthed Birds*. Head taxes and the 1923 Chinese Exclusion Act are cited as the direct agents that silenced the Chinese Canadian community: "The resulting isolation from the social, political and cultural mainstream of Canadian life spanned nearly a century and forms an important, although sometimes forgotten, part of our history" (Bennett Lee, 1–2). Later, using visual arts and film media, *Yellow Peril* targets the existing racial stereotypes of Asian Canadians. In its printed format, editor Paul Wong observes the psychological impact that existing stereotypes make on the behaviour of Asian Canadians:

> This in turn created an inferiority complex that has helped shape behavioural practice within our communities, and the way our community is viewed in the New World by the dominant culture.
>
> Behavioural codes include "try hard not to be noticed" and "be subservient to 'white people'." They are also evident in the ongoing stereotypical portrayal of Asian women in popular media as either being Susie Wongs or Geisha Girls. (6)

Publicly imposed inferiority on Asian Canadians and their self-inflicted subservience are among the important issues discussed in the anthologies.

The anthologists observe that the ongoing cultural assimilation in Canadian society constantly denies Asian Canadians a worthy double cultural identity. In the introduction to *Inalienable Rice*, the editorial committee points out that for Asian Canadians, personal success and upward mobility in society generally mean having to leave the communities:

> For Asian Canadians in general, moving upward meant leaving

> what communities we had and assimilating into the liberal white middle class. Only through encounters with others already questioning this process . . . on personal searches for a satisfactory sense of identity . . . were we able to break out of this syndrome of trying to become white. (Chu viii)

The editorial committee challenges the dominant Canadian cultural values based on the interest of "the liberal white middle class," from which the majority of Asian Canadians are excluded. *Inalienable Rice* also lists the damage inflicted by the dominant media on Chinese Canadians through the practice of "institutional forgetfulness": "The most basic deficiency of attempts to tell the early history of the Chinese in British Columbia is that these histories have been concerned almost exclusively with *white reactions* to the Chinese and hardly ever with the Chinese themselves" (Bennett Lee 6). Furthermore, Lee also observes the psychological damage: "It is one of the more damaging lies of liberal apologists that the Chinese were always passive, docile and slavish. . . . The assumption is that the Chinese somehow *deserved* to be abused because they were willing 'victims' . . . " (6). Targeting the historical damage and "institutional forgetfulness," the anthology provides a necessary forum for Chinese Canadian writers to deal with the community's hundred-year silence in Canadian society.

The anthology form is employed to undertake the political task to right the wrong. The editorial committee of *Inalienable Rice* perceives the struggles to establish a community literature as "epic struggles" to give voice to:

> a sense of empathy rather than sympathy, of *epic struggles* rather than unfortunate mistakes, of the central importance of the Asian Canadian experience to a realistic understanding of Canada, rather than its designation as a footnote to Canadian history, of a concern for the future of our communities rather than pat conclusions like "model minority" or "well assimilated." (viii, emphasis mine)

Traditionally and aesthetically, an epic is a long poem that gives expression to the ideals of a nation or race by depicting its historical journey. The struggle for Chinese Canadian literature is epic in that contemporary writers return to various historical spaces to write about the unrecorded experiences of early Chinese immigrants. This task was jointly taken by the first generation of Chinese Canadian writers, archivists and critics, whose endeavour produced the first anthology.

The "epic struggles" also specify the historical conditions for the birth of a community-based minority literature in English. Chinese Canadians have been prepared for a reterritorialization because the community had been historically suppressed as a racial minority for almost a century, and the accumulated resistance against the imposed deterritorialization is too strong to die out. The combination of these two conditions provokes the community, especially its native-born generations, with a psychological need to cry out in the dominant discourse. The publication of *Inalienable Rice* symbolizes the beginning of this collective transformation from silence to voice in the following two ways: first, the birth of Chinese Canadian literature in English is a sign of reterritorialization, especially because the first anthology opens up a forum for the participants to question the lack of representation of their experience in Canadian history and literature; second, *Inalienable Rice* envisages the collective nature of Chinese Canadian literature. The theoretical framework in *Inalienable Rice* is the prototype of Chinese Canadian literature, which since has had many applications.

Structurally speaking, the prototype of a mixed-genre configuration in both *Inalienable Rice* and *Many-Mouthed Birds* supports the collective basis of the enterprise. Instead of following a single-genre format as Canadian poetry and short story are traditionally anthologized, the choice of mixed genres for the two Chinese Canadian anthologies achieves "a thematic flow in which poem and essay, interview and proposal, visual and literary image have been mixed so that related ideas, feelings and points could be communicated on many levels" (Chu viii). The multi-level communication, which "stimulated more writing and became more of a beginning than a culmination" (Chu viii), treats both the reader and the texts with more respect, while the single-genre anthologies usually impose isolation by offering fixed models and patterns, paying tribute to dead giants in the genre.

A multi-genre configuration treats writings as discursive products rather than merely the products of the particular genre in which they are confined. A multi-genre format challenges the traditional critical concepts, such as that the essay is for issues and poetry for non-political sentiments. The poems included in *Inalienable Rice* illustrate that poetry can join the essays, photographs and interviews to express minority issues. Like prose and drama, poetry can voice resistance against dominant cultural hegemony as well as grant recognition to the historical contributions made by the Chinese labourer generation. Sean Gunn's sarcastic short poem "Assimilation" deals with the damage imposed by the white media on Asian Canadians:

> by any means
> bleach out your jeans
> and when they fade
> you've got it made
>
> and you wonder where the yellow went
> when you brush yourself with a permanent
> brighter than bright
> whiter than white
> ninety nine forty four one hundred percent
> and you wondered, where the yellow went?
> . . . .
> oh mirror, mirror on the wall
> who is the fairest, beneath it all?
> . . . .
> by any means
> bleach out your genes
> and when they fade
> you've got it made. (44)

While the poem begins with the metaphor of "bleached jeans," it ends with a desire to get rid of one's "genes," to make the Chinese Canadian look "fair" in the "mirror." The poem questions the powerful impact of popular culture in Canadian society.

In another poem, "And Then Something Went," Gunn explores the self-rejection widely experienced by Asian Canadians. Gunn, also a musician, combines poetry with music to investigate the cause of a young Chinese Canadian's suicide. He uses a fast rhythmic beat to engage the reader in an analysis of racial stereotypes and constraints. With short snappy sentences, simple diction and especially onomatopoeia (for example, "click click," "bam bam," and "pow pow"), Gunn involves the readers, especially those who are familiar with pop music, in a reading process. The poem is written in an unbroken stanza of more than a hundred lines, and the reader senses the intense rhythm that renders a metonymic experience of living under racial pressure until one cannot bear it any longer. "And then something went": the title of the poem completes the cycle. The two key lines in Gunn's poem, which I have quoted several times before, declare how the lack of a collective identity damages a minority Canadian: "criminal like man with no culture / very difficult to find true identity" (56); at the same time, Gunn brings the reader's attention to the racial stereotypes and clichés that have jointly killed the young man:

> here
> suck fortune cookie
> click click
> . . . .
> every day sammy tong houseboy
> one day he find no peter
> sammy tong shoot self in head
> click click
> beep beep
> . . . .

Because the poem implies performance, the reader who wants fully to understand the poem has to engage with the form physically by reading it aloud.

Paul Yee's short prose poem "Last Words II," which is collected in both anthologies, like Gunn's "And Then Something Went," addresses the need to reclaim the experience of early Chinese immigrants. It begins with two short stanzas: both use the imperative syntax, forming parallel and contrast. The poet starts by talking directly to the reader, asking "you" to choose either to forget or to remember Chinese labourers who are positioned collectively as the object of "your" choice:

Forget us
if you must.

But if you must
remember us . . .

Then, using the first-person "we," the poet describes the lived experience of the Chinese labourers who came to British Columbia by the thousands without their families to help build Canada in the nineteenth century. The use of "we" speaks to the collective experience of the labourers, who endured unusual physical and human hardships in addition to family separation:

We were young men

Broad of shoulder
and supple as bamboo.
We lived early mornings
Stretched and rippled
in the hazy fields
laid tracks to the horizon.
At break of work
We cooked rice
and ate as brothers.
There were our women,
they waited at home.
We waited,
but only the bosses came
the canneries came
the mines died
and cooks started up.

We could send
letters home. (*Inalienable Rice* 32; *Many-Mouthed Birds* 180)

In this short poem, Yee presents the heroic image of the Chinese railway workers as nation builders; their collectivity begets Chinese Canadian literature the same sensitivity as Yee effects in this poem. The editors of *Many-Mouthed Birds* put Yee's poem at the end of the anthology to further emphasize its significance—as Bennett Lee describes: "The question of identity, which in turn leads to an inquiry into the past, both private and collective" (3). The realization that "[b]y the development of our own Asian Canadian literature, both creative and analytical, we are setting out to bridge that separation from ourselves and other Asian Canadians" (Chu viii) further emphasizes the collective characteristics shared by all Asian Canadian literatures.

The strategy of dialogue and the literary trope of "searching for the bones," which are widely employed in Chinese Canadian literature, were both conceived as evident prototypes in Jim Wong-Chu's lyric, "Old Chinese Cemetery (Kamloops 1977/July)" published in *Inalienable Rice*. Wong-Chu's single stanza in this anthology describes the poet going through a phase of identity crisis. His search for an explanation leads him to the burial ground of the Gold Mountain men, where the bones of the community ancestors were deserted as their deeds were forgotten in Canadian history:

like a child lost
wandering about
touching, feeling
tattered grounds
touching, seeing
wooden boards
etched in ink
etched in weather
etched in faded memories
etched faded
forgotten,
I walk
on earth,
above bones of a multitude
of golden mountain men
searching for scraps
of haunting memories

like a child unloved
pressing his face hard
against the wet window
Peering in
straining with anguish
for a desperate moment
I touch my past (8)

The poem, as published later in Wong-Chu's collection *Chinatown Ghosts* (1986), has five stanzas. This single stanza in *Inalienable Rice,* however, makes the identity crisis more intense and the search more urgent.

The longing for a community literature in English is expressed metaphorically in Paul Yee's other poem "The Grass Dragon" in the first anthology:

Grass for our grass dragon
Yet to be awakened
Grass from the Fraser soils
Weave body to legend.
. . . .
to celebrate
our first dragon
Made in Canada.
We can only wait.
We can hardly wait. (39–40)

Woven with local materials by a team, "the grass dragon" symbolizes the birth of Chinese Canadian literature in English. The repeated use of "we" and "our" in this poem epitomizes "the collective self" as a predominant discursive paradigm.

However, in the formation of this collective identity, Chinese is only a modifier and it does not eliminate the differences among Chinese Canadians. Gunn's mini poem "Orientation #1" observes that "Chinese" is an adjective rather than a noun when used in Canada:

in the world today
Chinese
are people
who live in China

on the local scene
Chinese
are adjectives
that modify people (38)

As an adjective, a modifier, the word *Chinese* does not unify the differences among the Canadians of Chinese descent; thus, "Chinese Canadians" is a collective rather than a unified identity in Chinese Canadian literature. The diverse backgrounds of the contributors to *Many-Mouthed Birds*, such as their birth places which include Canada, Mainland China, Taiwan, Hong Kong, Singapore, Trinidad and Zimbabwe, further emphasize the collectively shared but non-unified Chinese Canadian identity.

While *Inalienable Rice* symbolizes the birth of Chinese Canadian literature, *Many-Mouthed Birds* presents its future. Its "relatively uncharted literary waters" embrace worldwide experiences, as Bennett Lee observes. Furthermore, these writings include a wide selection of genres including poetry, novel, novella, short story, and nonfiction. The configuration of *Many-Mouthed Birds* continues the opening-up principle, still testing "whether or not the results would reflect a sensibility which was identifiably 'Chinese Canadian' " (Bennett Lee). "Chinese Canadian" is not an imposed subject matter in the latest anthology (Bennett Lee); its entries include both traditional and experimental works, new and established writers, previously published and never published pieces. This selection represents a discursive practice that both challenges and redefines the identity formation of Chinese Canadians in a broader sociohistorical context, while searching for appropriate literary paradigms and expressions to embody their diversity.

Many-Mouthed Birds signifies a different collective endeavour; it is not merely a collection of individual writers chosen according to the taste of the editors. While some writings in *Many-Mouthed Birds* clearly generate identifiable Chinese Canadian sensitivities, others reveal different "priorities." "Chinese Canadian" does not totalize individual experiences, even though the anthology form does create a community basis for the anthologized. The prose entries in the second anthology illustrate this editorial practice. The mother in Garry Engkent's short story "Why My Mother Can't Speak English" depicts the character's forty-year isolation from the rest of Canadian society while working in the kitchen of her husband's restaurant in Chinatown. The mother's lack of social life reminds the reader of immigrant Chinese women's invisibility in Canadian society. This story finds its opposite in Winston Christopher Kam's short story "Mabel's Hockey Game." Set in Trinidad in 1960, it portrays a poor black servant woman, Mabel, whose interest in watching field hockey leads her gradually to enter the traditional, male domain of field hockey as an amateur referee. Although both stories depict an older woman as the heroine, the differences in the subject matter, plot, setting and characterization typify the varieties of prose entries in the second anthology.

The poetry selection in *Many-Mouthed Birds* supports the same principle of variety. Among the styles anthologized are concrete poetry, Haiku-like forms, and prose poetry. Some of the poems, especially the lengthy ones, will be discussed in Chapter Seven; however, Laiwan's bilingual poem, "The Imperialism of Syntax," which is the only entry in the anthology that has a Chinese component, deserves a special discussion here. Laiwan uses her poem to raise questions about the overwhelming power of the English language. By having the poem printed in both English and Chinese, with the Chinese version bearing an English title and the English version a Chinese title, the poet thus juxtaposes the dispossession of her language with the intercultural experience she lives as a Chinese African Canadian. If the small print of a footnote is read as part of the text, then the note best describes this intercultural experience, however ironic, which is embedded in many Chinese Canadian writings:

> "The Imperialism of Syntax" was written in english and translated into chinese. Being born in a british colony in africa, I am illiterate in chinese; english is my first language. I work with chinese translators as an exercise for me to perceive my dispossession of my origin and to research the impossibilities of accu-

rately embodying cultural meaning within translation. (57)

The experience of writing "The Imperialism of Syntax" is connected with the massive migration of cheap Chinese labourers in the middle and late nineteenth century. The poem focuses on the inevitable linguistic assimilation and humiliation that the Chinese immigrants experienced: "you had travelled long and far to be subject to another's language, / another's *syntax.* / Right away those rules of grammar were the forgetting of yourself" (58). While the footnote provides meaning for the poem, and vice versa, Laiwan's bilingual version of the poem explores the migration, colonization, and the inevitable linguistic dispossession experienced by thousands of people. This poem also gives the suppressed or lost heritage language an equal representation, even though this representation does not equal a linguistic repossession by the colonized.

Laiwan uses both poetry and essay to explore the impact of the language(s) in which one writes. In an essay paragraph titled "Ubiquitous China" that accompanies her photographs in the *Yellow Peril* exhibition, she expresses the same concern that English colonizes non-English speakers' minds and tongues through its syntax:

> English, with its history of imperialism and colonization of minds, is a syntactical problem. Its writing reinforces its history because it was the only language accepted in its colonies . . . I am dependent on english to deflate that which itself has created. I am dependent because it has become the *native* tongue that most of the reading world knows or wants to know. It is the audacious syntax that generates its own meanings and expectations within contexts it knows nothing about. (40)

The poet's own dependence on English for communication highlights her awareness of its power as a world language. Laiwan's prose paragraph also employs a Chinese translation as part of her strategies. The consistent bilingual practice in her writing reveals the poet's mixed sensitivities as a Chinese African Canadian, whose feelings cannot easily be expressed in either English or Chinese.

Mixed sentiments towards the English language are widely and similarly depicted in *Many-Mouthed Birds* as a collective, sometimes painful, intercultural experience. The title of Jim Wong-Chu's poem

"How Feel I Do?" deliberately disturbs the conventional English syntax in order to suggest its process of assimilation. It concludes:

like you
I too was mired in another language
and I gladly surrendered it
for english

you too
in time
will lose your mother's tongue (17)

The ironic word play of "mother's tongue" for "mother tongue" touches upon the material connection with one's mother tongue; thus, the loss of one's heritage language to the official languages, which are sometimes second languages to the dispossessed, could be seen as a cultural loss. The poem ends with a question in grammatically correct syntax, "now tell me / how do you feel?", suggesting that in due time residues of one's mother tongue will give way to the powerful English environment.

Several other poems and stories also depict the loss of the heritage language as part of the second- and third-generation Chinese Canadian experience. In "Why My Mother Can't Speak English," the mother who talks to her son about the news in the community newsletter suddenly remembers: "Ah, you can't read Chinese" (9). In her concrete poems *Sacred Texts*, Jam Ismail (the poet's name itself signifies an intercultural experience) describes the loss of the Chinese language among many overseas Chinese descendants:

in hongkong marie-clair said: you should say you don't know how to read, not, you don't know how to read chinese.
oh, sorry! the waitress apologized, rushed back with the english-language menu, & waited on bosan most sympathetically. (126)

The loss of the Chinese language is broadly depicted as a painful but unavoidable loss by the writers who were born as second and third generations in Canada or elsewhere in a non-Chinese-speaking environment. The phenomenon ironically confirms that adopting English as the working language is somehow not a choice but an inevitability due to either collective reterritorialization or linguistic dispossession.

The final making of *Inalienable Rice* and *Many-Mouthed Birds*, according to Eagleton's model of the "literary mode of production,"[3] illustrates the two stages in the development of Chinese Canadian literature. The literary mode of production includes the intrinsic features of textuality, such as genre, language and forms of depiction, as well as the extrinsic features that include the publisher, market distribution, and promotion. These components of the two anthologies indicate that they are literary products of different decades. *Inalienable Rice* alludes to "unalienable rights," the key phrase of the American Declaration of Independence.[4] Thus, it appeals to fundamental human rights that have long since become the inspiration of democratic societies. Because rice is the indispensable food for all Asians, the title comments on the social and racial equality that Asian Canadians are entitled to but were deprived of for many decades. The graphic design of the front cover further reinforces this effect. In the middle is a circle in which a rice bowl is flanked by a pair of chopsticks on one side and a knife and fork on the other. Outside the circle on the left is printed "50 lbs." and on the right "22.68 kg." Whereas the choice between chopsticks and knife and fork, or between the British weight measure system and the International System, is available for Chinese Canadians, a sense of double cultural identity is indicated as a sign of reterritorialization, especially in the birth of Chinese Canadian literature marked by the publication of this anthology. The first part of the title, "*INALIENABLE*," is placed around the top curve of the circle, and the second part, "*RICE*," is at the bottom. At the top edge of the cover is the advertisement, "*EXTRA FANCY*," inserted between three Chinese characters of equivalent meaning. At the bottom of the cover, following the description "packed for" appears the subtitle of the anthology: "*A CHINESE & JAPANESE CANADIAN ANTHOLOGY*." This cover design burdens an ethnic icon with tongue-in-cheek overtones to such an extent as to elicit a reaction against the interpretation of ethnicity as either inferior or superior. The 8 1/2 x 11-inch size of *Inalienable Rice* resembles more the format of a magazine than a conventional book. Its six-hundred-copy edition indicates the limitation of a community-based mode of production, marketing and readership. However, the birth of a new literary voice is fully signified in its publication.

Compared with *Inalienable Rice, Many-Mouthed Birds* demonstrates, intrinsically and extrinsically, a more professional mode of production. A long list of acknowledgements at the beginning of the book indicates some of the accomplishments of the writers in the anthology: excerpts from Sky Lee's novel *Disappearing Moon Cafe* (1990), from Fred Wah's Governor-General's Literary Award winner *Waiting for Saskatchewan* (1985), from other poetry and short-story collections, and from *Inalienable Rice* are anthologized here to present the scope and the development of Chinese Canadian literature. Contributors represent writers who live or have lived across Canada, as well as those who have come from various countries of birth. The cover design consists of a colour photograph of an Oriental face partially shaded among some leaves, and a 5 1/2 x 8 1/2-inch hardcover size fits the anthology neatly into a bookshelf. The title, "*Many-Mouthed Birds*," placed at the top of the cover, is well balanced by the position of the subtitle, "*CONTEMPORARY WRITING BY CHINESE CANADIANS*," printed with the editors' names near the bottom of the cover. As a metaphor, "many-mouthed birds" is no longer part of the cover photo, the icon. The phrase, which originates in Chinese and is translated into English, suggests a linguistic appropriation, an example of making English bear a linguistic characteristic from Chinese. Moreover, because the modifier "many-mouthed" and the modified "birds" are both plural in meaning and form, the title embraces plurality.

Many-Mouthed Birds entered mainstream literary production with advantages that *Inalienable Rice* lacked. That the second anthology was jointly published by Douglas and McIntyre (Vancouver and Toronto) and the University of Washington Press suggests its potential readership in both countries. The extrinsic advantages, provided by the professional mode of production and distribution, join the intrinsic features of the anthology to authenticate the collective signature "Chinese Canadians" on the cover of *Many-Mouthed Birds*.

Inalienable Rice and *Many-Mouthed Birds* entered mainstream Canadian literature to challenge the hegemony of the "monolithic, exclusionary systems of authority" conveyed by some of the existing Canadian anthologies, in particular, as Alan R Knight observes, by poetry anthologies (149). Knight further summarizes the hegemonic practices in Canadian poetry anthologies: "They exclude; they make a dyadic distinction between inside and outside. They leave no room for other systems or models" (149). The multigenre configuration in the two Chinese Canadian anthologies represents a different anthologizing model which aims at a plurality. And these two anthologies also reject the kind of patronizing practice that marginalizes minority writings, as exemplified in *Volvox: Poetry from the Unofficial Languages of Canada . . . in English Translation* (1971), edited by J Michael Yates. The choice of "unofficial", probably to create an ironic reference to the official language policy in Canada, inevitably backfires at those who chose to write in the heritage language. Also patronizing is the fact that the poets' original writings were excluded; the only valid versions of their voices were the English translations. The lack of an introduction that could have explained some of the issues, such as why the anthology was compiled, why its title was chosen, and why the original writings in the heritage languages were not included, further undermines the value of the publication by dismissing any collective efforts of the poets. In contrast, the fact that *Inalienable Rice* and *Many-Mouthed Birds* were both published and introduced by writers from the Chinese Canadian Writers' Workshop illustrates the strength of a community-based minority literature.

The publications of *Inalienable Rice* and *Many-Mouthed Birds* were long-awaited historical events for the community. They signified the collective social advancement and cultural development of contemporary Chinese Canadians. As landmark publications, they have helped to reclaim the community history, to define and redefine the Chinese Canadian identity in a dynamic community. As part of Chinese Canadian literature, the two anthologies join all other individual writings to make English bear witness to Chinese Canadian experiences. While the power of English is appropriated by Chinese Canadian writings, the anthology form is politicized; its traditional hegemony, founded on supposedly pure literary merits, is contested.

4. *Mythologizing the Collective History and Reclaiming "Chinamen":* Tales from Gold Mountain

The Chinese have cultivated the soil, raised vegetables, are employed in tanneries and at the canneries, in boot and shoe making, some in coal and gold mining and other labours. Having done these things, they have benefited the country. They have been producers—the one thing the country stands in need of.

Royal Commission 1885, p. 56

Folklore is that part of a people's culture which is preserved, consciously or unconsciously, in beliefs and practices, customs and observances of general currency; and in myths, legends and tales of common acceptance; and in arts and crafts which express the temper and genius of a group rather than of an individual.

THEODOR H GASTER, *The Standard Dictionary of Folklore, Mythology, and Legend, p. 399*

Canadian literature is said to be haunted by a "lack of ghosts."[1] In an article published in *Saturday Night*, Margaret Atwood, quoting Earle Birney at the beginning of her essay, takes issue with him regarding details of a many-faced, man-eating ghost figure called "Wendigo," a folklore character from the native tradition (81–90). While Atwood's equation between ghosts and folklore will be borrowed here, one questions whether Canadian literature is traditionally impoverished by a lack of multicultural folklores. According to folklorist Edith Fowke, the Canadian Centre for Folk Culture Studies was established in the 1970s to collect materials from various ethnic groups in addition to the Natives and the two founding nations. As a result, materials have been collected from over seventy different groups in Canada (270).

While folklore is an umbrella term that is widely used but difficult to define, the twenty-one folklorists in *The Standard Dictionary of Folklore, Mythology, and Legend* seem to agree in their contributions to the entry of "folklore." They propose an inclusive rather than exclusive approach to folklore, especially to its vast cultural application and media involvement. One is convinced from this that further distinction between myths, legends, folktales, and anecdotes, which are of primary importance to folklore (Leach 399), is almost unnecessary. Some of the definitions also include folk beliefs, superstitions, rhymes, folk songs, riddles, and proverbs. The medium involvement is as wide as the form and content: memories, storytelling, jokes, written records, dances, songs, crafts, arts, clothes, rituals, etc. (399).

While some critics adopted "motif" as a classifying principle to analyze folklore (Thompson 10; Baughman xi), Fowke uses a different principle in her book, *Folklore of Canada* (1976). She argues: "Although some national anthologies arrange the material by regions, in Canada it is more practical to arrange it by ethnic origin; hence there are sections on the native peoples, Canadiens, Anglo-Canadians, and the Canadian mosaic" (11). In her anthology, Fowke explains that the two criteria for her selections are "the size of the group, and the length of time it has been established in Canada. Our aim is to emphasize the traditions that have been preserved, adapted, or created in this country" (270). Her principles sound fair and reasonable because they emphasize the development of ethnic folk cultures in Canada after the groups have achieved reterritorialization. According to Fowke's two criteria, folk material from the Chinese Canadians should have been included. It is difficult to tell then why her anthology does not include them.

Facing the general lack of folk material about the Chinese community in Canada's archives and collections, contemporary Chinese Canadian writers have had to go further than traditional folklorists. They become the myth-makers themselves. This chapter focuses on Paul Yee's *Tales from Gold Mountain: Stories of the Chinese in the New World* (1989); it examines how Yee employs legend and myth to construct Chinese Canadian experience and cultural values. In his collection of tales, Yee develops a historic Gold Mountain milieu, a heroic journey motif, and a characterization of Chinese immigrants; he also records the adaptation of traditional Chinese culture to the

Canadian environment. The collection is illustrated by Simon Ng with powerful folk paintings to enhance the heroic images of the early immigrants and to emphasize the development of a minority people. While the stories contextualize the unrecognized contributions made by the Chinese immigrants to the development of the West Coast, they add an important missing chapter to Canada's cultural heritage. By writing the Chinese Canadian experience into the narrative of legend and myth, *Tales from Gold Mountain* helps to enrich the existing collection of Canadian folklore with an Asian origin and experience.

Yee's tales illustrate the discursive strategy in Chinese Canadian literature, which involves decoding the limited historical data and rewriting the collective experience. As a historian involved in the exhibition organized by the Chinese Cultural Centre (CCC) to celebrate Vancouver's centennial in 1986, Yee published *Salt Water City: An Illustrated History of the Chinese in Vancouver* in 1988, which included two hundred photographs and many first-person recollections of the community's past. Since it was the first time that many of the photographs were reproduced, the book constitutes the initial retelling of Chinese Canadian experiences by members of the community. The use of photographs and memories as document employs a strategy of testimony; it also rebuilds the community archives and therefore the community history. As historical photographs are always used by historians for anthropological and ideological justifications, the significant difference made by the CCC exhibition and Yee's subsequent publication of *Salt Water City* is that they entitled members of the Chinese Canadian community to re-decipher the photographs.

The connection between *Saltwater City* and *Tales from Gold Mountain* partakes in the intimate relationship between history and folk literature, such as legend and mythology. Discussing such a connection, Roland Barthes points out: "It is human history which converts reality into speech, and it alone rules the life and death of mythical language. Ancient or not, mythology can only have an historical foundation, for myth is a type of speech chosen by history" (110). Yee confirms the historical nature of his Gold Mountain tales: "These stories came out of my work in Canadian history, but they are part of the American past, too" (Afterword 63); he also points out that his resources include "old dates and dusty numbers" in the archives, as well as oral materials kept in the community, "memories . . . so sad and bitter that many want to forget them" (Afterword 63-64). Since history and myth are interrelated, the CCC's photo exhibition and Yee's subsequent publication provide him with the best materials for legendary and mythical fabrications.

Tales from Gold Mountain helps construct spatially and contextually what was missing from Canadian legend and myth—the minority Canadian experience. Based on the community's collective experience, these tales contest the proprietorship of Canadian folklore and history. According to Barthes,

> myth has the task of giving an historical intention a natural justification, and making contingency appear eternal.
>
> The world . . . comes out of myth as a harmonious display of essences. A conjuring trick has taken place; it has turned reality inside out, it has emptied it of history and has filled it with nature, it has removed from things their human meaning so as to make them signify a human insignificance. The function of myth is to empty reality. (142-43)

Yee's tales challenge the naturalizing effects of myth. These oppositional strategies start with foregrounding "Gold Mountain" in the title and then developing it into a milieu for all the stories.

Capturing the popular historical phrase *Gum-shan*, or "Gold Mountain," from the community's oral tradition, Yee uses it directly in the title of his collection. As a key signifier in the Chinese North American imagination, the phrase "Gold Mountain" stands as a historical testimonial. As a metaphor, the phrase connotes a romantic dream in a mythical land; and, to some extent, it is this romantic connotation that continues to signify opportunity and prosperity to generations of Chinese immigrants. As a historical term, "Gold Mountain" embraces the whole geographic area of North America, to which immigrants from all over the world come to explore its meaning and reality. In addition to its key-word position in the title, "Gold Mountain" as a Chinese immigrants' historical perspective of North America is also structured in the framework of Yee's book. The collection, which begins with "Spirits of the Railway" and ends with "The Revenge of the Iron Chink," emphasizes the historical presence of the Chinese immigrants in pioneer projects of the CPR and the BC salmon industry. This thematic framework contextualizes, thus testifies to, the unrecognized historical contributions made by the Chinese labourers to the frontiers of Gold Mountain.

Yee develops a Gold Mountain milieu from the following two perspectives: the physical world and the sociohistorical environment. Since the physical world is what traditional legendary heroes in myth have to face, Yee depicts the unfriendly physical environment as an initial challenge in "Spirits of the Railway":

> On both sides of the rushing river, gray mountains rose like walls to block the sky. The rock face dropped into ragged cliffs that only eagles could ascend and jutted out from cracks where scrawny trees clung. Never before had he [Young Chu] seen such towering ranges of dark raw rocks. (12)

However, this is not the only difficulty that challenges the Chinese heroes and heroines. Yee also depicts society, especially its racist discrimination, as the ultimate human hardship that the Chinese labourers have to endure. The social milieu is recounted directly in the workers' first-person voice to Young Chu, who came from China to look for his father at the CPR in the 1880s. The angry workers speak in a chorus: "My uncle was killed in a dynamite blast. No one warned him about the fuse." "The white boss treats us like mules and dogs!" "They need a railway to tie this nation together, but they can't afford to pay decent wages" (12). While the direct speech gives the tale an immediate personal perspective, the chorus recovers the collective voice and experience of the Chinese labourers, which are silenced in Canadian history.

"The Revenge of the Iron Chink," which closes the collection, contextualizes both the physical and the sociohistorical milieu of "Gold Mountain" in a fashion similar to "Spirits of the Railway." The writer depicts the BC salmon factory as another frontier industry in Gold Mountain about which the Chinese community has some collective memories. Yee describes the fish canneries as a wonderland initially:

> In the old days, all up and down the west coast of the New World, at the mouths of mighty rivers, scores of fish canneries, bigger than barns, sat perched over the water. When the tide went out, the canneries looked like huge caterpillars—long rusty roofs of corrugated tin covered plank board bodies that stretched over hundreds of stilt-like legs. (59)

However, this legendary setting clashes with the dehumanizing social environment captured in the story. An automatic canning machine, named "the Iron Chink" by the racist management, eats up hundreds of jobs held by Chinese cannery workers with a monstrous speed.

Yee also depicts what Chinese immigrants have experienced collectively in the Canadian job market. In "Friends of Kwan Ming," Kwan Ming and three other young men arrive in Vancouver in the same ship to look for their fortunes. ". . . everyone scattered throughout the port city to search for work. Kwan Ming hurried to the warehouse district, to the train station, and to the waterfront, but doors slammed in his face because he was Chinese" (27). Only jobs in the service industry are available to the Chinese since they appear less desirable to white men in general; Kwan Ming and his three friends find jobs as bakery worker, tailor's apprentice, innkeeper, and houseboy.

In addition to the CPR, the general labour market, and the salmon industry, which constitute part of the Gold Mountain milieu, Yee describes the historical development of the North American Chinatown as both conditioned and constructed by the dominant culture. "Gambler's Eyes" depicts the historical Chinese gambling halls, which provided recreational activities to the Chinese labourers because they were forbidden to enter mainstream entertainment facilities for many years. Yet, ironically, gambling halls in Chinatown were not free of discriminatory practices. The tale describes a blind gambler who travels from Chinatown to Chinatown, visiting gambling halls and winning wagers at the fan-tan tables. Eventually he is considered bad luck by other gamblers who forbid him to enter their gambling halls. The blind gambler then opens his eyes, revealing their "blue-green flashes—blue as sky, green as pine" (44). The blind man is not blind at all; he is a Eurasian. Again Yee chooses both the first-person voice and direct speech for the "blind" gambler to voice his experience as a Eurasian. Being shunned as a visible minority by the Chinese majority in Chinatown and by the Caucasian majority in Canadian society, the Eurasian has to hide behind "blindness" in order to survive:

> "When I was a child," he continued, "I could go nowhere with eyes like these. Storekeepers turned way. Children danced circles around me. White and Chinese alike, they mocked my mixed blood. So I shut my eyes and I opened my ears. As long as no one saw my eyes, they let me by." (44)

The Eurasian experience witnesses xenophobia and racism in Chinatown as part of Canadian society. With this well-situated irony, "Gambler's Eyes" is a self-examination of the Chinese Canadian community.

"Ginger for the Heart" and "Forbidden Fruit," which portray gender relationships in traditional Chinese culture, convey another important aspect of the Gold Mountain milieu from within the community. Using a romantic plot and similar narrative structure, Yee contrasts a nameless male character in "Ginger for the Heart" with a nameless female character in "Forbidden Fruit." In the former, the nameless male character exerts power over his female partner, Yenna, when he throws her love token, a piece of ginger, into the fire. Even if Yenna is portrayed as an independent and decisive character, her lover still attempts to control her simply because she is female. On the other hand, the nameless female character in "Forbidden Fruit" has no voice at all, nor any power. Throughout the tale, she remains silent in her relationship with her father, while the latter decides that she is not going to marry her lover. The power relationship between male and female in these stories indicate gender oppression in Gold Mountain. In direct speech, Yenna in "Ginger for the Heart" questions this male-oriented social order, in which Chinese women are kept at a subordinate position. Her voice cries out for change: "this is a new land . . . [m]ust we forever follow the old ways?" (38). The same message is issued in "Forbidden Fruit" with the death of the nameless female character. Positioning gender oppression with racism, xenophobia, the labour market, and other frontier experiences, Yee unfolds a multi-dimensional milieu in *Tales from Gold Mountain*. It is in this highly politicized sociohistorical milieu that the experiences of the Chinese Canadians is mythologized as a heroic journey in the New World.

Joseph Campbell notes that "father quest is a major hero adventure for young people" (129). Yee loads his character Young Chu's journey along the CPR construction sites with two tasks: one, to look for his father and two, to cross the traditional mythological threshold in order to achieve maturity. However, instead of contrasting the individual hero with the supporting characters, Yee positions Young Chu in a heroic group and highlights the collective heroism of the Chinese labourers. Using near rhyme and the classical poetic device of alliteration, Yee ritualizes the heroic crew:

> The crew pitched their tents and began to work. They *hacked* at *hills* with *hand-scoops* and *shovels* to *level* a pathway for the train. Their hammers and *chisels chipped* boulders into gravel and fill. Their *dynamite* and *drills thrust tunnels* deep into the mountain [emphases mine]. (12)

Here poetic devices magnify both the challenging wilderness and the heroic spirits of the railway builders, and at the same time they testify to Chinese labourers' deeds as nation-builders.

Yee also adopts and adapts the traditional ghost story to capture the horror of the accidents and the mistreatment of the Chinese workers at the CPR. Young Chu's determination to find his father leads him eventually to a half-finished tunnel haunted by ghosts. It is inside the tunnel that Young Chu finds his dead father in a pair of "blood-stained trousers and a mud-encrusted jacket" (14). In order to produce a first-person testimony to the horrifying accidents at the CPR, Yee makes the ghost speak directly. Farmer Chu's ghost speaks to his son about the hazardous conditions at the CPR which caused his death and about the white management's treatment of the Chinese, even the dead ones:

> His father's voice quivered with rage. "I am gone, but I am not done yet. My son, an accident here killed many men. A fuse

> exploded before the workers could run. A ton of rock dropped on us and crushed us flat. They buried the whites in a churchyard, but our bodies were thrown into the river, where the current swept us away. We have no final resting place." (14)

The ghost's account recovers the horror of numerous unrecorded accidents at the CPR; moreover it blends the heroic myth of "the father quest" with "the bone-hunting journey," a widely employed trope in Chinese Canadian literature. Young Chu's search for his father's bones symbolizes the journey undertaken by contemporary Chinese Canadians in search of the community history. "The bone-hunting journey" deconstructs the romantic connotation of Gold Mountain by unveiling historical racism and its victims; it also enhances the mythical aspect of Gold Mountain, filling it with ghosts refusing to be buried before their stories are heard.

Yee seeks a "final resting place" for the Chinese heroes in folk literature. "Spirits of the Railway" performs a symbolic burial ritual for the Chinese labourers who died in the accidents at the CPR; Farmer Chu's ghost instructs his son to perform the following ceremony:

> "Take chopsticks; they shall be our bones. Take straw matting; that can be our flesh. Wrap them together and tie them tightly. Take the bundles to the mountain top high above the nests of eagles, and cover us with soil. Pour tea over our beds. Then we shall sleep in peace." (15)

The metaphorical burial with chopsticks for the bones and straw for the flesh continues to underline the key signifier, "the bones," while suggesting that a symbolic burial may help to honour those who were wronged in history. The burial ground chosen by the ghost, at a height "above the nests of eagles," indicates an ancient ceremony of hero-worshipping; its detailed process, such as "cover us with soil" and "pour tea," signifies a sacred ritual for future tribal rebirth. Since burial rituals join the living with the dead in a continuous life circle, honouring the Chinese labourers at the CPR helps contemporary Chinese Canadians reclaim their heroic ancestors. Emerging from the tunnel after receiving instructions from his father's ghost, Young Chu matures as a leader. His transformation into leadership bears a resemblance to the conventions of the heroic myth.

Yee ends the tale with a genuine, mythical conclusion. After Young Chu performs the Chinese burial rituals on the mountain top, which becomes symbolically a monument dedicated to the Chinese labourers at the CPR, the rope he uses for climbing down the mountain subsequently transforms into a giant snake, a legendary dragon, ascending back to the mountain top to guard the graves. The transformation of the rope into a mythical creature signifies a discursive transcendence of the spirits after the burial rituals are properly performed in the language of folklore.

Using similar strategy, Yee constructs other tales in the collection in various Gold Mountain settings. In the closing tale, "The Revenge of the Iron Chink," instead of representing the Chinese cannery workers as mere victims of industrialization, Yee depicts the solidarity of the workers. Lee Jim, head of the Chinese crew, decides to teach the racist boss a lesson after his crew has lost its jobs to the automatic canning machine. The white manager is shocked to hear from Lee Jim that in the case of the fine salmon canned by "the Iron Chink" as a special gift for the Queen of England, Her Majesty will find Lee Jim's little fingers (62). "The Revenge of the Iron Chink" is a crude verbal joke; yet its punchline, that Jim's fingers are not in the cans, foregrounds the workers' struggle. Through this depiction, Yee positions the Chinese cannery workers in BC labour history and further in the resistant postcolonial world.

While the structure of the collection, represented by the beginning and ending stories, embodies Chinese immigrants' historical contribution to BC industry, the six tales framed in the middle of the collection cover two different aspects of Chinese settlement in North America. "Sons and Daughters," "Ginger for the Heart," and "Forbidden Fruits" challenge traditional male-oriented Chinese cultural practices; "The Friends of Kwan Ming," "Gambler's Eyes," and "Rider Chan and the Night River" render more representations of the Chinese immigrants on the frontiers. "Sons and Daughters" describes a rich Vancouver merchant Moy's moral dilemma caused by his abandonment of his twin baby daughters at birth and his simultaneous purchase of twin baby boys. Later in the tale, with Moy's purchased twin sons being sent back to China to look for wives after they grow up, Yee embeds the historical sex ratio imbalance among the Chinese in Canada. Since there were fewer Chinese women for marriageable Chinese men in Canada, many men had to go back to China to find wives, if they could afford the cost. The subtlety in Yee's use of historic data to build the Gold Mountain milieu politicizes the tale, and cuts like a double-edged sword against both gender and racial inequality.

In "Rider Chan and the Night River," Yee sketches Chinese participation in the exploration of the West Coast through Rider Chan's route as a courier: "It was his job to visit all the mining claims, all the shanty towns, and all the riverside camps throughout the gold countries" (53-54). The tale creates a Chinese frontier hero. Like a Western hero, Rider Chan is "strong, husky, honest and fearless" (53); he rides a swift gray horse; he helps the elderly and the needy; and he guards the moral order of Gold Mountain. Even the water spirit, who poisons Rider Chan's greedy brother and is killed by him, respects Rider Chan. Alluding to the Western genre, "Rider Chan and the Night River" verifies a minority hero on the frontiers and traces the presence of the Chinese in the New World back to the days of the Gold Rush. Overall, the six tales in the middle of the collection depict important aspects of Chinese cultural development in North America.

The tales are all illustrated by Simon Ng. The graphic images enhance the collective values produced by the texts. With folk-painting techniques, Ng highlights the visibility of the Chinese, such as their facial features—the slanting eyes and the light copper-colour skin. Ng also emphasizes the fashions of the Chinese in the nineteenth century, for example their hairstyle with the shaved front part of the head and a pigtail. By presenting these visible Chinese traits, Ng's iconography reclaims the innocence of their skin colour and hair style, which were read as signs of an alien and inferior race in Canadian history.[2]

Furthermore, Ng positions the Chinese heroes and heroines in the landscapes, establishing their presence within the physical settings of the Gold Mountain milieu. In "Spirits of the Railway" for example, Ng paints high mountain peaks in the background, a locomotive and a team of Chinese railway builders in the middle ground; while Young Chu's broad bare shoulders are positioned in the foreground, a sledgehammer in his hand portrays his role at the CPR as a nation-builder. For "The Gambler's Eyes," the gambling hall is sketched merely as a dark space filled up by the gambler's face. On the face is a pair of eye sockets painted blue and green and without eyeballs. Staring at the reader in the upper middle ground of the illustration, these empty sockets pose a poignant question to the viewer: Why is a Eurasian discriminated against in Canadian society?

Overall Ng uses the foreground and middle ground, especially the latter, to portray the heroes and the heroines, while the background space is employed consistently to construct either the physical setting or the sociohistorical milieu of Gold Mountain. Despite the fact that painting is a different medium from writing, Ng's illustrations play a constitutive part in assigning agents' roles to the Chinese characters and in rendering their perspectives of Canadian history legitimate. As part of the signifying process, Ng's paintings enact the role of certain graphics that Barthes calls "a kind of writing" and further "like writing, they call for a *lexis*" (110). Together with Yee's well-chosen lexicon, Ng's depiction and composition explore the power of the graphic arts in order to highlight the folk tales.

Regarding the role played by legend and myth in society, Joseph Campbell points out that they play a major role in "supporting and validating a certain social order" (31). "One thing that comes out in myths, . . . is that at the bottom of the abyss comes the voice of salvation" (39). The reason that legend and myth can convey "salvation" to those contextualized is because they verify the speaking subjects and the related history depicted in the context. *Tales from Gold Mountain* helps settle the ghosts, bury the bones, and revive the lost voices. "The salvation voice" merging from legend and myth as predicted by Campbell goes beyond the covers of the book. First of all, it helps the Chinese Canadian community reclaim its collective history and its Canadian identity. Secondly, with Chinese Canadians entering Canadian folklore, Gold Mountain legends challenge the existing body of Canadian folk literature. Furthermore, rather than being "emptied" of its history and filled with "nature," or being "removed" from "their human meaning" to "signify a human insignificance" as theorized by Barthes and quoted at the beginning of this chapter (142-43), Yee's folk tales give the voice back to those who were silenced in history.

Rewriting minority experience in various cultural forms, such as folklore, manifests how the marginalized people turn their historical silence and otherness into a meaningful asset and how they fight back against institutional forgetfulness. Such practice is not always recognized by mainstream critics. Ironically, in a promotion of Canadian multicultural literatures, the editor-in-chief of *The Canadian Fiction Magazine*, Geoff Hancock, who interviewed Paul Yee for an entry in *Other Solitudes: Canadian Multicultural Fictions* edited by Linda Hutcheon and Marion Richmond, continues to show a lack of interest in minority Canadian writings. The following is an excerpt from Hancock's interview with Paul Yee concerning the classifications of *Tales from Gold Mountain*:

> *Yet your book* Tales from Gold Mountain *uses Chinese tales and mythology.*
>
> That's a major confusion. When I wrote those tales, I was not writing Chinese mythology. I have not read a great deal of Chinese literature. My stories and tales came very much out of BC's history of industrial capitalism, and labour force, racism, the landscape, and the everyday folk culture that my people brought over here. The stories also came out of reading of Western folklore: Little Red Riding Hood, Hansel and Gretel, Sleeping Beauty. Book reviews have all commented on the Chinese tradition in my work, but I was not writing in a "Chinese" tradition; I was writing in a Western tradition.
>
> *Why was it important to write these stories for children?*
>
> I didn't write them for children; I was writing tales for anybody who wanted to read stories. I was writing to make history more accessible to more people. I do have a pedagogical motivation in all my writing. I want to teach things. Adults are resistant. Children are the future and they ought to recognize what the Chinese have done in Canada. It's the next generation that will change the social fabric of this country. (346)

Hancock's (mis)classification of a Canadian writer seems to be based primarily on an implied reading of the Anglicization of the writer's last name rather than the context of the stories. As an authority figure of an established Canadian literary institution, Hancock's mispositioning of Yee's tales with Chinese literature rather than with Canadian literature continues the historical stereotyping of non-white Canadians as aliens by mainstream Canadians. Secondly, Hancock's categorization of Yee's collection under children's literature instead of the genres of legend and myth, further trivializes the significance of *Tales from Gold Mountain* by dismissing its possible wider readership. Hancock's critical criteria speak to the lack of institutional acknowledgment of Chinese Canadian literature and constitute a mainstream negation of minority Canadian writings.

Yee's correction makes a political statement for all minority Canadian writers working in English. His clarification that he was "writing in a Western tradition," that he "didn't write [the tales] for children" but "for anybody who wanted to read stories" directly resists being marginalized by the mainstream critic. Furthermore, Yee's explanation that he "was writing to make history more accessible to more people" and "to teach things" to the public shows his awareness of the power of legend and myth. Yee wants to bring what Campbell calls the "light of salvation" to the future generations of this country, hoping that they will be able to share the kind of Canadian experiences that are perceived today as merely minority experiences. The reason why Yee chose this popular form is also made explicit here: pedagogically, folklore is more accessible than history for readers of any age. Legend and myth employ descriptive narrative, use enlargement techniques, and draw intertextuality from the existing motifs, such as the heroic journey and the father quest in Yee's tales, features that make folklore more feasible to be employed by minority Canadian writers to inscribe their cultural experiences.

Discursively, then, *Tales from Gold Mountain* is an ideological campaign. The collection exemplifies another endeavour of the community-based Chinese Canadian writers and myth-makers. The eight legendary tales and their illustrations help bring back the lost voices and banished ghosts from the community's unrecorded past. By developing a Gold Mountain milieu, Yee's tales contextualize the historical testimony embedded in the photographs collected in *Saltwater City*. Using direct speech, chorus, other narrative and structural devices, Yee empowers the Chinese characters and makes them the speaking subjects and historical agents in related events. With the help of Ng's illustrations, *Tales from Gold Mountain* effectively challenges the racial stereotype of "Chinamen" constructed by the dominant media and racist immigration documents. By ritualizing the historical experience of Chinese immigrants in English, *Tales from Gold Mountain* contextualizes the political, economic, marital, and familial status of early Chinese immigrants in North America. While the composition of the collection appeals to a wider readership, it posts, politically and aesthetically, a challenge to Canadian literature and folklore.

5. Bachelor-Man: *"A Silence Crying Out to Be Broken" in Canadian Theatre*

I had a woman's dreams! . . . I dreamt of a place where man is man and woman is woman, where that is understood with no deviousness. Where it is that simply with no confusions. Where eyes can meet and nothing else need to be said . . . I dreamt of a place where the nights are silken and where a man's touch brings no pain. I dreamt of a place where the nights are like velvet and where there are mutual shoulders for weary heads . . . where there are no dogs barking and no baby girls screaming atop garbage heaps . . .!

. . . I dreamt of love!

WINSTON CHRISTOPHER KAM, *Bachelor-Man*

Describing women's actions is not enough. In order for a feminist perspective to emerge, women themselves must be heard, must put their bodies and their words on the stage and on the page.

GAYAL AUSTIN, *Feminist Theories for Dramatic Criticism*

A BRIEF SYNOPSIS OF BACHELOR-MAN by the Playwright

Bachelor-Man is about a group of Chinese men who are forced to re-examine their relationships with their women and, in the process, learn about themselves.

The play is set in Toronto on Dominion Day, July 1, 1929. Six years previously, in 1923, the government had passed the Chinese Exclusion Act which curtailed further immigration of the Chinese to Canada. For those Chinese already here, mostly men, it meant a life without their women and families.

It is against this backdrop of the Exclusion Act and the Dominion

Day Parade outside that the play takes place. These men must cope without their women; they are the victims of white racism and they suffer an acute sense of alienation from the world at large. Theirs is an intense struggle to find a measure of self-worth and belonging in Gold Mountain.

This, however, can only be attained through some self-awareness. Queenie and her tragic life personifies that self-awareness. She is a mirror through which the men are forced to reexamine certain cultural traditions that have shaped their relationships with women. To their horror, they discover that these relationships were sometimes terrifying. They must confront the truth that they are no better and no worse than the whites who have pushed them into their ghettoes.

The play is gritty, but ends on a positive note. The men, through Queenie, rediscover the elemental beauty within themselves, a beauty which underscores a fragile humanity so common to all peoples.

—Winston Christopher Kam, 1985.

A Production Note

Bachelor-Man is a three-act play. All three acts are set on the same day, July 1, 1929, and in the same stage setting: the ground floor of John's tea/boarding house in Toronto's Chinatown.

Setting: the interior of a simple Chinese tea/boarding house; on the right-hand side corner there is a flight of stairs leading to upstairs bedrooms. In the main area, there is a counter; pots and pans are behind the counter on the wall; cups and teapots are on the counter; a table and a few chairs are arranged in the middle of the area.

Six actors: among them, one is much older and the other one much younger than the rest, who are middle aged; one disabled man with one arm.

Two actresses: both are middle aged; since they never meet, the roles can be cast on the same person.

*

In the history of English Canadian theatre, the few non-white heroes and heroines on the stage before the 1980s, such as Rita Joe and Louis Riel, were not created by playwrights from the communities depicted. Native and Métis heroes and heroines have been created, albeit only as tragic victims, but there have been to date very few mainstream English dramas involving Chinese characters as heroes or heroines. Yet Chinese characters have played minor roles to add decorative and exotic flavour to the drama. *The Stone Angel*, for example, adapted from Margaret Laurence's original novel and staged at Theatre Passe Muraille in 1992, depicts a minor Chinese character. Although the Chinese girl patient plays a foil and companion to Hagar, her role could probably be replaced by a young female character of any other race. Her Chinese ethnicity, however, does introduce a visible racial difference which helps portray the heroine, Hagar, especially her tolerance developed near the end of her life.

Confronting this mainstream theatrical tradition, in which Chinese characters play minor roles with little significance to their own development, *Bachelor-Man*, a three-act historical play written by Trinidad-born Chinese Canadian dramatist Winston Christopher Kam and produced by Theatre Passe Muraille in mid-November 1987, made a powerful breakthrough. *Bachelor-Man* put Chinese Canadian characters on the stage to tell stories about their own lives, thus marking "a silence crying out to be broken" (Kam 83, 93). This key line appears in the play twice and so articulates the thesis of this chapter.

Silence cries out from various aspects. First of all, in terms of subject matter, the play introduces Chinese Canadian experience into Canadian theatre, another mainstream discourse. Set in the ghettoes of Toronto's Chinatown in 1929, *Bachelor-Man* depicts the betrayal of Chinese immigrants by the Gold Mountain dream on the one hand, and on the other, it imposes a self-examination of the Chinese Canadian community by laying bare the internal silencing of women, gay men, Eurasians, and the disabled Chinese, all of whom are doubly discriminated against in Canadian society. However, *Bachelor-Man* is not just about silencing and the suffering of Chinese immigrants; as well, it is about a minority community that cannot be silenced any more. Using theatre, especially the theatrical conventions of mimesis, Kam stages the awakening of the Chinese Canadian community and its collective transition from silence to voice in Canadian society.

Kam's preference for drama is a discursive strategy. Since ancient times, the Aristotelian principle of dramatic mimesis[1] has been used by playwrights to stage a reinterpretation of history in order to reclaim a lost or denied identity. Following the communal tradition of drama, *Bachelor-Man* talks directly to the audience about Chinese Canadian history. By centring the play on a group of bachelors and two bound-feet women, the playwright reconstructs the isolation of Chinatown and its Gold Mountain dream. Moreover, by putting major historical events on the stage, such as the building of the CPR, Kam helps reclaim the community's collective contribution to Canada. And yet by having bound-feet Chinese immigrant women speak against their sexist male partners, Kam also makes the Chinese community reevaluate its own cultural baggage. *Bachelor-Man* examines some acute racial, cultural, and gender issues in Canadian society and gives voice to this silenced minority community, and especially to its doubly silencedmembers.

The subject matter of *Bachelor-Man* suggests a community-based Chinese Canadian drama. Set in a tea/boarding house in Toronto owned by a married bachelor named John, the play immediately provides the audience with a microcosm of the historical Chinatown and its bachelor society. More significantly, the historical time of the play is 1929, a dark era for Chinese immigrants, for it is six years after the Chinese Exclusion Act was passed by the Mackenzie King government and eighteen years before it was revoked.

From both the collective and individual perspectives, the playwright depicts how the Chinese were persecuted in Canada as a non-white, racial minority. The play begins on the morning of Dominion Day, 1929 with a newspaper headline highlighting the reinforcement of the anti-Chinese policy as a particular national-day holiday event: "Three wagonloads are taken in raid on Chinese club!" (Kam 3) Within this anti-Chinese social context, while the annual Dominion Day parade is taking place in the background, John's tea/boarding house becomes a hiding place for a group of Chinese bachelors. Inside the house, married bachelors recollect their fading memories about family life, while single men complain about their unfulfilled manhood. John, who knows that he will not be able to be reunited with his wife, shares her letter with his boarder, an old railway worker named Lian. Lian's is a typical life of the married bachelor: he has spent fifty years at the CPR, during which he has only visited his family in China twice—the first time for his wedding, and the second time for the birth of his first child. Kao, a native-born Chinese Canadian, who has lost an arm in World War One as a soldier in the

Canadian Forces, represents a different group of Chinese bachelors. Kao talks angrily about his disability, his bachelorhood and, above all, his resentment of the anti-Chinese national discourse. Though born in Canada, he is judged as unwanted because of his visible Chinese ethnicity: "There are too many reminders; the heat, the parade, July 1st . . . July 1st comes every year, you know. It's as certain as death. Only worse because it's always just around the corner waiting to mug you, and you know it" (15). By setting the play on July 1, which marks both Dominion Day and the Chinese Canadian Humiliation Day, Kam foregrounds the historical period during which the Chinese in Canada were collectively victimized.

The playwright also visualizes the historical survival of the Chinese bachelor community by creating a well-selected character profile and a close-knit relationship among the characters. The age gap among the six bachelors is set to suggest that at least three generations of bachelors regard John's tea/boarding house as their "home." Greeted as "Grandpa" by other boarders, Lian leads the bachelors in a practice of *Tai Chi* inside the tea/boarding house. As *Tai Chi* is normally practised in the open air, the fact that the characters are practising *Tai Chi* silently inside the house suggests a situational irony, emphasizing the conflict between the antagonistic social environment and the resistant Chinese community. The reiteration of the Dominion Day parade by different characters throughout the entire play produces a tension between the quietly shared *Tai Chi* exercises and the noisy goings on outside. While the former is a collective expression against anti-Chinese social pressure, the latter reinforces racist official discourse. Thus what is embedded in the contrasting atmosphere inside and outside of John's tea/boarding house suggests quite different racial experiences in Canada: while the Chinese were treated as an unwanted race, European Canadians were the race in power.

The play delivers historical evidence on the stage testifying to the betrayal of the Chinese immigrants by Gold Mountain. Although the play is set during a single day, the historical time touched by the characters' lives covers a period of half a century, from the mid-1880s to the late 1920s. Furthermore, with widely selected historical events, such as Chinese immigration, the CPR, head taxes, the immigrant detention camp, and the voluntary military service of the native-born

Chinese in the Canadian Forces in World War One, the playwright provides the audience with an opportunity to reread Chinese Canadian history. As a survivor of the CPR, Lian vividly remembers numerous unrecorded disasters:

> Dynamite! Explosions! Rocks! Pieces of flesh flying everywhere! Baskets tumbling down the cliff sides! Our brothers screaming . . . ! (*pause—softly*) And in the spring . . . in the spring . . . when the snow thawed, we'd find them . . . stiff and still clinging to their shovels . . . (44)

Lian also remembers a fellow Chinese labourer who is so homesick that one day he jumps into the ocean with a railway tie on his shoulders "sometimes I still see that man . . . under the ocean pounding spikes beneath the pounding waves building his railroad back to China" (42). John, owner of the tea/boarding house, points out to Lian that the latter is deceived by the Gold Mountain myth: "The Gold Mountain has betrayed you. You came here as a boy, you gave it your life, you built that damn railroad and look what's happened . . . ! There's nothing for you here!" (6) Canadian-born Kao is betrayed by Gold Mountain in a similar way: "I was born in this country and yet I needed a passport to live in it!" (13) Being a native-born Chinese, Kao is not exempted from racist discrimination, not even as a Canadian soldier fighting in WWI. In the trenches, he was not allowed by the white sergeant to bury the body of his friend: "Leave the fucking chink where he is!" (43) Since then Kao sees Gold Mountain as collective treachery against the Chinese: "I watch you brothers clambering off those ships eagerly paying your $500.00 to get to the Gold Mountain! And for what?" (13) "[W]hy did you come? The Gold Mountain is a lie! And you're fools all of you for believing in a lie" (42) Through personal experience, the playwright lodges a political campaign against national identity politics in Canada, which is historically based on white dominance.

Bachelor-Man also contextualizes personal life dilemmas in the Chinese community as a result of racial discrimination. In addition to exploiting the Chinese as cheap labourers on the frontiers, Gold Mountain betrays them in a personal way by keeping most of them bachelors for life without marital fulfilment. The playwright brings in the statistics of the sex ratio imbalance among the Chinese as a protest against the National Day celebration. A character, Asi, narrates the historical statistics of the Chinese population in Toronto in 1929: "There are about twenty-four hundred men and one hundred and fifty women in Toronto. Sixteen men to every woman . . . the Yin and Yang are out of balance" (36). Lian remembers a fellow named Yip who commits suicide in the immigrant detention camp by biting off his own tongue and swallowing it. Years later, bachelors in Chinatown still gossip sensationally about how Yip was killed by the pain in his loins because of the hardened semen. Kao uses a bitter self-mockery, "no arm, no woman" (13), to express his double loss as a native-born Chinese male trying to prove his loyalty to Canada. The above episodes, alluding to recognizable events in Chinese Canadian history, constitute the historic features of the play.

As a play, *Bachelor-Man* also complies with the basic features of Aristotelian tragedy.[2] Set in a period of less than twenty-four hours, and including the death of an innocent female character Mme Wu, *Bachelor-Man* not only depicts the tragedy of Chinese men who suffer both physical and psychological damage, but also portrays gender oppression as another human tragedy. It is through Mme Wu and her contemporary and successor Queenie that the playwright switches the focus of the play from bachelors to their female counterparts. By examining traditional Chinese cultural practice, the play discloses the "male homo-social connection" (Austin 48) as the social order in traditional Chinese culture.

By reconstructing the language spoken among the Chinese bachelors in the 1930s, the playwright unveils their various sexist practices against women. John and Lian, the two married bachelors with wives in China, simultaneously call their spouses their "rice-cookers" (5, 6, 52, 63). To the disabled veteran bachelor Kao, who is still a virgin, woman is a mystery. Asked by Kao to describe what a woman is, John and Lian choose to define a woman as part of the feudal marriage package created to serve her husband:

> JOHN: She makes you happy! She cooks your food! Washes your clothes! She happily inherits one-half of your problem . . .!
> LIAN: She gives you sons! The dream of every Chinese father! Sons. . .!

> JOHN: Big happiness . . .! Imagine, Kao. Imagine lying next to her, feeling her warmth, her soft skin against yours, tufts of hair as fine as silk . . . And her breasts! Like mounds of rice flour . . .
> LIAN: There's nothing like a woman, Kao. They are born to make us happy! (46-47)

The dialogue unmasks patriarchal social order and its male homo-social discourse. A married Chinese woman is expected to be a caretaker, a reproductive machine, a sexual toy and above all, an obedient wife—all to enable her husband's happiness. To further expose this male homo-social order, which is based on the possession and the exchange of women as gifts, Kam creates the tragic character of Mme Wu.

Mme Wu embodies the fate of traditional Chinese women, who were silenced at birth because of their gender. Her brief appearance on the stage in Act Two changes the focus of the play from the bachelors' lives to male-female relationships. The Wus are married through a traditional arrangement; the couple runs a small coffee shop in Toronto's Chinatown. When Mme Wu brings over a coffee ordered by a boarder in John's tea house, her appearance immediately sparks excitement among the bachelors. Nevertheless, instead of meeting her as a person, John greets her with a traditional male expression. In other words, instead of greeting Mme Wu, John greets Mr Wu's personal property: "Your husband is a lucky man, Mme Wu. To have a loyal wife like you . . . (*she tenses*). A totally obedient wife . . .? (*Suddenly she moans and covers her face with her hands. She trembles*)" (50). Kam uses his stage directions to further represent Mme Wu's life as a silence. Mme Wu responds to the bachelors' overwhelming interest in her presence with a whole paragraph of broken sentences, which suggest the quality of her life as a silenced object. The following paragraph speaks for the failure of her marriage and the Wus' cafe, her husband's self-oriented loyalty to Gold Mountain, and her faint hope for the future:

> You know . . . I . . . I've never been in a place like this . . . Never before . . . There're many places I've . . . I've never . . . oh . . . (*she chokes and her words fade. She looks around then in a strained voice*) It's so empty . . . Our cafe is empty too. Nobody comes to our

> cafe . . . Why is your teahouse so empty, brother John? I thought everyone likes you. You know how to please people. (*She begins to ramble haltingly*) I . . . Mr Wu . . . My husband? . . . he . . . he tries to please but he . . . he . . . Why does no one come to our cafe? . . . He's a . . . good . . . man . . . That's what they told me when we married! But . . . He . . . he's marching in the parade, you know. He's very proud of that . . . He wants to show his loyalty to the Gold Mountain so he's marching an entire block . . . He . . . he says it will make his life better . . . Oh! I hope so because then I . . . maybe I'll . . . (*pause*) It . . . it's always him . . . always him . . . always talking about himself . . . never . . . he . . . he . . . (*she chokes and suddenly darts for the door—fearfully*) Oh! I must go! He'll be looking for me . . .! (50–51)

The broken sentences in Mme Wu's one-and-only speech capture the silence and invisibility of the Chinese immigrant women in Canadian society. *Bachelor-Man* is one of the few plays that represents the dilemma of Chinese immigrant women before a Canadian audience.

However, Mme Wu is more than just a minor character who appears on the stage once and disappears for good. She is the playwright's theatrical prop. Her short visit in John's tea/boarding house reactivates the bachelors' earlier conversation about women, providing the playwright with an opportunity to expose the sexist nature of the bachelors' daily language. Mme Wu's visit reminds married bachelors Lian and John of their own "rice-cookers." Asi remembers his mother breast-feeding him and "[putting] beet sugar on her breasts" to make her milk taste sweeter (52). Other bachelors associate Mme Wu with a flower of their own choice, such as chrysanthemum or jasmine. While the bachelors see Mme Wu as a sexual being created to serve men, her broken sentences and her unbreakable silence on the stage indicate a traditional Chinese woman's dilemma in a patriarchal society and in its discourse. By staging Mme Wu's helplessness in such a society, in which she is disallowed any parts of speech except silence, *Bachelor-Man* presents racial discrimination and gender oppression as interwoven social practices.

However, Mme Wu's unique relationship with the bachelor characters makes her short visit, structually, a dramatic turning point for the development of the play. Following her appearance in John's tea/boarding house near the end of Act Two, the playwright not only shifts the focus of the play to male-female relationships, but also connects her with the Chinese women's collective. Although Mme Wu's untold experience is shared by generations of women, Chinese and otherwise, Kam chooses a prostitute named Queenie to voice the collective herstory. Queenie's double marginality, as a victim of sexism and as a social outcast, is employed in the play to help break through the historical silence endured by all women, especially obedient immigrant women like Mme Wu.

At first sight, Queenie appears to be Mme Wu's social and discursive opposite; however, as gender is an important part of speech in *Bachelor-Man* as in society, Queenie becomes Mme Wu's collective continuity. The connection between the two women characters is indicated in the transition of Queenie from a secondary character in Act One to a major role in Act Three, which is structurally scheduled after Mme Wu's short visit and disappearance from the stage for good in the last part of Act Two. After her transition from background to foreground, Queenie becomes the leading character in the play, as her name suggests. At the beginning of the play, when John opens the door of his tea/boarding house on the morning of Dominion Day, he calls Queenie a "smelly old hag" (Kam 7). But when the curtain rises for Act Three in the early evening of the same day, Queenie comes back to the tea house to challenge the male order. While resting her bound feet, she talks to the bachelors about traditional male-female relationships in Chinese culture. She points out the hypocrisy in the bachelors' self-pity, demonstrated by their hiding indoors on Dominion Day and their sense of superiority over their women: "I leave all the self-pity to you men. You plaster saints who have made it a part of your culture . . . Next to beating your women, self-pity is your favourite pastime" (63). After speaking out for the first time, Queenie's physical transition from background to foreground is followed by her identity transformation. She speaks no longer as a prostitute; instead, she speaks as a representative of the women's collective against gender oppression.

Queenie denounces the cultural and ritual activities that treat women as sexual commodities. She calls the bachelors' attention to a list of ritual events in Chinese culture in which women are physically crippled and sexually abused. The list is long enough to remind the bachelors of their personal involvement, such as binding women's feet, forcing grown-up women to marry boys, selling Chinese women in San Francisco, and even renting out one's wife for prostitution, an act which later causes Mme Wu's suicide. Queenie condemns John as an assimilated Christian pimp, "running this Christian whorehouse" (Kam 66) in his tea/boarding house. By examining these cultural activities, Kam points out that these traditions are not innate in humanity but are social and cultural practices constructed on the basis of gender inequality.

The connection between Queenie and Mme Wu is also embodied in the playwright's choice of the former as the messenger who delivers the news of Mme Wu's suicide. Queenie delivers her message in front of the bachelors:

> QUEENIE: . . . she's hanging from the rafters . . .
> JOHN: If this is a joke, Queenie . . .
> LIAN: But . . . why? Why would she do that?
> QUEENIE: She's a woman . . . (70)

Queenie's message underlines the collective experience shared by Chinese women. Furthermore, the playwright uses Kao's self-discovery to reveal the connection between gender oppression and the symbolic Oedipal relationship among men.

Feminist theorists inquiring about human relationships have repeatedly quoted Lévi Strauss's *The Elementary Structures of Kinship* on women being exchanged as gifts for male relationships rather than being partners in these exchanges. In her widely quoted article entitled "The Traffic in Women: Notes on the 'Political Economy of Sex,' " Gayle Rubin points out: "If it is women who are being transacted, then it is the men who give and take them who are linked, the women being a conduit of a relationship rather than a partner to it . . ." (174). Studying Lévi Strauss and Quebec drama in Canadian literature, Barbara Godard observes similarly: "the order of culture is founded on the exchange of women, a triangulation where woman is the token through which relations between men are enabled, an order of 'hom(m)osexuality' " (21). Godard further observes that the male homo-social connection is somewhat constituted by "the Oedipal configuration" in discourse (21), which homogenizes various social relationships with the dominant patrilineal paradigm of father and son.

Bachelor-Man displays the Oedipal relationship among the bachelors by unveiling their sexual lust for Mme Wu, and by exposing their common misconception of the female sex. Kao is shocked to discover that because of his complaints about his virginity, John and Lian have made an arrangement with Mr Wu to rent Mme Wu out for a night for him. Humiliated by her husband's willingness to make her a prostitute for money and for his friendship with other men, Mme Wu hangs herself. Ironically, John and Lian pay Mr Wu money taken from the boarders' daily donation, which is supposed to help pay passage fare for the wife of a married bachelor to come to Canada, in the event of the Chinese Exclusion Act being repealed. The irony is deepened when the two older men who made the arrangement for Kao show their total surprise and confusion when the latter is astonished and angry at them:

> LIAN: You don't understand . . . We did it for you, Kao . . . To help you. We don't want you to end up like the others . . . killing yourself . . .
> JOHN: Every day we watch you not knowing what to expect. You're always on the edge . . . doing crazy things . . . We were frightened for you. Can you blame us? We just wanted to help, that's all . . . It's the law, that's what! That damn law! (72)

The playwright uses the two older men's self-righteousness to underline the male homo-social connection as the cause of gender oppression of women. In the 1987 Theatre Passe Muraille production videotaped during a performance, the director inserted a powerful dramatic interlude between the curtains of Act Two and Act Three. Before the curtain falls at the end of Act Two, Mme Wu is seen standing on top of the roof of the Wus' Cafe. In the twilight of the evening, she is singing her swan song, sadly and helplessly, protesting against her life, being traded as a gift among men. When the curtain rises for Act Three, a mood of dramatic pathos hangs heavily in the air, creating the right atmosphere for Queenie to appear as a lead heroine.

As Mme Wu and Queenie are bound more by gender oppression

imposed on women than by gender itself, the dramatist inaugurates Queenie as the long-awaited heroine. Arising from Mme Wu's silence and suicide, Queenie comes forward to tell the stories of the Chinese women. Austin points out: "Describing women's actions is not enough. In order for a feminist perspective to emerge, women themselves must be heard, must put their bodies and their words on the stage and on the page" (40). By centring the second half of the play on Queenie, Kam puts the resistant voice of the Chinese women on the stage to reclaim the silenced herstory. Rather than ask the bachelors to pity Mme Wu, Queenie tells stories about her own life, which embody the untold stories of Mme Wu and many other Chinese women. Through Queenie's life stories, *Bachelor-Man* further addresses issues of the colonization of the female body and personal identity in patriarchal society. In her childhood, Queenie's feet were bound; her parents told her: " 'you'll advance in the world'; 'you'll have the prettiest of feet! You'll join the upper class!' . . . 'stand on the palms of emperors! . . . be a concubine! Of the emperor!' (74)" In her adolescence, her parents married her off to a wealthy old merchant in order "to settle for the second best" (75). In her adulthood, when she gave birth to her first daughter, she was immediately considered a failure by her husband, as was her baby daughter. Queenie remembers how death was awaiting the birth of her baby daughter:

> She was still moist, the cord still tied to her when he grabbed her by her tiny feet and tossed her into the garbage heap . . .! And all because she was a baby girl, a small happiness . . . (*pause*). I had failed, you see. As woman and wife. I didn't give him a baby boy! A precious baby boy . . .! (75)

After her baby girl's death, Queenie determines that she "is one piece of furniture you can't nail to the floor" (77) and runs away from her husband.

After a long journey from the gutters of Canton to the sidewalks of Gold Mountain, Queenie finds that she is still a sex slave. She has to wear a "corset" to make her "waist small and [her] breasts large" (85). Although Queenie shares the Gold Mountain dream with male immigrants of all nationalities, her dilemma is caused by sexual and racial discrimination. Queenie points out that the silencing of women saturates all cultural practices; as a result, many women are "born numb," and their "life is a general numbness":

> Sometimes even I wonder. Even as I sweep this floor on the Gold Mountain, I wonder. In the mornings, I wonder. At nights, I wonder . . . You never know for sure because all is confusion. And it's hard to think because your mind is not made to think . . . You see, you're born numb. Your life is a general numbness. You have an awareness and yet no awareness. You remember and you don't remember . . . (78)

Queenie's realization not only breaks through her own silence as a Chinatown prostitute but also the collective silence of the Chinese women, including Mme Wu. Through Mme Wu and Queenie, Kam puts the female body and herstory on the stage, thus concretizing the transition of Chinese women from subordination and silence to self-empowermen and voice.

The climax of *Bachelor-Man* occurs with Queenie's articulation of her dream as a battered woman. Instead of using dramatic action to bring the historical play to its climax, Kam employs the self-empowered Queenie to voice her dream, which includes a Canadian identity for immigrant women. This enunciation is made universal through Queenie's ironic self-deprecation of her own dream, which, however, is in fact a real dream for all women:

> *(a sudden self-deprecating laugh)* I had a woman's dreams! Fanciful dreams! I dreamt of romance! Oh! The conceit of this old cow! To dream of romance . . . ! I dreamt of a place where man is man and woman is woman, where that is understood with no deviousness. Where it is that simply with no confusions. Where eyes can meet and nothing else need to be said . . . *(short pause)* I dreamt of a place where the nights are silken and where a man's touch brings no pain. I dreamt of a place where the nights are like velvet and where there are mutual shoulders for weary heads . . . *(tremblingly)* where there are no dogs barking and no baby girls screaming atop garbage heaps . . .! *(pause)* Ha-ha-ha! I dreamt of love! Can you imagine me being loved? But . . . it's so important . . . to be loved . . . to know that you exist. (85)

Irony emerges from the difference between Queenie's daily life in the underworld of prostitution and her dream world where men and women are equals. Further irony derives from the poetic discourse used by the playwright to describe Queenie's dream world. Since Chinese women were not allowed to have their own dreams or ideals in feudal society, Queenie's articulation of her dream breaks through the symbolic order of the dominant discourse of her culture.

Queenie's suggestion "against tradition" (86) offers a political strategy for combating sexism and racism. She challenges the bachelors who are hiding inside John's tea/boarding house on Dominion Day and feeling sorry for each other as members of a deprived race. She calls upon the Chinese community to take public action in Canadian society:

> I knew then I wasn't going to hide any more feeling sorry for myself . . . I'll parade myself to the world . . . . Did any one of you see the parade this morning? I marched in that . . . . I wish Mme Wu was there with me . . . marching . . . on Humiliation Day . . . the day they took away your women . . . (86)

To demonstrate her pride as a Chinese immigrant woman, Queenie marches in the Dominion Day parade. This courage helps the community transform July 1 from Humiliation Day for Chinese immigrants to an antiracism and antisexism action day. The community's public demonstration raises its collective profile and marks Dominion Day, 1929, as the day whenceforth the Chinese Canadian community cannot be silenced any more.

Following Queenie, other characters speak out. They break through different types of political silence endured by various minority groups within the Chinese community. Because of his homosexual orientation, Huang probably has more reasons to hide inside John's tea/boarding house on Dominion Day. His homosexuality is referred to as "*kai-dai*" in Cantonese by other bachelors, meaning "man-love" (9), a crime in traditional Chinese culture. The playwright represents Huang's homosexuality as a result of his arranged marriage rather than as an original sexual orientation. Huang's bride, who is forced to marry him, "smack[ed] into the wall . . . cracking her skull open" (80) on the wedding day before he could possess her. Even more horrifying is that the villagers "bandaged her and told [Huang] to get on with it" (81). In other words, they told him to rape her, since she was already his sexual property. Huang's story exemplifies the traditional family-arranged marriage practice in feudal Chinese culture, including the way the brides would sometimes commit suicide on their wedding day. Although arranged marriages are usually interpreted and represented as undesirable in Chinese literature, there is no escape for the brides except in suicide. Sometimes both the bride and her true lover would commit suicide together, as in the Chinese classic, *Liang Shan-po yu Chu Ying-t'ai*, which bears a plot similar to that of *Romeo and Juliet*. Nevertheless, in most cases Chinese writers chose to have the bride end her life in order to protect her virginity, and her suicide usually occurs either before or during her wedding ceremony. Female rebellion in any social form is discouraged in traditional Chinese culture, which is founded on the male homo-social order of Confucianism. Thus Chinese literature continues to depict persecution of women and their passive resistance through different forms of suicide.

In *Bachelor-Man*, Kam borrows the same scenarios of family-arranged marriage and the bride's suicide, but he makes Huang, the victimizer, repent. As a co-murderer, Huang tells the audience about the tragic death of his bride, as well as the consequent impact on his own sexual orientation. By having Huang talk about his participation in the feudal marriage practice, Kam advocates Queenie's political strategy "against tradition." Furthermore, the death of Huang's bride has more impact on Huang's attitude against sexism than on his sexual orientation. Later, when the villagers find him another girl according to the "obligations" of the tradition, he refuses to participate. This resistance makes him a "troublemaker" for the patriarchal homosocial connections in society (81); he has to flee to Canada for survival. Unfortunately, he finds out that "these whites are as bad as these ignorant villagers" (82). Through Huang's story, the playwright contextualizes sexism and racism side by side as part of the tradition that should be challenged and abolished.

Kam's depiction of a Eurasian character, Kung, among the bachelors puts the silence of another minority group on the stage. Kung's mixed-race identity is gossiped about among the bachelors as much as is Huang's homosexuality. Since mixed parenthood is rare among the Chinese in Canada, Kung is referred to as a *"tchap cheung"* in Cantonese, meaning "bastard." The bachelors also deride Kung's parents for being from a lower class: "His father was the village idiot and his mother was some poor white woman" (40). If Kao's disability makes him a double loser with "no arm, no woman" (13), being a Eurasian deprives Kung of any recognizable identity in Canadian society. Kung narrates a Eurasian bachelor's experience: "I'm not white enough for white women and I'm not Chinese enough for Chinese women. Even the whores have their own standards" (33). For Kung, John's tea/boarding house becomes ironically the only "home" where he belongs; hiding among the Chinese bachelors gives him, paradoxically, a recognizable identity, even though it is a discriminated-against identity:

> You don't know what it's like outside . . . Bounced from one world to the next . . . Belonging to neither. Neither here, neither there, that's me. A half and half. An in between! A *tchap cheung*! (*pause*) This place was a god-send to me . . . I felt at home here. As if I truly belonged. I could be myself. You called me brother. No one ever did that before . . . (58).

Kung's mixed-race and cross-cultural experience becomes another structural prop for the development of the play, similar to Mme Wu's short visit to John's tea/boarding house. Kam brings the play to its conclusion by having Kung lead the rest of the characters in exploring the meaning of the Chinese character 好 meaning "good," and pronounced "hao" in phonetic Mandarin. Paired with Queenie, as her foil, Kung helps her bring justice to Mme Wu and to all other women who have been wronged by patriarchy:

> The image of *woman* and the image of *child* side by side means *good.*
> . . . A long time ago when our ancestors began to think and write they took the image of *woman* and the image of *child* and honoured them. They put the images side by side and said it was *good.* And whenever we think or speak or write the word *good,* you are honoured. They are cheering you in heaven, Queenie. They are saying it's not you they're ashamed of . . . (91)

The Chinese character "good" consists of two radicals: one is 女 pronounced "nü" and meaning "woman" or "female," the other radical is 子 pronounced "zi" and meaning "child." Thus, etymologically speaking, "female + child = good." The unexpected linguistic exploration of the formation of the character 好 signifies a "poetic truth," which refers to "a kind of truth that transcends empirical reality and resides in the mind and vision of the poet" (Vaughn 148). The use of a poetic truth suggests that at a deeper level of Chinese culture and perhaps in its subconsciousness, women are respected. Furthermore, as poetic truth usually embodies the playwright's "plea for freedom from verisimilitude" (Vaughn 148), Kam asks society to replace its racist and sexist reality with equality. Using this strategy, the playwright passes on a message to the audience that gender oppression is a cultural construct instead of an essential in Chinese or any other culture.

After the cause of justice is served, Queenie is rhetorically freed from her colonized identity as a Chinatown prostitute. Kam employs a conventional scene of recognition in which Queenie visualizes her own identity transformation: she seems to have achieved a higher level of spirituality upon hearing Kung's explanation of the formation of the Chinese character 好 .Queenie starts to see herself and her gender as equal partners in a would-be better Gold Mountain. To receive respect from a man is enough to make Queenie feel she has discovered a piece of genuine gold: "Is . . . is it possible . . .? Have I . . . . Have I found my gold in the Gold Mountain . . .? Have I . . . ?" (91) Upon the recognition of Queenie's identity transformation, the bachelors start to attack patriarchal cultural and ritual practices. Character Huang says that "we brought that darkness with us . . .!" Kao relates: "And it hangs over Chinatown like mustard gas . . ." (92). The self-examination of traditional Chinese cultural baggage brings the community to a stage of awakening, which prepares its members to emerge from the ethnic ghetto.

Bachelor-Man ends with a powerful image: instead of being unwanted objects, Chinese Canadians transform themselves into speaking subjects in Canadian discourse. Queenie and the bachelor characters organize a funeral ceremony to bury Mme Wu and with her their community's historical silence. Instead of paper money, which is usually used in funeral rites, the characters toss real money into the air, while marching slowly and methodically around the table on which Mme Wu's coffee pot is symbolically set (93). The youngest character, Asi, chants the mourning, while the rest of the characters repeat the same word "Hear!" as a chorus, except for John and Grandpa Lian, who are probably too old to change and stand by in confusion. The ritual ceremony not only buries Mme Wu as a person, but also her silence and her unfulfilled life representative of the collective experience of Chinese women: "We bury Mme Wu . . . and weep for her demise . . ."; "We bury Mme Wu but still we hear her cries . . ."; "We honour Mme Wu and all she might have been . . ." (93-94). With "the collective self" as her identity, Queenie, the awakened woman, takes over the leading role at the funeral ceremony, burying the causes of Mme Wu's suicide—sexism and racism:

> QUEENIE: We bury, John!
> *Lian hesitates then turns away in confusion*
> THE OTHERS: Hear!
> QUEENIE: And all people like him!
> THE OTHERS: Hear!
> QUEENIE: We bury them deep!
> THE OTHERS: Hear!
> QUEENIE: Beneath the parade's pounding din!
> THE OTHERS: Hear!
> *Silence. Short pause.* (94)

It is crucial that near the end of the play Kam brings the Dominion Day parade into the funeral rites. In the stage production, the noise of the parade, which exists continuously in the background throughout the play, finally starts to die out as the Chinese Canadian community collectively awakens to bury racism and sexism.

The mourning ritual for Mme Wu's death also signifies a personal healing for Queenie. This process starts to take place after Queenie has symbolically found her piece of "gold"—being appreciated as a person by the opposite sex:

> QUEENIE: Thank you, brothers . . . Ten years after I'm buried, disinter my bones. Clean them. Mend the breaks and heal the cracks. Make my feet whole again. So I can stand before my

> ancestors . . . the way they meant me to be. The way they honoured me . . . Do that for me . . . and the slate is clean . . . It's all I ask, brothers . . . I am a simple woman, after all . . . (94-95)

It is not coincidental here that in Queenie's oral "will" she leaves instructions about mending the broken bones in her bound-feet after her death. As "bones" is a key signifier in Chinese Canadian literature, Kam's insertion of the trope into Queenie's words immediately places her in Gold Mountain history. Her concern about the final settlement of her "bones" discursively positions Chinese Canadian women as equal partners in the community. With the reclamation of her identity, Queenie leaves the stage, and after her the bachelors one after another leave the tea/boarding house, except for its owner John, Grandpa Lian, and the regular worker Asi.

There are enough reasons to view *Bachelor-Man* as an epic drama which mixes history with mythology. The play fuses community history into Chinese mythology in order to communicate with the audience on the symbolic level of discourse. Throughout the play, references to the well-known Chinese classic novel *Journey to the West* are made by Kao and Asi (Act One, Sc. Two, 17; Act Two, Sc. One, 36; Act Three, 57). In the stage production, at the beginning of each act, the characters perform *Tai Chi* quietly under spot lights, following the rhythmic sounds of a pair of hardwood sticks. Against this choreographic image of a collective will, literary allusions to *Journey to the West* are narrated: Monkey King, Pigsy and Sandy protect the saint monk in his mythical journey to India to receive the Buddhist scriptures (37-38). The scene quickly blends the journey of the Chinese immigrants with the mythical quest of the saint into one ongoing search for truth. Among the characters, Kao sees himself as an incarnation of the brave Monkey King, one of the three animal knights, whose duty is to defend the saint monk and his sacred cause. This mythical connection increases as the play develops, until Queenie, Kao, Huang, and Kung are ready to leave the tea/boarding house while John and Lian exit upstairs. Asi sees a kinship among the four parties leaving for their further journey: "According to legend, the monk Tripitaka went off in search of enlightenment. And the three animal knight-errants, the Monkey King, Pigsy and Sandy protect him . . . protected *her?* . . . on the way . . ." [emphasis mine] (96). This final recognition establishes Queenie as a leader of the Chinese Canadian community at the symbolic level of Chinese mythology. The ending also denotes that the collective struggle against racism and sexism is a long journey to achieve the truth of humanity.

The production of *Bachelor-Man* generated some interesting reviews from various theatre critics since it was one of the few Chinese Canadian dramas that had been produced on the English Canadian stage. Among the reviews collected in the University of Guelph Archival Collections is a long article written by Lily Leung published in the December 1987 issue of *Dialogue*. Commenting on the characters, Leung writes: "they are not stereotypes—they are multifaceted roles" (13). Robert Lee, who acts the rather passive, but quite complex Eurasian character Kung, also comments on the individualized characterization: "How many times do you see a play where Orientals are real people instead of being the laundry boy?" (13) Although Kam's characters are representatives of different groups that have suffered discrimination in Canadian history, they are neither symbols existing on the abstract level of the language, nor stock stereotypes, nor racial stereotypes. Kam's characters are rounded in a sense that each of them has his or her own untold stories, and each is connected with the community's collective experience. Together these characters tell stories about the Chinese Canadians, who have experienced racist discrimination in Canadian history, and among whom some are even further discriminated against by their own community members.

As a historical play, *Bachelor-Man* takes the audience through a process of rereading Canadian history and Chinese Canadian community history. The impact of self-examination, which is also undertaken in other Chinese Canadian writings, should not be dismissed in the play. However, this process of reevaluation has invited negative response from Beverly Yhap, who comments in her review in the Winter 1987 issue of *Fuse*: "One could discuss the difficulties of rendering a subject that might be construed as being hostile to the very community it portrays. Then there is the question of political correctness. *Bachelor-Man* is certainly that—in fact too much, and too stridently so" (45). Contrasting Yhap's comments, the playwright himself remarks in an interview with Leung that the play does not try to be "correct" with either the Chinese or the whites:

> Although the play seems to open with the intent to "beat the white on the head with the history stick," Winston professes that the play does an about-face and subjects the Chinese to the same scrutiny: "When it comes to ignorance and stupidity . . . we are all the same—there is no difference between whites and Chinese." (Leung 13)

Had there not been the hundred-year anti-Chinese racism in Canadian history, *Bachelor-Man* would probably not be such a powerful voice. The same is true of the feminist critique undertaken in the play, which questions women's historical position as a second sex in patriarchy. To find fault with the political nature of this play is to deny the communal function of the theatre, which has never ceased to be political. Furthermore, using "political correctness" to criticize writings from the historically marginalized communities only ensures that the silencing of these communities, or of groups within communities, will simply go on.

6. The Collective Self: A Narrative Paradigm and Self-expression in Three Prose Works

It is clear that Chinese Canadian women have a lot to say and each of our stories is unique and multifaceted. An endless number of interwoven factors have come into play in our lives. We are neither passive victims of uncontrollable social forces—nor are we superhuman heroines.

Jin Guo

In a room at the back of the Chinese store, or sometimes above, like a room fifteen feet above the street din in Vancouver Chinatown, you can hear, mysteriously amplified through the window, the click-clacking of mah-jong pieces being shuffled over the table tops. The voices from up there or behind the curtain are hot tempered, powerful, challenging, aggressive, bickering, accusatory, demeaning, bravado, superstitious, bluffing, gossipy, serious, goading, letting off steam, ticked off, fed up, hot under the collar, hungry for company, hungry for language, hungry for luck.

FRED WAH

This chapter introduces three publications in prose narrative by Chinese Canadians: a collective memoir, *Jin Guo: Voices of Chinese Canadian Women* (1992), Sky Lee's novel, *Disappearing Moon Cafe* (1990), and Denise Chong's family chronology, *The Concubine's Children: Portrait of a Family Divided* (1994). Although different types of narrative are employed in these works, namely, interview, fiction, and nonfiction, their common setting—Chinatown—establishes the sociohistorical context as an indispensable component. Since all three works were written or collaborated on by women, to some extent they represent Chinese Canadian women's self-expression. While the community history and herstory made their essential contribution to the writings, the three prose works help to further verify the political paradigm of "the collective self" in the narrative of contemporary Chinese Canadian literature.

The publication of *Jin Guo: Voices of Chinese Canadian Women* challenges the myth that there have been no Chinese women in Canada until recently. Historically, Chinese women came to Canada as early as Chinese men. Though outnumbered by their male partners for many decades due to the Exclusion Act, Chinese Canadian women have a parallel herstory. On March 1, 1860, Mrs Kwong Lee, whose husband was a prosperous merchant from San Francisco, was the first Chinese woman to arrive in Canada; a Mrs Cumyow gave birth to the first Chinese baby born in Canada in 1861 (18); and numerous others came later as wives, daughters, mothers, paper brides with legal and illegal documents; and still more were born and raised in Canada. Winnie Ng, a community activist and a member of the editorial committee of *Jin Guo*, points out the necessity of compiling a collective herstory:

> I think back in '85 . . . [w]e kept our eyes open for any books or articles on Chinese Canadians. Basically, we couldn't find anything that reflected the voices of Chinese Canadian women . . . So we started this project. We were thinking of a booklet with photos and simple stories in plain English for immigrant Chinese women. The goal was to use their oral histories as a document—to give them the recognition for their contribution to the community. . . The idea got expanded. It grew into a national project—from a booklet to this book. (225)

The process of compiling *Jin Guo* was designed to help the women recover their memories. The use of a tape recorder during the interviews subscribes to a belief that since these memories have been preserved orally by the women in the community, they should be preserved in that manner when their oral history is transcribed into written word. Outlined in the "Introduction," this process is significant to the production of a collective text, especially because the participants could choose either English or Chinese for their interviews:

> We interviewed across Canada about 130 women in Chinese and

> English over a six-year period. Some were born in Canada and others immigrated from China, Hong Kong and other parts of the world. They ranged in age from nineteen to eighty-five. The interviewees responded to a set of standard questions. Over three hundred hours of conversations were collected. (11)

Because of their shared racial and gender background, the wide range in the age of the participants did not seem to affect how certain topics recurred in their personal memories. Their stories emphasize that racial identity as Chinese in Canada is essential to their experience as Canadians. Most women talked about being victims of anti-Chinese racism: paying the imposed $500 head tax upon landing in Canada (27, 35); being denied a teacher's licence, or a hotel room, or a residence in a white neighbourhood (29, 31, 107); or being called "Chinaman" by a school teacher (94). Collectively, they also remembered the overall denial of job opportunities to Chinese in Canada. Most of their families ended up in the service industry: restaurant, grocery, laundry, and Chinese stores (36, 50, 59, 141, 142, 146, 157, 160), with the exception of a very few who acquired jobs in the professions (59, 179).

Jin Guo also testifies to the commonality of gender-related experience. Since for many decades the anti-Chinese immigration laws forbade married Chinese labourers from bringing their families to Canada, many women who eventually were allowed to enter Canada to be reunited with their husbands or fathers had to deal with various family problems caused by decades of separation and, in some cases, with the husbands' second families in Canada (42, 51, 122). Several women talked about the xenophobia in the Chinese community that discriminates against inter-racial marriages and Eurasian offspring (51, 63, 83, 181).

However, the images of the Chinese women are changing as their roles in the community have changed. While their grandmothers' and mothers' generations came to Canada as paper brides for Gold Mountain men (60, 67), contemporary Chinese Canadian women, immigrant and native-born, are directly involved in political organizations, and campaigning and lobbying for the collective causes of the community (47, 48). Their leading roles are recognized both in the community and in Canadian society. For example, Jean Lumb was awarded the Order of Canada in 1976 and the Queen's Jubilee Medal in 1977 for her leadership as a community activist. Today, reexamining the traditional male-oriented Chinese culture, many women call themselves "Chinese Canadian woman" to suggest a liberation from the feudal bondage based on a traditional marriage and family relationship. Velma Chan puts the sensitivity of this new identity in words: "I'd call myself a typical Chinese Canadian woman, which is pretty hard to define. I think a woman has to maintain her own identity by being independent. The education here certainly broadens your horizons, so that a woman can better maintain her position" (165). The fact that it is hard to define this double identity as a "Chinese Canadian woman" connotes a process of gradual identity formation.

In fact, most women are proud of their double cultural identity. They see that their being Canadian cannot exclude their Chinese identity in this country. Winnie Ng sees her own identity transition in relation to her involvement in the community:

> For me, the whole identification of myself as a "Canadian" has been a very gradual process . . . But once you get involved in working in the community, eventually there's a process of moving from identifying yourself as an immigrant to identifying yourself as a Canadian of Chinese origin. Having two children here sort of prompted that process—and the fact that those labels, at a certain point, are arbitrary. (167–68)

Although labels are arbitrary and restrictive, tentative and appropriate naming is necessary in order to give recognition or to signify a stage of development. Romona Mar points out that Chinese Canadian culture is yet to be named: "It is not solely Chinese, nor is it white Canadian. Our culture is a blend of both" (176–77). This "blend of both" includes the collective struggle to protect Chinatown from being wiped out from city expansions in both Toronto and Vancouver (54). It also means that "we need to have correct images of ourselves, but that means that we have to be more vigilant monitoring the images which appear, or more often than not, the images which do not appear" (177). Mar's observation concerns the representation and objectification of the historically marginalized people by the mainstream media. The power of naming and of composing the community history should be collectively possessed by the community. If Chinese Canadian culture is a "blend of both," the project committee points out that this blend should change the situation that Chinese Canadians "are not even represented in Canadian literature" (227). Sharon Lee expresses her wish to see "all of our community art and writing . . . become part of the mainstream culture" (97); Lee's novel *Disappearing Moon Cafe* written under her pen name Sky Lee, which will be considered in detail below, was the first Chinese Canadian novel that ever caught mainstream critical attention.

Jin Guo is the first written document to transcribe the oral history of Chinese Canadian women into English. The repetitive and colloquial features of the transcript keep the women's personal voices alive and their individual identities intact. Margaret Chan's story is historically significant to early Chinese immigrant women's experience because she came to Canada as early as 1910 at age eight. The denial of her teacher's licence after she had received her teacher's diploma in Victoria testifies to racist discrimination that prevented Chinese from entering the professions for many decades. Though she did not live to see her life story in print, passing away in 1989 three years after the interview (27), Margaret's personal voice is preserved in *Jin Guo*. The transcript reads vividly, as if the speaker were talking directly to the reader. The following passage about her unhappy marriage typifies the colloquial feature of the written transcript:

> I worked as a housemaid. So I have to go wherever he goes. But those days I was *stupid*. I should not have gotten children for him—I should have run away fast. There are other people like me, but I try to go the narrow, straight way, and try to behave myself—by being stupid as I was. I have too much hindsight, no foresight, you follow me? (29-30)

The personal voice in Margaret Chan's testimony illustrates the respect of the editorial committee of *Jin Guo* for the participants of the book, whose lived experience makes up the valuable resource of the collective herstory. By retaining the personal verbal traces in the interviews, *Jin Guo* offers a documentary representation of the lives of the Chinese Canadian women rather than a fictional reproduction.

These life stories, however, do provide writers with raw materials which can be further developed in various literary genres.

*

Published earlier than *Jin Guo*, Sky Lee's novel, *Disappearing Moon Cafe*, has been "hailed as the first novel to deal with the experience of Chinese immigrants in Canada" (Romell 58). It is also the first contemporary Chinese Canadian novel that has caught mainstream critical attention. Paul Yee calls Lee's novel, "a milestone," because "it will lead the way for other Chinese Canadian writers to break the code of silence" (Romell 59). As Yee predicted, four years later the publication of Denise Chong's family saga, *The Concubine's Children*, further confirms the role of the community's history in the development of its contemporary literature.

Disappearing Moon Cafe blends family genealogy and community history into one narrative space. The title of the novel, which is the name of a family restaurant, signifies the sociohistorical setting in which Chinese were relegated to the service industry, especially to cafés and restaurants. Using a traditional Prologue/Epilogue structure, Lee frames a historical period from 1892 to 1939 through the memories of Wong Gwei Chang, one of the community's leaders. Wong Gwei Chang, who dies in 1939, eight years before the Chinese Exclusion Act was revoked, does not have an opportunity to testify to the experience of the Chinese bachelor labourer generation. However, Lee's narrative framework highlighting the significant historical events in Wong Gwei Chang's life, achieves the discursive effect of retrieving part of the unrecorded experience from the memory of the dead. Moreover by ending Wong Gwei Chang's memory in 1939, the writer sends out a message that the campaign to reclaim Chinese Canadian history is long overdue.

Lee uses various narrative techniques to connect community and individuals into one historical reality in which "the collective self" emerges as a double identity construction for the Chinese Canadians. "The collective self" also indicates that the historical silence and invisibility of the community still affect contemporary generations: they cannot gain a more respectable identity in today's society unless their collective history is recognized as part of Canadian experience. The transformation of the community's hundred-year silence into speech involves a process of decoding silence and retrieving unrecorded experience. Structurally, the seven chapters depicting the four generations of the Wongs are framed between a Prologue and Epilogue which are set in Wong Gwei Chang's memory. This double structure suggests a process of decoding historical silence by contemporary Chinese Canadians. The transition from silence to voice is also embodied in the double narrative voices in the novel: the writer uses the first-person voice for her narrator Kae Ying Woo and the third-person narrative voice for Wong Gwei Chang's memory. The relationship between the two narrative voices indicates a rereading and re-writing of the community history by a contemporary Chinese Canadian, a woman writer.

Thematically, dialogue between early Chinese immigrants and contemporary Chinese Canadians is activated by the historical bone-hunting journey. The powerful trope of "the bone-hunting journey" is foregrounded in the Prologue as a resistant force. Historically, the bone-hunting journeys were organized by the Chinese Benevolent Association in British Columbia in the 1890s; in the novel, Wong Gwei Chang is chosen by the community to undertake this task in 1892. Lee presents Wong Gwei Chang's participation in the bone-hunting journey as a learning process to discover the railway builders' heroic deeds. Wong Gwei Chang cannot envision the relationship between the bones and the men who gave their lives to the CPR construction until he sees where their bones are scattered:

> By then, he understood. By then, in the utter peace of the forests, he had met them all—uncles who had climbed mountain heights then fallen from them, uncles who had drowned in deep surging waters, uncles who had clawed to their deaths in the dirt of caved-in mines. By then, he wasn't afraid and they weren't alien any more. Like them, he would piece himself together again from scattered, shattered bone and then endure. (13)

Through Wong Gwei Chang's emotional changes during the bone-hunting journeys, Lee presents the bachelor labourers at the CPR as the heroic ancestors—"uncles"—of all Chinese Canadians. The bone-hunting journey symbolizes an educational process necessary for contemporary Chinese Canadian writers, before they can set off to reclaim the experiences lived by the community ancestors. As a literary trope, the bone-hunting journey is a protest against mainstream Canadian history, in which the historical event of importing as many as 17,000 Chinese railway workers to build the CPR is seldom mentioned, let alone the harsh living and working conditions, and the heavy death toll suffered by the Chinese labourers.

Another historical event highlighted in Wong Gwei Chang's memories is the successful boycott organized by the Chinese community in Vancouver against the "Janet Smith" bill in 1924. The depiction of this event recalls the prosecution of a Chinese houseboy as the suspect in a white maid's murder. During the trial, the community activists and leaders meet in Wong Gwei Chang's restaurant, Disappearing Moon Cafe, to discuss the strategies which concerned not only the fate of the houseboy, but that of Chinatown, because "[u]nder the strain of bigotry, they were outlaws. Chinamen didn't make the law of the land, so they would always live outside of it. In fact, it was a crime for them just to be here" (211). The writer captures the mainstream presentation of the trial: "A no-good chinaboy sniffing after white women's asses" (76), illustrating that it is the houseboy's race rather than his crime that was judged and sentenced by Canadian law. The boycott organized by the Chinese community successfully defeats a further legislative attempt to pass a bill which would sentence the whole Chinese race to being criminals by prohibiting white women from working in close proximity to the Chinese (227). The outcome of this historical event, highlighted in Wong Gwei Chang's memory in the Epilogue, celebrates the power of the community and underlines "the collective self" as a shared historical identity for Chinese Canadians.

The bone-hunting journey symbolizes an educational process for contemporary Chinese Canadian writers who need to return to the historical time and space before they can reclaim the lived experience of the community ancestors. By taking a symbolic bone-hunting journey, contemporary Chinese Canadian writer Kae Ying Woo not only retrieves the community history, but also the lost kinship. In the Prologue/Epilogue, the storyteller captures Wong Gwei Chang's lingering memories after the stroke. He remembers a short period of his life that he shared with a Native woman, Kelora Chen, during his bone-hunting journeys in 1892, which led to their marriage in the Native tradition. However, it is only in the Epilogue that the reader finds out that Wong Gwei Chang, who was later called by his mother to China to do family duty, actually enters a family-arranged marriage with Lee Mui Lan. After Wong Gwei Chang comes back from China, he finds a little boy named Ting An at their old hut, but Kelora has died during his absence. This underdeveloped episode, reviewed in Wong Gwei Chang's mind before his death, not only expresses his longing to be reunited with Kelora, but also uncovers the lost kinship between the Chinese and the Native peoples in British Columbia that probably can be traced as far back as the Nootka Sound settlement in 1788 mentioned in Chapter One.

Furthermore, Lee's development of Ting An adds another perspective to the connotation of the bone trope. Ting An works in Wong Gwei Chang's family business for several decades and mates secretly with his daughter-in-law Fong Mei. Though he helps to produce the third-generation for the Wongs, Ting An is a skeleton in the Wong's closet. His eventual decision to end his non-status at the Wongs, to get married, and to change his last name back to his mother's maiden name "Chen," speaks the revolt of the silenced. Ting An's Native identity brings his rebellion up to date with the Native peoples' situation in Canadian society today. In the Epilogue, Lee presents Ting An's rejection of Wong Gwei Chang's last attempt to keep him in the Wong family by promising him the pending, nonexistent father-son relationship:

> "I am your father," Gwei Chang had to answer. "I gave you my name because you're my son." Ting An smirked at him.
>
> "Don't you know that you are my son?" Gwei Chang asked.
>
> "A Chang, you have always treated me like family," Ting An said hesitantly at first, then continued with too much deliberation. "All these years, I wanted to thank you for the protection of the Wong name, *sir*. I will always be very grateful to you for all that you have done for me." (233; emphasis mine)

The use of "sir" emphasizes Ting An's lifetime identity as a hired worker in Wong Gwei Chang's business rather than as a son in his privileged family. By uncovering the prejudice against illegitimate offspring in the Chinese community, Lee attacks not only patriarchal and patrilineal values, but also the exploitation and mistreatment of the Native peoples by the rest of Canada, including sometimes the Chinese Canadians.

Ting An's final outcry demonstrates the power of the silenced which cannot be appropriated by a discursive regularity or a social legitimacy. In this case, the legitimacy is a traditional Chinese cultural value deriving directly from the institution of marriage and male lineage. The following conversation captures Ting An's irreconcilable resistance to the internal discrimination within the Chinese community against interracial marriages and mixed-blood offspring:

> After a while, Gwei Chang said, "Keep the Wong name. It is yours. Eventually, I'll find you a real wife from China . . ."
>
> "A real wife from China," Ting An repeated in disbelief. He shook his head from side to side, as though something rattled in his head. A suspicion perhaps, but he kept interrupting himself. His eyes narrowed at Gwei Chang, only to dart away a couple of times. Then a bewildered expression, as though he realized something for the first time in his life.
>
> . . . Finally, he turned to Gwei Chang, his eyes wicked with hate.
>
> "Like your real wife from China?" he asked. "Not a dirty halfbreed, buried somewhere in the bush?" (233)

Ting An's final declaration of his identity as a half-breed, a Eurasian rather than a Wong enhances "the collective self" as an identity constructed from a different angle. This episode is positioned in the Epilogue, as Wong Gwei Chang's final remorse before death, and so it brings home a self-imposed criticism of racial phobia in the Chinese community.

Another personal relationship highlighted in both the Prologue and the Epilogue is Wong Gwei Chang's lifetime friendship with a bachelor labourer friend Lee Chong. In the Prologue, set in 1892, Wong Gwei Chang and Lee Chong are seen in their heroic journey shipping the bones of the deceased railway workers on a home-made raft down the water route to Victoria. In the Epilogue, when Lee Chong comes to say goodbye to Wong Gwei Chang, who is sick in bed after a stroke, the writer takes the opportunity to remark on the harsh lonely life of the old bachelor generation: "Lee Chong still lived alone in Chinatown. One tiny room, kitchen and toilets at the end of a long, narrow hall. That was the way he lived" (228). As one of the few married and rich businessmen among his peers in Vancouver's Chinatown, Wong Gwei Chang still remembers those bygone years, during which they survived together as closely as family members could ever be: "year after year, right or wrong, they had always been loyal to each other. How many lonely, softhearted nights, respectfully attentive to the would-be heroics of laundrymen and gardeners, they had all played surrogate wives to each other" (226). Wong Gwei Chang regards his generation as the pioneers of this country who are yet to be recognized: "They'd been coolies all of their lives, dogs of famine. But in the freedom of this young land, old coolies could almost make-believe that they were generals" (219).

Lee's strategy of double narrative voices—the narration of Wong Gwei Chang's memory in the third-person voice and Kae Ying Woo's in the first-person—exemplifies the process of rereading community history by the contemporary generation. In this process, Wong Gwei Chang is not a speaking subject but a silent historical document for his great-granddaughter to decipher. These voices not only maintain Wong Gwei Chang's memory as a strong force of "resistance," which can never be fully reconstructed in words, but also the vulnerability of early Chinese immigrants, whose silence is interpreted and represented in the mainstream Canadian discourse that originally ordered the silencing. Therefore, the combination of the beginning of the Prologue, "he remembered" (1), and the very ending of the Epilogue, "[h]e closed his eyes, the heavy chant of the story-teller turning to mist in his head" (237), indicates that the writer is in control. Lee's decision to make Kae the storyteller, who chooses to tell the stories of her mother's side instead of her father's, because "[her] mother's side is more vibrant, to [her] way of thinking" (20), further emphasizes the power of the writer. As the storyteller, Kae Ying Woo opens the closet, exposing the skeletons and releasing the ghosts in order to reclaim their denied identities. In addition to Ting An's hidden identity, which is a skeleton in the Wong family genealogy exposed by Kae Ying Woo, she also reclaims the "bones" of the Wong women from the patriarchal house.

Lee reclaims the four generations of the Wong women from being further wronged by patriarchy—"Temple of Wonged Women"—as the writer puns later (209). In traditional Chinese society, a woman's value and identity relied heavily on the reproductive capability of her body, especially on the number of male heirs she bore. As the wife of the richest Chinese businessmen in Vancouver's Chinatown, Lee Mui Lan came to Canada in 1924 at age forty-four with no personal identity of her own, except "the mother of Gwei Chang's only son. Stamped on her entry papers: 'A merchant's wife.' A wife in name only, she relied heavily on him for her identity in this land, even though the hard distance remained on her husband's face. And this she could only bear in silence" (Lee 28). Kae also finds out that her grandmother Chen Fong Mei came to Canada as a paper bride. Her entry in Canada costs her in-laws head tax at immigration and money to bribe the investigating government officers in order to secure her landing status. As a paper bride, Fong Mei is expected to be a reproductive machine by her mother-in-law, Mui Lan, who

> wanted a grandson to fulfil the most fundamental purpose to her life. A baby with a brow as clear and as promising as his future. A little boy who came from her son, who came from her husband, who also came lineally from that golden chain of male to male. The daughters-in-law who bore them were unidentified receptacles. (31)

Thus unless Fong Mei has children, especially sons, she has no identity in the family. Realizing that her identity crisis comes from being barren for five years after her marriage, Fong Mei gets pregnant and gives birth to two daughters and a son in eight years by secretly having a sexual liaison with Ting An. Lee presents Fong Mei's change from having no identity to a powerful position in the family by using her reproductive capabilities as a means of survival and personal development:

> Fong Mei produced only a girl, who, tiny as she was, gave her mother enough omnipotence to vie for power and launch a full-fledged mutiny (as one can do only from deep within the ranks). First, Fong Mei learned to drive a car; next, she took her share in the family business and turned it into the most lucrative one of all—real estate. (134)

It is in the "Temple of Wonged Women" that Lee locates the voice of resistance of the Chinese Canadian women. From her mother's old housekeeper, her nanny Seto Chi, Kae Ying Woo learns that her aunt Suzi is the most wronged of all. Suzi, without knowing that she and her boyfriend Morgan were both descended from Ting An, is to be sacrificed in the temple of patriarchy. The writer locates the historical cause of Suzi's tragedy: "Since 1923 the Chinese Exclusion Act had taken its heavy toll. The rapidly diminishing chinese-canadian community had withdrawn into itself, ripe for incest" (147). Personally, Suzi is persecuted by her mother's parental authority and guilt about her own past. After losing her baby at birth, Suzi commits suicide, sending a strong protest against societal control of women's reproduction in the institution of marriage and legitimacy.

By allowing Fong Mei to recant, Kae Ying Woo frees the ghosts of both mother and daughter from the "Temple of Wonged Women." Fong Mei's ghost not only rights the wrong that is done to her daughter Suzi, but also repudiates the representation of masculine experience and male lineage as the dominant social force and expression:

> (The ghost signals for silence. She wants to go on.) Fong Mei: "what if I had refused to have children for men and their namesake? Then my daughters would have been free to have children for their own pleasure as well, and then how free we all would have been! . . . What is this Wong male lineage that had to be upheld at such a human toll? . . . I forgot that they were my children! I forgot that I didn't need to align them with male authority, as if they would be lesser human beings without it. (189)

Fong Mei's recantation calls on women to free themselves from historical bondage, which is prolonged, in part, by a self-imposed slavery. At her mother's awakening, Suzi's ghost cries out for justice: "All this bondage we volunteer on ourselves! Untie them! Untie me!" (189) Lee alludes to a technique that is often used in classic Chinese literature in which ghosts of the wronged souls are allowed to come back to settle accounts. By doing so, Kae Ying Woo sets the victims free from the patriarchal temple by reclaiming each individual experience as part of the collective:

> they were ungrounded women, living with displaced chinamen, and everyone trapped by circumstances. I prefer to romanticize them as *a lineage of women* with passion and fierceness in their veins. In each of their woman-hating worlds, each did what she could. If there is a simple truth beneath their survival stories, then it must be that women's lives, being what they are, are linked together. Mother to daughter, sister to sister. Soon or later, we get lost or separated from each other; then we have a bigger chance of falling into the same holes over and over again. Then again, we may find each other, and together, we may be able to form a bridge over the abyss. (145-46, emphasis mine)

It is not so incidental here that Lee uses the phrase "a lineage of women"; the phrase envisions a female saga which is based on the women's collectivity.

By rewriting the Wong family saga, Kae Ying Woo appropriates the traditional male-oriented genealogy. From the lineage of women, Kae Ying Woo relocates her own lost identity. Kae Ying Woo is the great-granddaughter of Wong Gwei Chang and Kelora Chen. She is the granddaughter of Fong Mei and Ting An. On her father's side, she is the granddaughter of a poor Chinese waitress Song An and an unknown gambler grandfather. The revelation of the unrecorded illegitimate kinships, which actually keep the community together through shared motherhood, undermines the superiority of patriarchy and male lineage. Kae Ying Woo's acceptance of her old nanny Seto Chi as her "other mother," her "(trans)parent" (127), establishes female connection as a different social order from that of the traditional father-son lineage. Thus, it is crucial for the narrator to conclude that "family sagas" in the traditional sense cannot convey her characters' experiences: "No wonder no one writes family sagas any more!" (128). Lee indicates that the traditional definition of legitimacy and the type of discourse that reinforces male lineage are both oppressive to women's experience and inadequate for representing women's lives. Only by undermining the traditional family saga with a female saga in which wife, paper bride, mother, daughter, wet nurse, surrogate mother, waitress, business woman, and victims of incest and suicide are all regarded as contributors to the final making of the herstory, can "the collective self" emerge from the "bones" of her female ancestors to construct a valid identity for Kae Ying Woo.

As a shared identity for Chinese women, "the collective self" is composed not only thematically, but also narratively. Lee employs an overall episodic narrative mode of short passages. Instead of following a traditional chronicle, Lee tells her stories in a great number of episodes; their length varies from half a page to ten pages. These episodic entries appear to be assembled almost freely, repetitively, and unchronologically over one hundred years, representing a free interaction. By putting these episodic entries in a continuous process of interaction, the writer brings past and present, individual and collective into one narrative space. This interplay also combines community events with personal lives, assigning women's experiences an equal position and undercuts the male orientation and male dominance in traditional family saga. Moreover, the episodic structure allows the writer to juxtapose the outcomes of the historical events with the reinterpretations of these events from a contemporary point of view. Without telling the complete story chronologically, the episodic narrative breaks up the traditional narrative order. The climaxes of the stories and the outcomes of the historical events are deferred until several chapters later and sometimes even until the Epilogue to avoid any realistic illusions. Overall, the episodic narrative in Lee's novel facilitates the dialogues between past and present, self and collective, male and female, without further arranging them. The interactions gradually and effectively define contemporary Chinese Canadians, whose personal identities are derived from the collective history and herstory of the community.

The linguistic interaction between English and the translated Chinese also contributes to "the collective self" as a double identity for Chinese Canadians. Lee inserts some phonetic and morphemic translations of Chinese words as intrusive elements in the predominantly English syntax. These non-English units not only create a thematic uncertainty with their foreign textuality, but also posit a linguistic hybridization between the two languages and two cultures. Since the insertions of Chinese phonetic and morphemic translations are limited to stories of Kae Ying Woo's great-grandmother, grandmother and their generations linguistically and culturally, they indicate the isolation of early Chinese immigrants, especially the women. For instance, when Mui Lan defends her arrangement to hire the waitress in the restaurant to be a surrogate mother for her future grandson, she says to her daughter-in-law Fong Mei, "no one can accuse the Wong family of having 'a wolf's heart and a dog's lung' " (61). The Chinese metaphor *langxin-goufei,*[1] literarily means having a wolf's heart and a dog's lung. While the idiom suggests that a person who is less humane is animal-like, the metaphor might not be appreciated by an average English reader, because wolf and dog are not necessarily immoral creatures. However, the word-by-word translation of the idiomatic Chinese saying provides the reader with a linguistic flavour of the Chinese language. Its insertion into the English syntax interrupts the semantic order of English. Concurrently, Lee chooses contemporary English for Kae Ying Woo's generation, indicating the bilingual skills and linguistic assimilation of the fourth generation into mainstream culture. Merging the two cultures and languages into mutual appropriation indicates the reality of contemporary Chinese Canadian community.

From the subtitle of the Prologue, "Search for Bones," to that of the Epilogue, "New Moon," *Disappearing Moon Cafe* presents the journey of a contemporary Chinese Canadian woman writer. Kae Ying Woo realizes the freedom she gains from rewriting the collective history, and especially from composing a herstory for the "Temple of Wonged Women." Her exclamation that "[a]fter three generations of struggle, the daughters are free!" indicates that after reclaiming the community history in which its women have an indispensable place, the 1990s is a new era for Chinese Canadian women (209). Regarding the subtitles of the Prologue and Epilogue together with the body of the novel in the middle, the reader can see that the embedded narrative paradigm of "the collective self" works as a unifying force throughout the novel. Kae Ying Woo's lesbian lover, Hermia Chow, sees the unity of this double identity for contemporary Chinese Canadians:

> Do you mean that individuals must gather their identity from all the generations that touch them—past and future, no matter how slightly? Do you mean that an individual is not an individual at all, but a series of individuals—some of whom come before her, some after her? Do you mean that this story isn't a story of several generations, but of one individual thinking collectively? (189)

The identity transformation of the Chinese immigrants to Chinese Canadians is also embodied in the physical transformation of the original Chinese restaurant, "Disappearing Moon Cafe, 50 East Pender Street, Vancouver, British Columbia" (23) to the famous Chinese Cultural Centre at the same address today. "The collective self," which emerges from various Chinese Canadian writings and becomes a significant narrative paradigm and self-expression, needs to be applied to the discussions of Chinese Canadian literature. Without the perspective of the connection between the community history and its literature, Graham Huggan's essay on Lee published in the special issue of *Canadian Literature* exemplifies the kind of reading that aims to fit minority experiences into the straightjacket of mainstream universality.[2] Applying "the collective self" as a critical approach to Chinese Canadian literature, the reader can see that the collective is created by the individual(s) of the community, the identity of the individual(s) emerges from the collective and from creating the collective. This powerful and effective identity construction model will continue to see more applications and elaborations in Chinese Canadian writings. Denise Chong's family history, *The Concubine's Children,* is already one such example.

*

Set mainly within the boundaries of Chinatown in Vancouver and Nanaimo, and partly in Chang Gar Bin, *Kwangdong* province (*Guangdong* in phonetic Mandarin; Canton in English), southern China, *The Concubine's Children: Portrait of a Family Divided* is a family saga. It begins with an article published in *Saturday Night* in October 1988, in which Denise Chong describes her trip back to Chang Gar Bin with her mother. Chong's initial journey to meet her relatives in China leads her to discover and recover both her family history and the collective history of the sojourner generation of earlier Chinese immigrants, regardless of their gender. Similar to Sky Lee's choice of Kae Ying Woo as the narrator in *Disappearing Moon Cafe*, Chong positions herself as the contemporary point of view. From this perspective, she traces the fifty years' lived experiences of her grandmother May-ying, grandfather Chan Sam, her mother Hing Chan/Winnie Chin, and her own childhood, and includes some accounts of her grandparents' family in China. By establishing May-ying as the provider for both families in Canada and China, *The Concubine's Children* not only frees one woman from being further wronged by the temple of patriarchy as a concubine, but also reclaims the historical role played by the Chinese women in the development of the community. Since Chong's chronology is based on her family history, generically speaking her narrative would belong to the genre of nonfiction. However, as the author deliberately mixes fact with fiction, *The Concubine's Children* defies a narrowly defined genre description. Furthermore, by foregrounding the role of the writer in her narrative, Chong emphasizes research as a process to recover and to reconstruct historical data. From her narrative, "the collective self" emerges as an underlining paradigm and an identity construction model, as it does in Lee's fictional family saga.

Similar to the use of the Prologue/Epilogue in *Disappearing Moon Cafe*, Chong uses a "Foreword" as a structural device to highlight the personal and collective need to recover the family history. Like Lee, Chong perceives her writing as a process of breaking through the historical silence which has enclosed both her family and the Chinese community. Chong's research and writing project started initially from a pile of "old black-and-white photographs" kept at the bottom of "the cedar chest upstairs in [her] parents' bedroom" after her grandparents passed away (ix). In reality, the urgency is more pressing because Chong observes that the historical evidence about her grandparents' generation is disappearing fast from the communities in both Canada and China. The development of a global economy is rapidly wiping out local historical landmarks:

> Nanaimo's old Chinatown was already gone, burnt to the ground in 1960. In Vancouver, I stood at the wicket where Chan Sam once bought passage to China; I sat at the counter at the B. C. Royal Café, where May-ying once worked; I climbed the dark staircases of the rooming houses where my mother once lived. But in the echo of my footsteps, the wicket was torn down, the cafe was closed and the rooming houses were overtaken by a skid row drug culture. The decline continues as the newest wave of Asian immigrants, those with money enough to flee Hong Kong before it becomes China's in 1997 . . . I found the south of China to be changing even more rapidly. (x-xi)

The urgency to recover the unrecorded family and community history becomes even more pressing after she starts her project: "[e]ven as I researched and wrote the book, I felt as if the window of opportunity to get a glimpse of the past was closing" (x-xi). Urged by both personal and collective needs, Chong keeps open the windows to the past through the family photographs kept in her mother's bedroom.

Chong's approach to the family photographs challenges the traditional way that photographs are presented as a reliable, final testimony. Though she sees these photographs as silent historical data, extremely valuable to her research, she regards them as elusive as words can be in terms of signifying the absolute truth. In "Foreword," the writer notes that some of the photographs were originally taken by her grandparents "to record a moment for posterity" (ix), especially those taken for more formal and ceremonial occasions, in a studio; thus she underlines their function as a means of representation. In fact among the thirty-seven photographs inserted in the middle of the memoir, at least a dozen are studio products. Therefore, what those historical photographs can truly testify to is clarified: on the one hand, the studio photographs represent the photographer's preferable postures in his studio, and, on the other hand, since some photographs were later cut and pasted in the album by Chong's mother Winnie, they speak to her need to reconstruct her memory. By underlining the various manipulations of the photographs, Chong makes no attempt to disguise the disparity that lies between the "powerfully suggestive voice" deriving from the cut and pasted photographs (ix), and the reality that is shut out initially by the camera or later cut off by her mother's editorial scissors.

The historical reality to be reinterpreted and recovered lies between what remain as the historical documents and what is deleted from the documents. In other words, what is represented in the documents is only part of the historical reality; what has been deleted from the existing documents is also a part of the reality, known as lived experience, existing in personal memories or lost to the indefinite space between the written and unwritten. The search for the existing documents leads Chong to Chang Gar Bin in two trips with her mother, during which she not only meets her relatives in China, but also locates some valuable historical records—a small package of letters written by her grandfather to his other family in China during the last few years of his life. Knowing that these letters can only offer an incomplete knowledge about her grandparents, as do the photographs cut and pasted by her mother, Chong sees the significant role played by herself in terms of processing the available historical data and reconstructing the family saga.

In her foreword Chong foregrounds her writing project as a collectively-based "family project" (x). This critical approach draws from the community's oral tradition based on the historical circumstances that "poverty, the lack of education, and the claustrophobic existence of being excluded from the larger white society—lent [the community] itself to a legacy of oral history" (x). In Chong's family, out of many conversations between her mother and herself starting from her childhood in Prince George, BC. (3), she begins "to order the past" (x). These family talks start to break through the historical silence of the community by recovering its lost memory. The oral tradition, which preserves bits and pieces of personal memories through "vivid accounts of conversations" (x), is carried on, by and large, by women in the community, as testified to in *Jin Guo*.

Secondly, Chong observes the relative truth of her presentation in comparison to the historical truth lived by the elder members of her family. Also in the foreword she notes that "[t]here are as many different versions of events as there are members of a family"; thus "[t]he truth becomes a landscape of many layers in an ever-changing light; the details depend on whose memories illuminate it" (xi). Chong's clarification that only a relative historical truth can be represented in writing offers the reader a critical approach to her preference for the third person omniscient narrative, which is used more often in fiction than non-fiction. She notes "[i]t seemed that the most fair and honest way to do that was to tell the story as an omniscient narrator. This involved some necessary interpretation of events and some reconstruction of dialogue" (xi). Chong's omniscient narration, which is based on "interpretation" and "reconstruction," suggests that nonfiction discursively overlaps fiction. This critique also reminds the reader of the limitation of words and accounts for the disparity between verbal representation and lived experience. By calling the reader's attention to the limited power of words, Chong emphasizes the indispensable subjective contribution made by the researcher, the writer, and the reader, who all participate in the process of deciphering historical silence as contemporary historians. As far as her own experience in writing the family saga of her grandparents is concerned, Chong says: "I approached it as one might approach the task of restoring a painting—the original canvas was someone else's. Of course, in the very act of writing a book, I myself bring another shading of truth" (xi). The metaphor of restoring an old painting also illuminates the subtle relation between nonfiction and fiction, and between a historical truth and the narrative account about such a historical reality.

The title of *The Concubine's Children* illustrates how Chong employs the narrative perspective as a political strategy to challenge history. Concubines are historical products of patriarchy in a feudal society. In traditional Chinese society, concubines are usually bought by rich old men, "the more concubines a man had, the more prestige and social status he garnered" (8). It is also believed that the concubine's youth and virginity would rejuvenate her aged or dying husband. In some cases, if the first wife fails to give birth to a son, a concubine is chosen to carry out the reproductive task for the family. Like many other concubines, May-ying possesses youth and unusual beauty, but unlike most who were sold to local rich old men, she was bought by a married bachelor in Gold Mountain. While this feudal cultural practice allows rich and privileged men to have more than one wife, or to abandon their wives, concubines are their husbands' personal properties that can be disposed of at any time. Therefore by aligning her family with her grandmother rather than with her grandfather Chan Sam, Chong's narrative reclaims the socially and culturally marginalized concubine as the head of her family.

Furthermore, by mixing the feudal cultural practice of polygamy with the bachelor culture in historical Chinatown, *The Concubine's Children* explores the ironic fruit of the Gold Mountain dream. Whereas most Chinese labourers remained single all their lives, or were separated from their wives and children in China for life, Chan Sam is one of the few who had a concubine in Canada and a wife in China. Being an average, uneducated peasant, had he continued to live in China, Chan Sam could have never afforded a concubine. However by immigrating to Canada, he obtains the liberty and opportunity to pursue the dreamed privilege of a rich man. Chan Sam not only fathers two families, one on either side of the Pacific Ocean, he also builds the most impressive house in Chang Gar Bin, which stands there two generations later as a testimony to the illusion that there is "wealth to be found in Gold Mountain" (70). This illusion, which is gradually established through Chan Sam's three home visits, ironically disguises the bachelor labourers' meagre opportunities in both Canada and the United States.

Chong's depiction of Chan Sam's three home visits details the power of the Gold Mountain dream. Chan Sam visits his home village three times after he came to Gold Mountain in 1911 (18); each home visit marks a special stage of his life: the first time, his first wife dies; he returns to visit her grave and to take a replacement wife, Huangbo; the second time, he takes his concubine May-ying and their two Canadian-born daughters, Ping and Nan, back to China for their education; the third time, he goes by himself to build a house with May-ying's money and to produce a son with his at-home wife. Chong highlights Chan Sam's second and third visits, showing the reader how a successful overseas father and husband is honoured because he remembers to "return home in brocade" (18, 41) and to "bring so much . . . as to reach the roof of the cart and make the ox carrying it sweat" (41). The author details the load of furniture and other consumer products shipped from Vancouver to China for Chan Sam's visits. In the shipment accompanying his second visit:

> [t]here were three large wall mirrors and two dressers—a tall one, and a commode dresser with drawers on either side and a three-way mirror in between. A stool went with it. Of particular fascination was a metal crib, for no villager could believe the luxury of furniture for children. . . the girls each had with them their down comforters, made in Canada.
>
> Chan Sam had a love of clocks. Though hardly necessary to a peasant's life, to him they were the important symbol of a gentleman. He brought home several, including a large mahogany Regulator wall clock, and two smaller ones of jade and gold. He brought wool blankets that were the trademark of the Hudson's Bay Company in Canada, the country's oldest store.
>
> The villagers were invited to sample the family's favourite overseas foods. There were crates of sweetened condensed milk, crackers and raisins . . . (43-44)

Among the commercial products and the construction tools that Chan Sam ships home for his third visit are:

> a red wagon for Ping and Nan, a wind-up Big Ben alarm clock for each of them . . . made in Peterborough, Ontario . . . RCA Victor phonographs along with some Cantonese opera recordings, made in New York by famous opera stars.
>
> The most essential part of his shipment were tools required to build the house. North American tools, even those as basic as spades and saws, would be better than the tools made in China that he would have to buy or borrow. Better tools, he reasoned, would improve the workmanship. (66-67)

With the furniture, bedding, food, and tools made in the West, Chan Sam demonstrates, in front of the villagers, the material success of the Gold Mountain dream, through which a ragged and uneducated Chinese peasant can become a rich gentleman. Furthermore, what he wants to build in Chang Gar Bin during his third visit with the imported tools is not an ordinary peasant's family house but a symbolic monument with "western architectural touches, whose balustrades, porticos and balconies decorated at least two stories, sometimes three," which will glorify "overseas fathers like him, standing in judgement of the generations of squat, crumbling one-story adobe houses huddled at their feet, offering proof that going abroad was the only hope of raising one's family above the peasant class" (73). The superiority of the West is even demonstrated in Chan Sam's rejection of the Chinese tools and his disapproval of the local brick-making craftsmanship during the construction of his house (75).

Chong also depicts how the Chinese relatives preserve the Gold Mountain myth as a material success as they preserve the house. Thirty years after her grandparents passed away, Chong sees both the myth and the cliché of the Gold Mountain dream in the house built by her grandfather:

> the surreal western scenes overhead on the porcelain panels that my grandfather had commissioned. The scenes of wealthy Hol-

lywood, San Francisco's Golden Bridge and the pristine sea and mountain-scape of Vancouver evoked none of the feeling of the dingy rooming houses of my grandparents' time or of the frontier logging and pulp mill town that Prince George was when we moved there. (253)

Conversing with her Chinese relatives, Chong learns that the Gold Mountain myth lives extensively in their imagination. It has never changed since the days when May-ying was sold to be a concubine in Gold Mountain: "People living in *Gum San* have wealth and riches; they have to push the gold from their feet to find the road" (8). Fifty years later, Chong's aunt, Ping, talking about her possible future visit to her country of birth, Canada, says seriously that her disabled half brother Yuen should also come, because "[w]ith his crooked feet, he can rake in the gold and you and I will follow behind and pick it up!" (258). In addition to the cliché and misrepresentation of Gold Mountain, what disturbs Chong and her mother most is that their Chinese family's Gold Mountain dream excludes May-ying, their provider. In the letters written by Chan Sam to China, May-ying is presented as a drinker and a gambler; as a result of this representation, she is remembered by her own daughter Ping simply as a "foreign lady" and an unworthy mother (252, 253).

In order to help complete the partial knowledge of the Gold Mountain myth, Chong documents the anti-Chinese sociohistorical milieu in North America. She identifies the historical and psychological reasons why early Chinese immigrants became lifetime sojourners in Canada. In Chapter Two, Chong includes a short description of Chinese immigration, including the 1840 Gold Rush in California, the discovery of the second Gold Mountain in British Columbia, and the anti-Chinese immigration laws in both the United States and Canada which prevented Chinese immigrants from becoming naturalized and from being reunited with their families in North America (12-15). Chong also depicts the discriminatory labour market, in which Chinese labourers received only a fraction of what was paid to the white and "Hindu" (Indian) workers. They had to pay for segregated bunkhouses and lived in appalling conditions: "To cram in more bunks, rooms were crudely partitioned, windowless and no bigger than six feet by eight, with makeshift bunks three deep on each side. Like a game of musical beds, there were more bachelor men sharing the monthly rent than there were bunks" (19). Because Chinese labourers were not allowed to make Canada their chosen home until the Chinese Exclusion Act was revoked in 1947, they could only sojourn in this country while dreaming about returning to China, if not alive, then perhaps after death. Some bachelor labourers managed to go home for family-arranged marriages, while others remained single all their lives. Some of them managed to go home a few times to father one or two children, to buy a few *mau tin* of land (16), or even to build a house as Chan Sam did. However, people in Chang Gar Bin will never know whose money built the house, since May-ying's role as the provider is never mentioned in Chan Sam's letters. To reclaim May-ying's role, Chong writes: "The house that they cherished as a monument" to Chan Sam had actually been built on May-ying's back, "on the wages and wits of waitressing and the life that came with it. . . . it stood for everything that had been so misunderstood about her" (254). Only by recovering what is deleted in Chan Sam's letters and what is never recorded in any other written documents, can Chong and her mother Hing/Winnie reclaim the historical invisibility of May-ying as the breadwinner of Chan Sam's two families. Like Kae Ying Woo in *Disappearing Moon Cafe*, Chong's bone-hunting journey leads her not only to discover her own identity as a concubine's granddaughter, but also that of her grandmother, May-ying, as the sole provider for Chan Sam's two families in Canada and in China.

The Concubine's Children comprises a three-generation herstory of Chinese Canadian women as an indispensable part of community history. Like Queenie in *Bachelor-Man*, whose improperly bandaged feet made her value drop so that she is sold as a concubine by her parents, May-ying is also sold as a concubine to Gold Mountain. Though her buyer and future husband Chan Sam had to purchase a birth certificate and pay for her passage, upon landing in 1923 she is immediately contracted as a waitress at Vancouver's Peking Tea House to help recover the cost of her importation into Canada (24). Her working experience and her lower social status prevent her, paradoxically, from becoming the gender and cultural stereotype—an obedient Chinese housewife like Mme Wu in *Bachelor-Man*. May-ying not only earns more money from waitressing than Chan Sam does from his occasional unskilled jobs, but also excels in playing mah-jong when Chan Sam uses their home as a mah-jong parlour in the evening (36). Living in the self-enclosed Chinese community, May-ying shares the sojourner mentality[3] and other cultural practices in the community. Since it is common for husbands to show up on their wives' pay days to collect their wages, May-ying allows Chan Sam to borrow her wages for his third home visit and even lets him send her wages and tips as regular remittances to China long after the house is completed and after their official separation. By depicting these historical circumstances, Chong recovers May-ying's pivotal role in the family and in the survival and development of the community.

Besides honouring her economic contribution, Chong reclaims May-ying's independent spirit. Her public image as a lower-class waitress in Chinatown, or as a wanton woman in Chan Sam's eyes, is made to contrast with her self-image as an independent modern woman. Traditionally, a Chinese waitress is called *kay-toi-neu*, a "stand-at-the-table-girl," who is considered "almost to be one and the same as a prostitute" (25-26). May-ying's gambling habit gives Chan Sam enough reason to complain to his at-home wife that "[May-ying] is a woman who is more like a man" (76). Ironically, during Chan Sam's third home visit, which lasted for two or three years, May-ying is identified in Nanaimo's Chinatown as a member of the married-bachelor community even though she is a married, single mother with a child. Her gambling and other related behaviour, such as drinking and occasional sleeping around, become equally acceptable because she "simply did what most men on their own did—indulged in one of Chinatown's few diversions" (80-81). The ironic image of May-ying becoming a married-bachelor woman is extended by her public appearance of wearing "a custom-tailored three-piece suit" and "a man's tie and cap to match" (123). Chong politicizes her grandmother's choice of the masculine dress:

> When May-ying was seen dressed in this way in the gambling dens and around Chinatown, it was as though she was making the statement that she was taking her rightful place in a man's world; that a woman who made her own living, who didn't depend on a man for support, should be respected. Perhaps more than anything, her masculine dress was a statement that a

> woman could do as she pleased with her life. As if to prove some solidarity, she convinced two other women friends to do the same, to wear men's suits and matching caps. They called themselves "The Three Sisters." A photograph of the trio . . . stood on May-ying's dresser . . . (123-24)

The irony that independent women have to look like men emphasizes the significance of appropriate representation. For many decades, since Chinese women came to Canada, the lack of representation of their subculture in Canadian discourse denied their existence and deleted their roles in the community.

In addition to depicting her grandmother's masculine suit as a silent statement, Chong constructs May-ying's declaration of her own independence. After she decides to cohabit with a professional gambler, Chow Guen, instead of marrying him, she makes an open statement to Chan Sam against being sold one more time as a piece of sexual property. The following episode well illustrates May-ying's rebellious spirits:

> "If you want to go live with him, go then," Chan Sam said. "I won't stop you, on one condition. Chow Guen has to pay me three thousand dollars." He was proposing to do what he would have done had he been in China, sell her to another man. The amount he named was more than most Chinese saved during a lifetime in Canada.
>
> May-ying practically spit her words out. "I am not for sale. You are such a greedy man. How could you?! He'll never pay you, and I'll do exactly what I want to do." (125)

Following this declaration, May-ying continues to live as a sojourner and a married-bachelor woman. She follows Chow Guen to different cities at her own expense, until seventeen years later when she is abandoned by him at age fifty because of her drinking problems. Chong's depiction of May-ying's search for independence represents the awakening of Chinese Canadian women.

In addition to the relationship between husband and wife in the Chinese Canadian community, *The Concubine's Children* explores the relationship between mother and daughter. Chong does not romanticize her grandmother by making her a super-heroine; rather she presents May-ying as a historical being whose mentality and behaviour are constructed by her cultural environment. Living in a male-oriented culture as a concubine, May-ying is disappointed by the birth of her third daughter Hing, whom she was expecting to be a son. At one point May-ying even cuts Hing's hair and dresses her like a boy in order to have an official picture-taking (90). The photograph of the mother and her "son" foreshadows the daughter's "childhood filled with fear and confusion" (91). During the many years when May-ying is waitressing to support the two families, she drags Hing through the Nanaimo and Vancouver areas, moving from cheap rooms to even cheaper ones without having a home of her own. One of the shocking experiences that Chong records at least three times is that Hing sees her mother in bed with different men on various occasions (108, 114, 162). Once they even make love in the same bed where Hing was supposedly asleep (108). The lack of privacy in Chinatown and the neglect of growing children force Hing painfully to judge her mother's misconduct.

Chong also depicts how traditional Chinese culture treats children as their parents' personal property, similar to the way married women are possessed by their husbands. May-ying's wish to have a son who can take care of her in her old age leads her eventually to buy a baby boy for $300 (117); moreover, her daughter Hing is made to take care of this brother, Gok-leng. Even when Hing moves out of her mother's rooming house in Vancouver at age eighteen and renames herself Miss Winnie Chin (166), she is still her parents' property. Upon Winnie's marriage, her mother asks the future son-in-law for a $500 bride price, as if her daughter were a piece of property which she preserves the right to sell (179). Similarly, Chan Sam sells the birth certificates of his two elder daughters, Ping and Nan, who never came back to their country of birth after being taken back to China for their education (191-92). For some time the relationship between the parents and Winnie becomes so ugly that they even sue each other for money (209-210). At May-ying's funeral, Winnie cannot even cry, nor does she want a piece of her mother's jewellery (232-33). Ironically, the only object she takes back from May-ying's rooming house is "a chenille bedspread," a previous year's "Christmas present, unused, its original tags attached. Woodward's would take it back"

(233). Later, by cutting her mother's photographs, Winnie attempts to edit out her mother's lived experience to soothe her own painful memory of their relationship.

The death of May-ying, who is killed in a car accident, is presented less as a personal tragedy than as part of the collective tragedy of the sojourner generation. May-ying, who is wronged even in death by the false identity of her bought birth certificate, signifies the historical tragedy of her generation. The *Vancouver Sun* reports the accident twice, but "[t]he name was wrong, and so was her age; only the address of her rooming house was correct" (229). May-ying's personal collection kept by the police, which contains an amount of $40.94 in coins and a receipt from B. C. Collateral for her jewellery, are not a measure of her life's achievement (232). But these coins and receipt bespeak the financial hardship that her generation experienced.

May-ying's failure to find gold in Canada is not portrayed as a personal failure, but part of the collective betrayal of the Chinese immigrants by the Gold Mountain dream. In Chan Sam's case, after selling the birth certificates of his two daughters in China and failing to sell his crippled son's right to come to Canada, he has to acknowledge to his son that his forty years of toil abroad have come to naught (211). Long before May-ying's death, Chan Sam dies of cancer, confined to a straitjacket in the basement of Vancouver General Hospital. His membership number "1091" in the Chan Society on Pender St is crossed out and an equivalent of the twenty Canadian dollars remaining in his account after the funeral is sent to China as the last remittance from Canada (214). A few months after May-ying's accident, Jang Noong, an old bachelor and a loyal friend of May-ying and Chan Sam, dies of a stroke and is buried a pauper (234). Later Chow Guen, May-ying's gambler lover, has a stroke and retires to a nursing home in Prince George, having left enough money to cover his funeral and to send four thousand dollars back to his family in China (234). The sojourner generation is dying out. After being mistreated for many decades in Canada, together with all the bones that could not be shipped back to China, ironically, most of the sojourners "made Canada their new home" (190), willingly or unwillingly, if not in life at least in death.

With the sojourner generations dying out, new generations succeed them in the Chinese Canadian community. By stepping into the narrative directly as herself—Denise—in the first-person singular voice (195), the writer brings the "family project" up to date. Growing up in a non-Chinese neighbourhood at Prince George Airport, she cannot renew her Chinese identity, but for her grandmother May-ying's occasional visits, especially for the Chinese food she cooks for the family during the visits. Contrasting May-ying's "Chineseness" is her daughter Winnie's "Canadianness": she serves "roasts on the table, enriched the milk in our glasses with extra cream and introduced cheese into her cooking . . . Lasagna, along with cinnamon buns, pound cake and apple pie, became one of her specialities" (224). From the daily food she prepares, the daily language she speaks at home, and the self-image she fosters in her children, Winnie brings up her children with assimilation in mind. Denise's career, as a senior economic adviser to Prime Minister Pierre Trudeau, certainly signifies success in the mainstream (238). However, her mixed cultural identity—as a Chinese Canadian—is addressed as a problem, which relates to her mother's growing up.

Chong's psychological struggle to come to terms with the "Chineseness" in herself illustrates the identity crisis that sometimes arises for native-born or second-generation Chinese Canadians. She is emotionally disturbed when she decides to look for her Chinese relatives at the end of a two-year job posting in China:

> The photograph of the two young girls, my mother's two sisters, that lay among the pile in the cedar chest kept coming to mind. A feeling that I had to stand on the same soil dogged me. It was not a sense of "Chineseness" I was after; I had stopped trying to contrive any such feeling following Mother's early advice—"You're Canadian, not Chinese. Stop trying to feel something." I didn't know why I wanted to, only that I could not leave China without going to the village of my grandfather's birth. I also knew that Mother had to accompany me. Persuading her was the hard part. (238)

While knowing one's roots and looking for living relatives seem perfectly natural, Denise's self-inflicted denial of her "Chineseness" embodies a typical minority Canadian experience—the pain of cultural assimilation. The narrator's self-image incorporates her mother Winnie's experience as a second generation Canadian-born Chinese, one whose ethnicity and Chinese name are rejected in Canadian society (92).

The perceived conflict and confrontation between "Chineseness" and "Canadianness" reflects a problematic dichotomy in Canadian culture. Rather than perceived as an advantage, a double cultural identity for racial minorities is viewed generally as a negative in Canadian society. This viewpoint is also related to another well-established dichotomy, East vs West. In the map of today's global politics and economy, the East is presented as a state of raw materials and cheap labour force awaiting Western money and technology. This dichotomy explains why Denise and her mother Winnie carry a fear shared by the relatives from the West in terms of what their Chinese family would want from them:

> It was a well-known travellers' tale that poorer Chinese relations cared less about blood ties than about the foreign-made color television, the VCR, maybe even a washing machine or refrigerator that their "rich" overseas relations could bring in as part of their special duty-free exemptions. The bigger the gift, the more money it cost, the happier were the Chinese relations. Mother invoked more deep-rooted suspicions: "Somebody could be fooling me, trying to get me to go to China." (240)

Ironically, their "Canadianness" turns into an obsession with material wealth that an average Chinese peasant does not possess. If the above list of electrical equipment details their Canadian fear, ironically, the list updates the illusion of the Gold Mountain myth presented by Chan Sam several decades before in his home visits. In that sense, perhaps the illusion of the Gold Mountain dream will continue to live with the Chinese in both China and the West as long as the "Canadianness" keeps presenting itself as a material resource and contrives to impose ideology on the Chinese. However, "Canadianness" vs "Chineseness" is a dichotomy as arbitrary as other ideological labels. This seemingly logical dichotomy is deconstructed by what Winnie's eldest sister Ping remarks upon their reunion: "You and I drank the same mother's milk"; Winnie's own answer that "I can see

Mama in you," and "even your voice is like hers," has the same effect of ridiculing her earlier fear of meeting her Chinese relatives (244).

Whereas "Canadianness" vs. "Chineseness" forms a traditional, ideological dichotomy, the Chinese Canadian experience lived by each individual is a concrete historical reality. Out of thousands of these lived realities emerges again "the collective self" as an effective narrative paradigm, which is capable of embodying and representing the shared experience of the community as a racial minority group. "The collective self" justifies the sacrifice made by May-ying, Chan Sam, and many others, because the Gold Mountain dream continues to bear fruits for contemporary generations. The two women who came to Canada under the names of "Ping" and "Nan," with the birth certificates purchased from Chan Sam, regard themselves as step-daughters of the family. They continue to visit the tombs of May-ying and Chan Sam, observing the Chinese tradition of grave-sweeping and ancestor worship during the festival of *Ching Ming* every spring (264). "The collective self" also explains to the reader why Chong feels the urge to recover her family history under the current title: the reclamation of May-ying's role as the contributor in the family economy establishes Chinese immigrant women as agents. At the same time, this reclamation constructs an identity for Chong as May-ying's descendant. Near the end of the book, Chong's insight about the continuity between mother and daughter underlines "the collective self." As a unifying force, this paradigm bridges the gap between lived experience and the narrative that represents that experience from across the generational boundaries:

> I believe it was Mother's doing. A mother's stories to her daughter ultimately stirred a feeling in me that the life we lead begins before, and continues after, our time. I owed it to Mother, and to Chan Sam and May-ying, to find the good among the bad, and pride among the shame of their past. The lost history that Mother and I recovered gave the past new meaning, perhaps enough to be a compass to provide some bearings when her grandchildren chart their own course. (266)

The above quotation sounds similar to an earlier statement by Sky Lee's character Hermia Chow in *Disappearing Moon Cafe*, who sees an individual not merely as an individual, "but a series of individuals—some of whom come before and after the individual person" (Lee 189). The insight shared by both writers also illuminates "the collective self" as a writing process, through which contemporary Chinese Canadian writers are connected.

Given how little is written in Canadian discourse about early Chinese immigrants, especially about independent immigrant Chinese women, *The Concubine's Children* offers an extensive representation of their lives. Chong's narrative proposes new meanings to her grandparents' lived experience, so that it can continue to live in the reader's imagination. In this sense, the fruitful labour of pioneer Chinese immigrants, of both men and women, is finally recognized.

I began this chapter by citing *Jin Guo* as a historical resource of memories retrieved from several generations of Chinese Canadian women who testified in their chosen languages. The repetitive and colloquial feature of the transcript not only recognizes their shared experience, but also acknowledges orality as a living tradition in the Chinese Canadian community and especially in women's subculture. By retrieving unrecorded experience from personal memories, *Jin Guo* celebrates the collective advancement of contemporary Chinese Canadians as continuous with the harsh survival battle waged by early generations.

The historical silence of the community also induces a resistance in contemporary Chinese Canadian writings against being further silenced or denied visibility. Dialogues between the contemporary speaking subjects and the elders in the family and the community, which include dead Golden Mountain men and women, become a predominant literary trope in prose narratives of both fiction and nonfiction. In Lee's novel *Disappearing Moon Cafe* and Chong's family memoir *The Concubine's Children*, the narrator's first-person voice initiates the dialogue with the older generation, as well as interprets the extant historical data, such as family photographs and letters. Through dialogue, contemporary subjects both reclaim the denied community history and relocate their own worthy, double cultural identity. Moreover, *Disappearing Moon Cafe* and *The Concubine's Children* demonstrate an awareness that writing about the Chinese Canadian women's experience is an indispensable part of composing the community history.

Various narrative techniques are employed in order to delineate the Chinese Canadian history and herstory. Lee adopts the episodic narrative mode to disrupt the traditional chronological narrative order. Chong's narration follows a chronology, but she switches the settings from Chinatown in Vancouver and Nanaimo to Chang Gar Bin in southern China. These narrative techniques bring the individual and the collective, men and women, immigrants and their families, from historical enclosures into contemporary time and space. Out of the on-going narrative interactions, "the collective self" surfaces again and again as a self-expression, as it does in other Chinese Canadian writings. In this paradigm, the self, although acting as the speaking subject, is always comprised of and contextualized by the collective, at the same time, it constructs and presents the collective from the contemporary point of view. While the self and the collective become mutually constitutive in the Chinese Canadian literature, the resistant discourse starts to right the historical injustices imposed on the community. In all three works, no individual is held responsible for his or her personal failure in Gold Mountain, and the collective survival is commemorated.

Disappearing Moon Cafe and *The Concubine's Children* were both shortlisted for the Governor-General's Literary Award, and both won the City of Vancouver Book Prize, in the 1990 and 1994 competitions respectively. Mainstream recognition helps broaden the readership for Chinese Canadian writers, yet the purpose of reclaiming the collective history and herstory is more than just to earn mainstream "mention" (New 4). If *Disappearing Moon Cafe, Jin Guo,* and *The Concubine's Children* are read and appreciated by Canadian readers of any race, then this racial minority experience will truly become a significant part of Canadian experience and heritage.

7. Dialogue: A Discursive Strategy in Chinese Canadian Poetry

Poetry is capable not only of serving as a means for the expression of personal identity or even nationalist sentiment. Poetry, as a part of the cultural institutions and historical existence of a people, is itself an arena of struggle. BARBARA HARLOW

Alone and on the edge of their world, far from the centre. This kind of edge in race and family we only half suspect as edge. FRED WAH

Some critics consider poetry a nonpolitical form because of its classic antiquity and economic form. Terry Eagleton's observation supports this critique: "For poetry is of all literary genres the one most apparently sealed from history, the one where 'sensibility' may play in its purest, least socially tainted form" (*Literary Theory* 51). Since poetry usually foregrounds the signifier rather than the context, compared to other literary genres, it has the effect of "pushing communication into the background . . . asserting that language is 'being used for its own sake' " (Easthope 16). However, Antony Easthope also argues that as a certain kind of discourse, poetry is a "means of representation," which "is not a neutral vehicle." As such, poetry "is already 'shaped' for ideology and is therefore itself ideological" (7, 22). Describing resistance poetry, Barbara Harlow points out: "Poetry is capable not only of serving as a means for the expression of personal identity or even nationalist sentiment. Poetry, as a part of the cultural institutions and historical existence of a people, is itself an arena of struggle" (33).

In Canadian literature, poetry is a mainstream genre. George Woodcock remarks in his chapter on Canadian poetry for *Literary History of Canada*: "Nowadays poetry is not merely—in numbers of titles—the most published of all genres in Canada; it sells more reliably than fiction, and poets, recently derived, have become something very near to culture heroes, especially among the young" (286). Many of the founders of Canadian poetry in the 1960s have long since become monumental figures in the literary canon; some are also mainstream critics and educators, teaching Canadian literature in the universities. The economic and career fulfilment for mainstream Canadian poets underlines the potential of poetry which can go beyond the capacity of a literary genre; it is a channel through which social development can be achieved for individuals as well as for communities.

A literary community is a product of the surrounding world. It usually takes several decades for a literary community to develop the quantity and quality of writers and readers, and it can only do so if the overall political and economic timing is right. According to Woodcock, for today's mainstream Canadian poets, who emerged in the 1960s, the establishment of the Canada Council in 1957, which "encouraged and sustained poet-edited magazines and poet-directed presses," made a historical contribution as a financial and political patron (*Literary History of Canada* 15). Although one cannot underestimate the struggle that the mainstream poets have undergone in the last few decades, these developments have taken place in the politically supportive, culturally and linguistically friendly environment of their mother tongue. The overwhelmingly white Canadian poetry anthologies do not reflect racial and cultural diversities in Canada, not to mention the linguistic diversities other than English and French. Thus through "the Canadian poetic renaissance" (Woodcock 307) led by A J M Smith in the 1940s, to its flourishing in the 1960s and its academic establishment in the 1970s, racial issues were seldom depicted or considered by Canadian poets or critics.

This literary scene began to change in the late 1980s and in the 1990s for several reasons: one, the Native peoples' resistance against five hundred years' European colonization; two, the establishment of large non-white minority communities because of the changes in Canadian immigration patterns; and three, encouragement from the official multicultural policies in the last two decades. Minority writers and poets are currently undergoing a similar journey to that travelled by mainstream Canadian poets in the 1960s. Nevertheless, for the non-white poets, the journey will probably be much longer and more difficult, simply because barriers are everywhere: the overall biases of Canadian history towards these communities, the linguistic barriers for some of them, and the psychological challenge for members from the historically marginalized groups who have never had a voice in Canadian culture. Now that the first-generation writers from these communities are making their appearances in the publishing world, one expects them to establish different, but equally important, components of Canadian poetry, ones that have been missing from the official canon.

This chapter examines dialogue as a political and poetic strategy that is widely used by Chinese Canadian poets, such as Jim Wong-Chu, Sean Gunn, Paul Yee, Laiwan, Jam. Ismail, Fred Wah, Lucy Ng, Evelyn Lau, and others. Through dialogue with the dead railway workers, deceased community ancestors, family members, and above all with the reader, these poets are engaged in a continuous process of rereading the community history, relocating the collective values, and redefining the Chinese Canadian identity. Their efforts also include seeking poetic forms and tropes that can best represent their sentiments and lived experience. In this chapter, the poems collected in the two anthologies and discussed in Chapter Three will not be reexamined, although generically speaking, they do belong here. However, discussions of Laiwan's bilingual poem, "The Imperialism of Syntax," and Jam. Ismail's *Sacred Texts* will be continued.

JimWong-Chu's poetry collection *Chinatown Ghosts* (1986) explores the Chinese Canadian tradition and history as viewed from the interior of Vancouver's Chinatown. The opening poem, "tradition," depicts a certain kind of Chinese food, *zong zhi,* as it is pronounced in Mandarin, which is traditionally served during the memorial festival in spring to commemorate the legendary hero Qu Yuan of the Han Dynasty (206 BC–220 AD). The poem is a dialogue between the reader and "a bundle of rice / wrapped in leaves / forming triangles"; this unknown object, which contains a Chinese ritual and cultural tradition, calls the reader's attention to the signifier as a cultural artifact rather than as merely an arbitrary sign. Using a first-person persona, the poet describes the process of discovering this somewhat exotic food in slow-motion details:

I pull the string
unlocking the tiny knot
releasing the long thin strand
which binds

I tug at the dry green leaves
holding the sweet rice within

peeling it back
I begin to open (11)

The object for the ending verb "open" is actually the title "tradition"; thus the poem reads cyclically, suggesting a symbolic process of discovering and rediscovering a cultural tradition. The closing line, "I begin to open," structurally embeds an implied oxymoron; rhetorically, it suggests an open ending instead of a closure. The reader senses a need to continue reading in order to discover this different tradition. Since this is the first poem of the collection, the "tradition" to be discovered and rediscovered can be related to the title of the book, *Chinatown Ghosts*, a Chinese Canadian history to be reclaimed as a part of the tradition.

Wong-Chu uses dialogue metonymically in his search for the community's history. His poem, "old chinese cemetery: kamloops July 1977" discussed in Chapter Three, vividly encapsulates the dialogue between a searching poet and the bones of the Gold Mountain men. Another poem, "scenes from the mon sheong home for the aged," describes the lifetime physical and psychological damage that is done to a Chinese road construction worker after he survives an accident caused by a white engineer's mistake. The poet narrates the old man's memory of the accident after many years:

this was a fuller page
of his life

he remembers the road building accident
in 1910

his body among the rubble

blood of dead men ran
thick as pig
so thick
he had to lift his head
to breathe

the *gwai low* engineer
gave wrong instruction
with the dynamite

"I lucky"

the break in his leg
did not pop the skin (28)

The old man is driven mad by his vivid memory of the accident. The few sentences he can speak in English, for example "Where is my china?", indicate his life and the life of his generation as isolation and silence. A similar poem, "fourth uncle," depicts a dialogue between the I-narrator and a Chinese labourer in Victoria, a village relative, whose last dream after a lifetime struggle as a bachelor labourer is to die near the Chinese cemetery:

you said
you travelled and worked
up and down this land
and now you have returned
to die

to be buried
beside the others
in the old chinese cemetery
by the harbour
facing the open sea
facing home (19)

The above dialogues between the poet and the Chinatown ghosts help to recover the silenced lives of the Chinese labourer generation.

Dialogue can transform the power relationship between the dominated and the domineering. In his sarcastic narrative poem "equal opportunity," Wong-Chu uses repetition as a rhetoric device to engage the reader in such a practice. By foregrounding economic competition as the main cause of racism in the pioneer days, the poet engages the reader in a dialogue with frontier history:

> in early canada
> when railways were highways
>
> each stop brought new opportunities
>
> there was a rule
>
> the chinese could only ride
> the last two cars
> of the trains (14)

Later, underscoring the perverse logic of racism, the poet ridicules the bizarre change in the railway regulations:

> until a train derailed
> killing all those
> in front
>
> (the chinese erected an altar and thanked buddha)
>
> a new rule was made
> the chinese must ride
> the front two cars
> of the trains (14)

The poet repeats the same lines of another accident that "claimed everyone in the back"; so the final offering of "equal opportunity" to all passengers, and the ruling that "the chinese are now allowed / to sit anywhere / on any train," are results of accidents (15). Using repetition to ridicule racism, the poet contests its practice in Canadian history. Centred within Vancouver's Chinatown, Wong-Chu's lyrics, which attest to Chinese Canadian experience, suggest that poetry is not sealed from history. On the contrary, history is inscribed in the poetic discourse.

The investigative and interrogative features of Wong-Chu's poetry are also exemplified in other Chinese Canadian poems, in which various forms of dialogue occur. Sean Gunn's poem, "And Then Something Went," which was discussed in Chapter Three, is a dialogue between poetry and performative media. Laiwan's poem "The Imperialism of Syntax," collected in *Many-Mouthed Birds* and briefly discussed in Chapter 3, is a linguistic dialogue between English and Chinese since the poem is published in both languages. The poem focuses on the inevitable linguistic assimilation involved in the survival of Chinese immigrants:

> you had travelled long and far to be subject to another's
> language,
> another's *syntax*.
> Right away, those rules of grammar were the forgetting of
> yourself.
> Those letters never pronounced before
> Became the subject of your ridicule.
> The bitterness on your tongue became hidden in need for
> survival
> a proof of assimilation,
> the invisibility of yourself . . .
>
> Now you are here
> do you remember your syntax, your language
> that which would be the remembering of yourself? (58)

The poem underlines the process of cultural assimilation through linguistic assimilation, which occurs daily wherever the official languages are spoken. Through its grammatical rules and syntactic order, English colonizes the mind and the tongue of the non-English speakers; at the same time, it ridicules their willingness to be assimilated. However, Laiwan's poem also exemplifies the resistant nature of postcolonial poetry. By writing about non-white or non-European experience, postcolonial poetry helps dismantle the power of the imperial syntax with its resistant context.

Published in both Chinese and English, the two versions of Laiwan's poem stage a postcolonial irony. While the heritage language is gradually losing its function to the overwhelming mainstream languages, the heritage culture remains a resource of psychological resistance. Since the two versions of Laiwan's poem are printed physically back to back on the two sides of the same page, the linguistic dialogue between them becomes quite a complex experience for different readers. First of all, the poet cannot read Chinese; therefore the Chinese version, which is not exactly a word-by-word translation from English, challenges her as a postcolonial agent whose "dispossession of [her] origin," as footnoted, is hardly reclaimable (57). Secondly, since most English readers cannot read Chinese, the linguistic dialogue between the two versions cannot function equally in the reading. Thus, to a unilingual English reader, who looks at the Chinese print with awe and curiosity, the Chinese version stands as a linguistic barrier. Looking at the English version, a unilingual Chinese reader feels what the poem describes: "*shengyingdi fayin, chengle rang ren xiluodi / xiaoliao*"—"Those letters never pronounced before / became the subject of your ridicule" (57-58; phonetic Mandarin is mine). Therefore, for a unilingual reader in either case, the linguistic dialogue between the two versions of the poem can only converge as an imaginary and intellectual dialogue between the poem and the reader.

A bilingual reader, however, will have a different experience in reading the poem. Comparing the two versions, the reader discovers the English title, "The Imperialism of Syntax," is translated into Chinese as "*zhi min hualedi wenhua*" (phonetic Mandarin is mine), meaning "the colonized culture." In other places, especially in the third stanza, the Chinese syntax is not as clear as the original English lines, because the word-by-word translation is done syntactically rather than semantically, which is how the translator translated the title. Thus the poem debates the level—semantic, syntactic, or phonetic—at which poetry can be properly translated. Regarding translation as a linguistic dialogue between signs and objects/concepts, translation of poetry not only translates words verbally, but also transforms cultural concepts intellectually from one language to another. Overall Laiwan's poem raises important questions for other Chinese Canadian and postcolonial poets.

The agony of a postcolonial subject using the colonizer's language is somehow assuaged in Jam. Ismail's poem *Sacred Texts*. Born in Hong Kong and living in two British colonies, Hong Kong and India, before immigrating to Canada, another postcolonial space, Jam. Ismail writes the resistance of the colonized into her poetry. The excerpt from her volume *Sacred Texts* included in *Many-Mouthed Birds* exemplifies a deconstructive approach to the imperialistic language at all linguistic levels: semantic, syntactic and phonetic. *Sacred Texts*, as it is ironically named, disfigures the traditional formats of poetry or prose by deliberately violating the rules of capitalization, spacing, punctuation, paragraphing, structuring, and typesetting. Phonetically, the group of poems follows the colloquial flow of English in the colonies, contesting the sacred position of the written words in Western culture. Some of Ismail's poems read like casual conversation caught by an eavesdropper, while others sound like episodes of humorous dialogue among friends. Personal names appear in the context; among many participants in the conversation, "bosan" and "dai ji" appear frequently.

Ismail's poems are numbered in itemized paragraphs. In print, they look like a list of things, equally spaced. Some of her paragraphs seem without particular topics, while others depict a slice of life, or a slice of a much bigger phenomenon which reveals an ironic space for postcolonial subjects. For example, the paragraph marked "b.7" offers a glimpse at the unmeasurable space between semantics and the subconscious: "Staring at the typo 'accumiliate' made by a chinese from / zimbabwe, bosan grimmed: yeah, accumulate + / humiliate" (128). The playful combination of "accumulate" and "humiliate" in this specific space questions whether a linguistic signifier is a transparent sign. The poem marked as "c.1" has a confusing subtitle printed deliberately in a box for emphasizing:

ratio quality

young ban yen had been thought
italian in kathmandu, filipina in hong
kong, eurasian in kyoto, japanese in anchorage, dismal in
london england, hindu in edmonton, generic oriental in
calgary, western canadian in ottawa, anglophone in
montreal, metis in jasper, eskimo at hudson's bay
department store, vietnamese in chinatown, tibetan in
vancouver, commie at the u.s. border.

on the whole very asian. (128)

The phonetic closeness between "ratio" and "racial," which could be a mispronunciation, satirizes the identity confusion in society. These two paragraphs capture the psychological paranoia in a racist world that is based on face-reading.

Rhetorically and stylistically, *Sacred Texts* challenges the conventional format of prose, especially its rigid concepts of beginning, middle and ending. It also defies the traditional ideal of poetry constituted by versicle stanzas. Rather than following the rigid grammatical rules of English, which help preserve the imperialistic tradition, Ismail distorts the English syntax in order to challenge the ideology of hegemony inscribed within. Her nontraditional syntax indicates liberation and freedom for a postcolonial subject. And her tongue-in-cheek attitude and sometimes sarcastic humour mocks the narrowly conceived identity concept that is traditionally based on race and genealogy.

The subject matter of identity is also explored by Fred Wah as a recurrent topic in his prose poems written over several decades. Among Wah's dozen poetry collections, his Governor General's Literary Award-winning collection, *Waiting for Saskatchewan* (1985), exemplifying this on-going quest, will be studied in this chapter with his recent poems from *Seasons Greetings from the Diamond Grill. Waiting for Saskatchewan* consists of four groups of prose poems under the subtitles of "Breathin' My Name with a Sigh," "Grasp the Sparrow's Tail," "Elite," and "This Dendrite Map: Father/Mother Haibun." Together they form a lengthy dialogue between the speaking subject/the son and the deceased father/the "you." George Bowering observes this depiction in his introduction to Wah's other poetry collection, *Selected Poems: Loki Is Buried at Smoky Creek* (1980): "The death of his father causes the poet to bring to life his memories of earlier life with the no longer breathing Wah" (15). The opening poem of *Waiting For Saskatchewan*, starting with the title line, begins a chain of Wah's frequently-used signifier, foregrounding his mixed origins and family genealogy in this composition:

> Waiting for Saskatchewan
> and the origins grandparents countries places converged
> europe asia railroads carpenters nailed grain elevators
> Swift Current my grandmother in her house
> he built on the street
> and him his cafes namely the "Elite" on Center (3)

The beginning of the poem also illustrates Wah's poetic style of using fewer punctuation signs and more noun parallels. Wah only uses one set of quotation marks, a few commas, and some capitalization in this poem. He parallels his nouns to each other, such as "origins grandparents countries places" and "europe asia railroads carpenters." Without using verbs regularly to designate the relationship between the nouns as either subject or object, Wah positions the parallelled nouns as equal entities in the line. Thus, rather than creating a traditional syntactic order of subject + verb + object, Wah's parallel nouns and run-on lines produce a nonhierarchical relationship among the words, a paratactic sentence.

Exploring the difference between the hypotactic sentence and the paratactic sentence, Stephen Fredman notes in *Poet's Prose*:

> A hypotactic sentence fulfils our normal plot expectations: . . . there is a logical connection and subordination among the grammatical elements of the sentence plot and an outcome in which the plot reaches a denouement or completion. Like any familiar plot, the hypotactic sentence can be diagrammed hierarchically; it has a logical order. The plot of the paratactic sentence works by a continual sidewise displacement; its wholeness is dependent upon the fraternal bonds of a theoretically endless proliferation of familial resemblances rather than the dynastic bonds of

> filiation. Thus the conscious sentence writer can subvert, deny, or replace the authority of the hypotactic sentence through the alogical plot and the aural structure of the paratactic sentence. (30-31)

Wah's use of parallel, unrelated nouns shows that he is a conscious sentence writer. These parallel nouns not only subvert the traditional logical order expected from a hypotactic sentence, but also create a fluid context that allows the reader to generate different meanings.

This fluid context probably indicates a personal sentiment, which might be read as an analogy to Wah's mixed-blood genealogy of Swedish and Chinese immigrant ancestors in Saskatchewan. By mixing the boundaries of prose and poetry to create a prose poetry, Wah finds a metonymic form which helps him explore the duality of his Eurasian identity. He also employs dialogue to engage the reader in a similar quest for meaning(s). A short poem about the impact of his father's death, which triggers the poet's major personal crisis, leads him to search for his mixed identity:

> Father, when you died you left me
> with my own death. Until then I thought
> nothing of it. Now I see it's clear cut
> both genetic "bag" as well as choice. I know now
> I'd better find that double edge . . . (6)

The search for "the double edge" is expressed in a direct dialogue between the poet as the first-person "I" and the father as the addressee "you." Although the "you" never answers, his silence provokes the speaking subject "I" with a consistent presence for many years: "when you die it snows"

> father it is fall
> the leaves turn
> . . . .
> I'm over forty now . . .
> . . . .
> father
> again it is another season,

. . . .
your name is my name
our name is bones
bones alone names (10, 14)

The Eurasian "bones" shared by the father and the son—the father is half Chinese and the son a quarter—binds Wah's poetry with other Chinese Canadian writings by its predominant literary trope of "bones," through which his Chinese genealogy and identity become locatable.

The search for his "genetic 'bag'" as a Eurasian leads the poet to take a physical journey to China. *Grasp the Sparrow's Tail* is a travel diary written during Wah's trip to mainland China via Japan, Taiwan, and Hong Kong in search of his family's "bones." Each journal entry consists of two parts: an italicized prose passage recording the daily travel agenda and a poetic passage printed in normal font. This format itself embeds and embodies different dialogues: dialogues between the fonts, between the travellers (his wife Pauline, pp. 37, 38, 53), between the physical and psychological journeys, and between prose and poetry. While the poet's search for his genealogical roots in Canton is received doubtfully by the Chinese, since a Eurasian is not considered a Chinese, his mental dialogue with his father continues during the trip:

> *So what have I got going besides this "father" list? . . . I've misplaced the family information my mother gave me so I can't check out actual possible connections still here in the Canton region. I mention this to the guides and the others in our tour group, tell them my father was sent here as a child to be raised and educated by his Chinese relatives.*

You were part Chinese I tell them.
They look at me. I'm pulling their leg.
So I'm Chinese too and that's why my name is Wah.
They don't really believe me. That's o. k.
When you're not "pure" you just make it up. (43)

The poet's mental dialogues with his father challenge the traditional genealogy based on racial linearity. While his father's meaning is further explored in "Elite," especially in "Elite 9," during the trip the poet sees his father everywhere among the Chinese (Wah 44)—from the rice fields in Canton, to a construction site in Zhengzhou near the Yellow River, the coal-mining town in Taiyuan, a Buddhist temple in Datong in northern China, and to a single window in Huhhot of Inner Mongolia(45, 46, 51). In a direct dialogue, he tells his father "[w]hat always gives you away is your haircut, your walk, or the flash in your eyes" (44). Through the typical Chinese haircut and mannerism, the narrator seems to find kinship with many ordinary Chinese.

However, the more the poet sees his father among the ordinary Chinese, the fewer illusions he has about his dispossessed origin. Wah depicts the cultural dispossession which is happening on a global level; his own disillusionment is revealed near the end of his journey. When his trip ends up in the national capital, the narrator seems to see less and write less. Regional differences are lost in Beijing where images of ancient Utopia are mixed with signs of a modern tourist industry: "Lotus fields everywhere. Look at the hats they wear. Everything happiness and longevity"; "*everywhere, the masses, the people from New York airing their teeth*" (54-55). Wah's poetic travelogue, *Grasp the Sparrow's Tail,* named after a movement in *tai chi,* ends magically at the entrance hall to Chairman Mao's mausoleum. Here the poet not only links the huge oil painting of Mount Kun Lun in front of his eyes with the mountains along the Kootenay River in British Columbia in his home town, but also links his search for his father and his family genealogy to the late great Chinese leader Mao Tsedong. The group of poems ends with a simple dialogue between the poet and his father, and with Mao, since the identity of the "you" is not fixed in the context:

Mao, in front of me
the things you cared for too

river, mountain
a town, the whole
blue sky (56)

It is in this simple ending that the poet merges all the noticeable differences between past and present, East and West, China and Canada, Chinese, Caucasian and Eurasian, his father and Mao, into the eternal latitude of poetry, which is probably the only space that is capable of embracing all the differences.

The search for his family genealogy and Eurasian identity is continued in the ten prose poems collected under the subtitle, *Elite*, included in *Waiting for Saskatchewan* and later anthologized in *Many-Mouthed Birds* (169-179). The *Elite* poems begin with an implied oxymoron: "Swift Current Saskatchewan is at the centre" (59), which typifies Wah's style of prose-poetry. It also marks the significance of the prairie town to the poet and his poetry. "Elite" is the name of the Chinese family cafe opened by Wah's grandfather in Swift Current along the CPR. Like other Chinese cafes and restaurants, such as the Disappearing Moon Cafe in Sky Lee's novel, and the tea/boarding house in Winston Christopher Kam's drama, "Elite" is a historical ethnic setting, within which the poet relocates his family history in the history of the Chinese Canadian community. Here "elite" is marked on the title page to be mispronounced as "ee-light" (Wah 57), which ironically foregrounds the linguistic interactions among the settler groups in the prairie, as well as the Chinese immigrants' longing for acceptance.

In *Elite*, the poet continues to use dialogue as a strategy to engage the Eurasian son, the persona "I," and his already deceased Eurasian father, the "You." Speaking the first-person voice, the poet transforms his father's silence into answers to his own questions about their mixed genealogy. "Elite 3" explores the lack of a clearly defined racial identity for Eurasians in either Canadian or Chinese society:

> I know when you came back from China you must have felt more Chinese than anything else. But I remember you saying later that the Chinese didn't trust you and the English didn't trust you. You were a half-breed, Eurasian. I remember feeling the possibility of that word "Eurasian" for myself when I first read it in my own troubled adolescence. I don't think you ever felt the relief of that exotic identity though. In North America white is still the standard and you were never white enough. But you weren't pure enough for the Chinese either. You never knew the full comradeship of an ethnic community. So you felt single,

> outside, though you played the game as we all must . . . I don't think you felt there was anyone else in the world like you. (62)

Delineating his father's double immigration, the poet reclaims his father's silence. At age five, his father is sent from the Canadian prairie to Canton to be educated; and at nineteen, he comes back from Canton to Swift Current, Saskatchewan. His double immigration and twice being made "languageless" are fully recounted in "Elite 9." The poem consists of one unbroken sentence, protesting against the Canadian immigration detention camp at Victoria for jailing returning Asian Canadians before their status in Canada could be clarified. In "Elite 9":

> When you return from China via Victoria on Hong Kong Island and they put you in jail in Victoria on Vancouver Island because your birth certificate had been lost in the Medicine Hat City Hall fire and your parents couldn't prove you were born in Canada until they found your baptism records in the church . . . when you arrived in China in 1916 only four years old unable to speak Chinese and later in the roaring twenties when each time Grandpa gambled away your boat passage so you didn't get back to Canada until 1930 languageless again with anger locked up in the immigration cells on Juan de Fuca strait . . . did you see islands? (69)

The use of one unbroken sentence achieves a totally different dramatic effect from the parallel nouns used earlier in Wah's poems. While the overlapping, nonreflexive parallels disrupt textual and grammatical closures, the one-sentence paragraph without punctuation builds up a syntactic momentum and tension so as to give the reader a metonymic experience of the father's silenced anger, which needs to be discharged.

Besides immigration experience, Wah also depicts the on-going struggle of a Eurasian family in Canadian society. The multiracial Canadian society is mocked by its own miniature at Swift Current: "The ethnicity here feels so direct. I mean the Chinese are still connected to China, the Ukrainians so Ukrainian, in the bar the Icelanders tell stories about Iceland, the Swede still has an accent, the

French speak French . . . What is a Metis, anyway?" (62) In this setting, "Elite 4" and "Elite 5" capture the Eurasian family's ongoing endeavour to become mainstream Canadians. "Elite 4" depicts the father taking time off from work in order to go to the church on Sundays with the family:

> You were proud, then, of the fact you were going to church and you made a point of telling some of the customers in the restaurant that you had to go to church. That was after you had stopped desiring China . . . I think the church thing was white responsibility and you did it for that and a sense of our family in that community. (63)

In "Elite 5," "that community" of mainstream Canadians, who go to church on Sundays, shifts to the ice hockey arena, in which the I-narrator posits his silent father for a place of belonging:

> I think you were the manager or something, you helped out. The brim of your hat is turned down, Chicago gangster style . . . I've always been "proud" you were part of that team. The Swift Current Indians were my first hockey heroes and their movements over the ice instilled a sense of body and mind-set which I have carried with me all my life. Even though you never played hockey I know you had the invisible movement of the game inside you too. (64-65)

The irony that the father never plays ice hockey except in the son's imagination expresses the son's growing-up experience as a Eurasian—searching for identifiable mainstream Canadian images, including stereotypes.

"Elite 10," which concludes the series, summarizes the family's struggle to establish itself in business. Wah depicts the entire family business history within, again, one unbroken long sentence that runs for a page and a half without punctuation until its ending. The family's business experience exemplifies Chinese immigrants' slim opportunities in Canada after the CPR was completed. The part of the job market that is open to the Chinese is exclusively self-employment in the service industry: restaurants, cleaners, cafés, and motels. The unbroken one-sentence poem provides the reader with a linguistic opportunity to share the family's persistent search for a better opportunity, which is eventually exhausted as the poem ends with: "finally the Holmes Motel in Cranbrook in the early sixties where that was the end of the deals the cafés the houses the driving the building the running right through it, for you, that was it" (71).

The omission of punctuation in both "Elite 9" and "Elite 10" intensifies the resistance of the silent father—"you"—as a partner in the dialogue. Although his silence is displaced by his son's interpretation of that silence, the physical existence of "you" throughout the text still maintains some of its provocative power, and arouses pathos in the reader. In talking to his father, especially by transforming the latter's silence into words and his life into poetry, the I-narrator relocates a Eurasian family history and his personal identity in the collective history of the Chinese Canadians. With this conclusion, a political irony emerges, cutting even more deeply than the I-narrator's childhood preference for his father's participation in mainstream Canadian cultural activities, such as church and hockey. Although a Eurasian descends from a mixed parenthood of a European and an Asian, the I-narrator's eventual association with the Chinese Canadians rather than with the European Canadians denounces the racist attitude of the dominant culture.

The last group of Wah's prose poems in *Waiting for Saskatchewan*, "The Dendrite Map: Father/Mother Haibun," embodies a dialogue between the two poetic forms: *haiku*,[1] and prose poetry. However, the poet replaces the rigid Japanese poetic form of *haiku* with a prose paragraph written with parallel nouns. In addition to exploring a loose *haiku* style, Wah does not attempt to offer "a specific spiritual insight" (Holman 247) when he concludes his poem. Instead his last line suggests a second thought, which is sometimes ironic and other times irrelevant. In this group of poems, besides talking to his deceased father, the poet occasionally talks to his mother. In "Father/Mother Haibun #1," his search for an explanation of his mixed genealogy continues:

> . . . my Grandfather which made my life "racial" not that he actually came to be there but simply him here/there and her, my Grandmother, her Salvation Army Englishness really solid in the

> middle of his flux but both of them cutting "geo" out of their world thus Maple Creek Moose Jaw North Battleford Medicine Hat somewhere in England and Canton China places in their lives much more than in their world, you, my father, almost too, thus me . . . (75)

Here the poet underlines the Chinese blood in him and his father, which makes them experience "racial" minority status in Canada. This political statement also explains why he often seeks to talk to his father, instead of to his mother, about the family genealogy. However, as Wah's serious statement is often balanced by his ironic disengagement from a narrowly constrained meaning, the poem ends with a loose, unfinished *haiku* line printed in bold letters: "**Two weeks late I turn the calendar, crave for ripe tomatoes**" (75). The concluding line is totally detached from the main prose passage about his grandparents who made him a Eurasian. It dismisses the reader's expectation of finding the "truth" in conclusion. In "Father/Mother Haibun #11," the narrator talks to his mother about the family genealogy:

> Mother somewhere you flying over me with love and close
> careless caress from Sweden your soft smooth creme skin
> only thoughts from your mother without comparison the
> lightness of your life / blood womaness which is mine . . . (86)

The depiction of his mother's fair European skin continues to underline racially divided Canadian society in which people are defined by their skin colour. Although the poet's family has mixed blood, it is the Chinese blood in him and his father that makes their lives "racial" and binds them to the Chinese Canadian community by the "bones."

A group of new prose poems, "Seasons Greetings from the Diamond Grill," published in *Canadian Literature* in 1994, continues Wah's tireless search for family genealogy and for the place of Chinese Canadian culture in prose poetry. As he usually does, Wah begins his poem with an oxymoron to capture the irony of the visible but slightly off-centre place of Chinatown in Canadian culture:

> On the edge of Centre. Just off Main. Chinatown, at least in most cities, is always close to the centre but just on the edge of it,

> because of the cafes. In places like Swift Current, Regina, Calgary, Vancouver, the Chinese cafes are clumped together in a section of town usually within a few blocks of the hub. Not way out. Not rural. Downtown. but on the edge of. In smaller towns like Red Deer, Nelson, Fernie, the cafes are more part of the centre. (8)

The paragraph is an ironic dialogue between the polemic concepts of the centre and the margin. The borderline in between seems to be decided by the size of the city and by the attitude of local white Canadians toward minority groups and their cultural products. As Chinese food has become more and more cosmopolitan these days, Chinese cafes and restaurants are conveniently located at the near-centre scene in Canadian cities. Contrastingly, Chinese stores are located somewhat off the centre, geographically and conceptually. Instead of the cafes or the restaurants, the poet depicts a Chinese store as the focus of his poem, thus discursively transforming the margin into a centre. It is in this marginalized centre that ethnic Chinese culture is not only well preserved but also actively engaging the community. Wah describes the Chinese store as a cultural centre that does not signify marginality to its subjects:

> . . . the Chinese store—a room really, smoky, dark and quiet, clock ticking. Dark brown wood panelling, some porcelain planters on the windowsill, maybe some goldfish. Goldfish for Gold Mountain men. Not so far, then, from the red carp of their childhood ponds. Brown skin stringy salt-and-pepper beard polished bent knuckles and at least one super-long fingernail for picking. Alone and on the edge of their world, far from the centre. This kind of edge in race and family we only half suspect as edge. (*Seasons Greetings from the Diamond Grill*, 8)

The paradox that the margin is also a centre emerges from the rich texture of life in the back of the Chinese store. This time Wah uses a long list of paralleled adjectives, and present and past participles to capture the passionate voices behind the Chinese store:

> . . . you can hear, mysteriously amplified through the window, the click-clacking of mah-jong pieces being shuffled over the table tops. The voices from up there or behind the curtain are hot tempered, powerful, challenging, aggressive, bickering, accusatory, demeaning, bravado, superstitious, bluffing, gossipy, serious, goading, letting off steam, ticked off, fed up, hot under the collar, hungry for company, hungry for language, hungry for luck. (*Seasons Greetings from the Diamond Grill* 8–9)

While the margin is depicted as preoccupied as the centre by human desires and emotions, the polemic difference between them is dismissed. Furthermore, the traditional power relationship between them is also conceptually displaced by the new paradigm of similarity.

Wah's recent poems also speak more provocatively against racism in Canadian society. The poet calls the reader's attention to street racism, such as a child's name-calling: "Until she called me a 'Chink' I wasn't one. That was in elementary school." With another similar situation of name-calling, the I-narrator is completely victimized:

> The old Chinamen had always just been friends of my dad's. . . I went fishing down by the boat-houses with one of them. . . We were walking back up the hill with our catch of suckers and some kids started chiding Chinky, chinky Chinaman and I figured I'd better not be caught with him any more. (*Seasons Greetings from the Diamond Grill* 10)

Wah captures what racism sometimes does to a victim. As racism undercuts the victim's self-esteem with shame, sometimes the victim adopts a similar discriminatory attitude against other victims:

> I became as white as I could, which, considering I'm mostly Scandinavian, was pretty easy for me. Not for my dad and some of my cousins though. They were stuck, I thought, with how they looked. And I not only heard my friends put down the Chinks (and the Japs, and the Wops, and the Spiks, and the Douks) but comic books and movies confirmed that the Chinese are yellow (meaning cowardly), not-to-be-trusted, heathens,

> devils, slant-eyed, dirty, and talk incomprehensible gobblydee-gook. Thus "gook n. Slang. 1. A dirty, sludgy, or slimy substance. 2. An Oriental. An offensive term used derogatorily." (*Seasons Greetings from the Diamond Grill* 10)

This paragraph maps out a chain reaction of racism starting from probably an innocent child's name-calling in the street. The poet digs into society to reveal the nature of name-calling, which is never as simple as it looks. Like the comic books, the movies, the popular slang, the dictionary, and the language, which are all products of the existing culture, racism is a cultural product.

Wah continues to search for his family genealogy and through it, for a Eurasian identity in the new poems. If in *Grasp the Sparrow's Tail*, the poet's travel diary in China, traditional genealogy based on pure racial lineage is deconstructed, in *Seasons Greetings from the Diamond Grill*, genealogy becomes fictitious between the poet and the reader: "Who am I thought I might say to my friend Charlie Chim Chong Say Wong Liu Chung, the chinese poet. He said he could tell me more about my father than I can imagine" (*Seasons Greetings from the Diamond Grill* 9). The tongue-in-cheek humour continues with the exploration of the narrator's family name:

> Like my name. This chinese doctor I go to for acupuncture always gets it wrong. He calls me Mah. And I say no, it's Wah . . . He says Wah just means overseas Chinese. So I'm just Fred Overseas.
>
> I tell him my dad was really Kuan Wah Soon. He says my family comes from Canton region. Then he smiles. He knows so much. (*Seasons Greetings from the Diamond Grill*, 9)

If the poet's father was called "Kuan Wah Soon," his family name should be "Soon" instead of "Wah," which was part of his father's first name. However, since what really matters to Wah's poetry is not the location of his origin but his search for genealogical connections, this illusive origin remains a resource of his poetry.

Wah's fascination with genealogy produces more poetry when he depicts his relationship with his daughters. As the mixed blood in his family keeps mixing, the poet illustrates how arbitrary and subjective racial stereotyping can be:

> Strange to watch your bloods. Like one of those sped-up movies of a cell dividing under a microscope. For just a split second your body'll do something Asian—like poised over a dish of Lo Bok with your chopsticks. There's just a brief Chinese glint in your eyes that flashes some shadow of track across your blond and ruddy Anglo-Swedish dominance . . .
>
> And I've watched you both closely at times to see if I can detect any of that Nordic gloom my grandparents brought over from Sweden. Once in awhile during your teenage years I worried that depressive despair might overwhelm you as it has me from time to time. But what foolish stereotyping, to generalize about an ethnic quality like that. (*Seasons Greetings from the Diamond Grill* 10-11)

Seasons Greetings from the Diamond Grill ends metaphorically with a simple analogy of bread and butter as daily necessities for everyone: here traditional butter is replaced by a mixed, cheaper, and perhaps better product called "oleomargarine," ironically and symbolically, "for the world's starving, the mix of the century" (*Seasons Greetings from the Diamond Grill* 11). By selecting a simple metaphor as a solution for the complex racial issues in society, Wah sends out an unmistakable message to readers of all races in Canada that an understanding of each other is necessary as it is in a family.

The search for a family genealogy is also a subject of Lucy Ng's prose poetry, entitled "The Sullen Shapes of Poems" published in *Many-Mouthed Birds* (Ng 160-168). Similar to *Waiting for Saskatchewan*, Ng's poems are dialogues of a third-generation Chinese Canadian daughter with both her parents about their family's history. They begin with the first-person narrator talking to her father about his visit to mainland China, recognizing the psychological connection with the origin:

> Father. . .
> . . . .
> Sometimes dreaming or reading, I think I know
> what you must have felt when you climbed that
> Great Wall or wandered through those magnificent

rooms, finger-deep in dust. Did you feel the
pain of recognition—thirty years gone—as
you chanced upon this, the undiscovered country,
its imprint in your heart? (160)

Another poem begins with a dialogue with the narrator's mother, an immigrant woman, who plays a double role both at home and in the community:

Mother, I remember the quiet house—you on your
knees, curved over the bathtub scrubbed white
like the back of a beluga whale . . .
. . . I wondered
how you could do it—your back broken
after six hours crouched in the fields
and then the strawberries stolen when you
went to pee. You came home angry hands
stained red. (163)

A third poem touches upon the life of her grandfather—of the first generation from her family to emigrate from China. Upon his death, her grandfather left his descendants a few solid pieces of heirloom to build a family with:

When grandfather died he left: four benches, two
shoe racks, three bookshelves, a cabinet and a
potty chair for the baby (in the hole he'd dropped
the green plastic beach bucket . . .
its handle broken). . .(166)

During his lifetime he expresses his emotional connection with China by painting his toolshed "vermilion, the colour, too, of the rooftops he'd /left behind in China" (166).

A fourth poem depicts the family observing the Chinese remembrance ritual for the narrator's uncle who is buried in Canada. The ritual consists of burning paper clothes, paper shoes, paper money, and serving wine and food for the dead in front of the grave. Ng's detailed descriptions portray Chinese immigrants' commitment to

Canada, whereas their connection with Chinese culture becomes part of their cultural heritage in Canada.

> Mother says, Don't crumple them, Uncle
> likes his clothes well pressed. I imagine
> him in the other world receiving his new
> suit eagerly, straightening the lapels,
> and pulling the hat over one eye the
> way detectives do in those black and white
> movies. Afterwards I think—I should have
> poured him another whisky. (165)

Ng also depicts the limited opportunities faced by Chinese immigrants in Canada. The group of nine poems ends with a list of service businesses that the family has undertaken: "Chinese cafe, grocery, laundry—skipping rope / rhymes—you want something different for me / Poet? you say. What's that?" (168). This line sounds similar to the experience described in Wah's "Elite 10" in *Waiting for Saskatchewan*. The recurrent depiction of limited opportunity for Chinese immigrants raises a collective voice of protest against the racist labour market in Canadian history. Using the same narrative strategy of engaging the deceased family members in on-going dialogues, both Wah and Ng construct their family genealogy as a part of community history.

In addition to the dialogues between the narrator and her parents, Ng uses the first-person plural pronoun "we" to engage the reader in a discovery of Chinese Canadian cultural practice. By blending Chinese tradition with Canadian customs, Ng's poems weave valuable ornaments from both cultures into a new tapestry of Chinese Canadian culture. The following poem is about the first New Year after the family settled down in Canada, "the second mainland," or "home," as her father calls it "after Hong Kong and Trinidad (mere islands)" (161).

> The first New Year we danced in the kitchen
> scented with the perfume of joss sticks
> till Father said, Stop. And so we lined up in
> front of the table to give thanks: apples

and oranges, a pair of fat fish, a roast
chicken, vermicelli for long life and
steamed brown sugar dough clusters like
shiny grapes, sweet and rubber textured.
All the time the lucky red signs
above our heads like Canadian flags.
Mother said, Bow.

One bow. Two bows. Three. (162)

The rich texture of Ng's prose poem is not only woven with different names of ornaments, but also with different rituals and customs for the New Year. The symbolic meaning of the New Year is employed here as a significant setting to renew Chinese tradition in Canada. Ng's poem speaks positively about the Canadian culture in which ethnic minorities, such as the Chinese, can preserve their heritages and at the same time absorb new elements from mainstream and other minority cultures.

Besides naming the Chinese ornaments and customs in English, Ng also blends the prose with Japanese *haiku* sensibility and concludes with an informal *haiku* line; thus her poetry includes a dialogue of poetic forms. In the short prose part of her poem, her narration is built around a carefully selected event, which describes in detail how the Chinese immigrants rebuilt their homes in Canada. The informal *haiku* line at the concluding position provides her prose with a depth and sometimes with a new dimension. The poem about the Mother's Chinese vegetable garden reminds the reader of the textuality of a water-colour painting:

In the summer there was the garden—rows
and rows of vegetable greens, leafy clumps;
long furred beans and tender-crisp snow
peas, vines laced round the wood stakes you
drove . . . into the earth. Neat crisscrosses x x x x x. This is
a Chinese garden x x x x x. This is
a Chinese garden. The wind tipping your hand,
your straw hat, gently. (164)

The harmonious green vegetable garden tranquillizes the reader's mind, while Mother's hard work to build such a garden in Canada is emphasized with the ten crisscrosses across the lines. The poem ends with an amusing *haiku* line, recommending Mother's Chinese philosophy of natural recycling: "I remember you spraying piss water; life green life" (164).

By cultivating the different experiences of a three-generation Chinese immigrant family, Ng's group of prose poem presents a reality shared by many Chinese Canadian families: migration from mainland China, or from Hong Kong, or from Trinidad, or from Africa, and eventual settlement in Canada. After two generations' struggle for survival, the third generation starts to see some growth, even the birth of a poet, or an artist. The group of poems ends with the image of the ancient Chinese poet Li Po of the Tang Dynasty (618-907 AD) writing "brushstroke of calligraphy on water"; this connection recognizes the literary tradition of Chinese culture as a heritage that all Chinese descendants can inherit whatever their nationalities. The poem concludes with a meditative *haiku* line: "You gave me these: a river, a boat /a bridge. The sullen shapes of poems" (168). Ng's conclusion, which lists three solid nouns, implies a ritual passage that all immigrant groups have to go through before achieving a reterritorialization in a new land. Several generations after the initial settlement, the Chinese Canadian community has seen the birth of its first-generation writers and its community literature in English.

Community history, family genealogy and cultural heritage become significant components in the poetry written by most Chinese Canadian poets. However, these collective characteristics should not be regarded as restrictions to limit what Chinese Canadian poets ought or ought not to write. Born and raised in Canada, writers who belong to the second, third or fourth generations never needed a boat to cross the oceans to Canada, neither did they experience the difficulties of linguistic and cultural dislocations as did the first generation immigrants. Influenced by the dominant Western ideology of individualism, a few might even want to cut ties with their community. Vancouver poet Evelyn Lau did this by running away from home.

Some of Lau's poems first appeared in various magazines, including academic periodicals, such as *Ariel, Michigan Quarterly Review,*

Queen's Quarterly, and *Southern Review*. Later they were published in three collections: *You Are Not Who You Claim* (1990), *Oedipal Dreams* (first published in 1992; republished in 1994), and *In the House of Slaves* (1994). In 1990, with *Oedipal Dreams,* Lau became the youngest writer ever nominated for the Governeror General's Literary Award.

Lau's three poetry collections depict prostitution and sadomasochism as does her prose, which will be discussed in the next chapter. Despite the subject matter, which distinguishes Lau from most other Chinese Canadian poets and from Canadian poets in general, her poetry demonstrates the shared poetic strategy of dialogue that is widely employed by many Chinese Canadian poets. Unlike other Chinese Canadian poets who use dialogue to investigate racism, or to search for family genealogy and personal identity, the dialogue in Lau's poetry is carried on between a first-person female persona and a second-person male addressee. While "I-versus-You" becomes a dominant narrative paradigm, her poetry depicts the experience of a female subject in the sex industry.

You Are Not Who You Claim typifies Lau's poetic paradigm of I-versus-You. The poet uses dialogue to question the sexual relationship between a young female would-be poet and various professional adult males. Lau describes the "you" in detail to remind the addressee of the schemes he uses to manipulate an otherwise innocent relationship with the young female subject. The opening poem, entitled "Role Models," depicts the "I" already a sexual object and the "you" a manipulator:

> You arrive on my doorstep
> I seem a small thing to sacrifice
> . . . .
> you watch teenage girls cross the road, your eyes
> weave stockings to fit their legs
> they carry their breasts like welcome burdens
> your daughter stands in a doorway and you hunger
> for her, the body she must have stolen
> while your back was turned
> . . . .
> you insist you are my saviour
> how can I help but know the truth

and love you for your lies (*You Are Not Who You Claim* 5)

As the "role models" (a term that ironically explains the title) eventually become sexual predators of the "I," the collection exposes the masks worn by the respectable "you," who is sometimes a "lawyer," a "literary lion," a "psychiatrist," and at other times a "drugged" addict, or a "john" (7, 8, 11, 13, 23). The social statuses of the sexual exploiters are mapped out in several poems, when "[t]he neons burn holes into the city's fabric / glaring at the man of the streets" (23), and the "you" everywhere corners the "I" and corrupts her. Lau also lists various games played by the "you," such as "promises," "handful of words," "kisses," and "hug[s]," leading the "I" to sexual exploitation:

Now you sprawl, legs open
in a cafe doorway in the west end
shirt deliberately unbuttoned, a showcase
of chest hair gleaming gold (9)

Listening, I feel again your weight on the bed
springs obeying laws of gravity (8)

you unknot the secrets of your silk tie and
I breathe in sloped shoulders
a mountain of belly (11)

The I-versus-You paradigm presents the "I" as a desirable and disposable sexual commodity. Although gender and sexual confrontations are depicted in Lau's poetry, the power relationship between the "You" and the "I" remains unchanged—the "you" consistently overpowering the naïve and vulnerable "I."

Since the "I" and the "you" are bound by the traditional power relationship between the two sexes, there is an accusatory moral tone in Lau's first poetry collection. When the "I" is a junior, almost like "your daughter stands in a doorway," the "I" accuses the "you" of being a manipulator. However, occasionally when the "I" changes to "you," and the "you" changes to "he," the accusatory overtone disappears. When that happens, prostitution and writing ironically merge into one poetic syntax of harmony: "your thighs straddle his shoulders like run-on sentences" (*You Are Not Who You Claim* 45). In this case, the moral paradigm of I-versus-You is undermined by an inclusive and unifying pronoun "we" as exemplified in the title of another poem "What We Do in the Name of Money" (*You Are Not Who You Claim* 45). As Lau's street experience grows, her poetry becomes a callous witness to her life.

Although the I-versus-You paradigm remains the basic poetic structure in Lau's second collection of poetry, *Oedipal Dreams*, the tension between the narrator and the addressee starts to dissolve. The relationship between the "I" and the "you" becomes an equal business partnership:

> you had written me into your appointment book with initials
> that were not my own.
> I counted the hours into my purse and wrote the important names
> into a black book in the bathroom. (*Oedipal Dreams* 14)

Without the I-narrator's accusation of the "You" as in Lau's first poetry collection, the power relationship between the female narrator and the male addressee reaches an equilibrium in *Oedipal Dreams*. In this collection, her depiction of doctors and psychiatrists reading Freud and sexually exploiting the young female patient (14, 18, 20, 25, 46) may astonish the reader; it does not irritate the "I" narrator. An assignation is presented as a social event, with a sense of reunion rather than moral degradation: "your eyes never rest, I watch our complexities / twine like sunburnt arms in their shallows" (20). At the same time, financial reward is accepted as a justification for the trade of body:

> . . . from that day on all my money began to smell of you
> even that hundred dollar bill.
> I struggled to breathe you into me. . .
> (*Oedipal Dreams* 21)

> two days later I snuck back
> to bi-weekly cash instalments
> and expensive tax-deductible gifts
> to hold you in my arms and . . . (*Oedipal Dreams* 28)

In this collection, sometimes the "I" narrator seems even more callous than the "You" and offers the latter a mirror of self-reflection. For example, an ironic reflection occurs when the narrator enters the house of a married john:

> you do not see the three wedding photos on the dresser
> where his arm holds a woman who looks happy
> even though she is standing in a park by the edge of a cliff
> with a good view (*Oedipal Dreams* 27)

Sometimes when the first-person I-narrator changes to the second-person "You," the self-reflection allows the persona to see her own Oedipal nightmares:

> but before long it seemed that something ended,
> the light rusted, you rose dazed from a year as if
> from a long sleep and dreams of love,
> dreams twisting into nightmares.
> and there was the silver afternoon, the metal plate of the day
> tearing aside the blanket of your Oedipal dreams,
> tearing him away till the day was dull and the room empty
> and the sky unmoved. And you sat in the middle of your bed,
> not a child, with Daddy grey and bent in the bathroom mirror
> looking terribly confused, his fingers tapping ten anxious
> thoughts,
> old as myth. (*Oedipal Dreams* 46)

Early in her work her representations of prostitution are charged with anger, but in her later work the anger is absent.

Lau's latest poetry collection, *In the House of Slaves*, continues the same theme of prostitution with an emphasis on S & M. In this group of poems, the I-versus-You relationship presents the I-narrator as a torturer or a dominatrix, who is physically in control, while the addressee "You" is a passive sex slave, who is financially in control, even though this relationship is not always clarified. Although the "I" narrator is in fact confined inside the houses owned by her "slaves," Lau's poetry is loaded ironically with details of the powerful female dominatrix in S & M role-playing. Thus she generates a self-deceptive image of her temporary power: cuffs are buckled and unbuckled; knots are tied and untied; her slave is punished or set free. Ironically, in the particular male-female relationship based on sex games, the parties are unusually friendly and civilized: "At the door we exchanged Christmas presents, the red packages from you so many they spilled over my arms" (*In the House of Slaves* 21). Set in the private houses which the "I" narrator frequents for business, Lau's latest poetry further develops male and female stereotypes in the sex industry.

Among the few reviewers of Lau's latest poetry collection, John Moore points out that her characters are not individuals but stereotypes: "Poets who go hunting for metaphors and archetypes on such marginal ground run the risk of succumbing to the sensibility of the subculture they try to exploit, as Lau does here. Instead of archetypes, we get stereotypes" (Moore D18). Lau's own explanation also offers a clue to the logic in her writings: "My experience of sexuality has been, for the most part, some form of prostitution" (Inwood B15). Lau's limited experience in life, which matches the restricted subject matters in her writings, emphasizes the connection between life and art, which, in a very different way, is illustrated by the writings of other Chinese Canadian poets who found their topics from community history and family genealogy. Lau must have realized that her writing, which has been entirely about her experience of the sex trade, starts to gain her such a reputation. She tells a reviewer: "I promise this [*In the House of Slaves*] is the last thing I write about S & M" (Andrews D16).

Despite all the differences between Lau's poetry and the poetry written by the community-based Chinese Canadian poets studied in this chapter, there is one discursive strategy that they do share; that is, using personal or collective experience, or both, as a resource for poetry composition. When poetry is employed as a medium for collective and individual experiences, its "purest, least socially tainted" "sensibility" is challenged.

In this chapter, I have illustrated the discursive strategy of dialogue that is widely adopted by the Chinese Canadian poets to portray different subject matters. Dialogue provides the poets with a narrative space in which they investigate, question, reclaim, and redefine community history, family genealogy, personal identities and experience. Dialogue is usually issued by the first-person narrator, whereas the addressees could be deceased community or family ancestor(s), bones of Chinese railway labourers, or the reader. In most cases, the addressee, "you," remains silent or unable to reply. However, the consistent presence of the "you" provokes the narrator with a desire to transform the former's silence into words. Jim Wong-Chu's lyrics connect the silence of the Chinese labourers with the identity crisis suffered by contemporary Chinese Canadians. *Chinatown Ghosts* rewrites part of the existing Canadian history by recognizing early Chinese immigrants as nation-builders and community ancestors. Fred Wah's prose poems search consistently for a family genealogy in the collective history of the Chinese Canadians. So do Lucy Ng's prose poems. Fred Wah, Laiwan, and Jam. Ismail write resistantly to disengage the syntactic order of the English language and the cultural hegemony signified through its rules. Paul Yee's poems, "Last Words II" and "The Grass Dragon," which are discussed in Chapter Three, also involve the reader in a joint effort to reconstruct the forgotten Chinese Canadian community history in its literature. Evelyn Lau's poetry explores the experience of a female sex worker with sometimes an ironic reflection.

The body of Chinese Canadian poetry demonstrates once again the discursive practice of employing a mainstream literary genre to reinterpret minority experiences. Since most of the Chinese Canadian poets use the poetic form to describe experiences, or to define and redefine concepts, such as origin and genealogy, Chinese Canadian poetry demonstrates narrative strategies of reflection and conceptualization. These strategies explain why many of the poets chose the more innovative and flexible form of prose poetry rather than verse. By fusing the generic boundaries of prose and poetry, poets who choose prose poetry have access to both, and yet are not exactly bound by either. In addition, Chinese Canadian poetry also demonstrates the significant role of the speaking subjects, or the first-person poetic personas, who are contemporary Chinese Canadians. Similar to the first-person narrator in an autobiographical novel or a nonfiction work, the I-narrator/persona in many poems discussed in this chapter refers back and forth to the poets' identifiable personal data for recurrent topics. This poetic practice emphasizes the personal and autobiographical references as relevant historical components of poetry as they are of other literary genres.

8. From Testimony to Erotica: The Split Subject and Oedipal Drama in Evelyn Lau's Prose

Of all women they are the most submissive to the male . . . There is no feminine type, however—virgin, mother, wife, sister, servant, loved one, fiercely virtuous one, smiling odalisque—who is not capable of summing up thus the vagrant yearning of men.

SIMONE DE BEAUVOIR

Porn, I suggest, is the representation of the eroticization of relations of power between the sexes.

ALISON ASSITER

Born in 1971 to a Chinese immigrant family in Vancouver, Evelyn Lau is probably the youngest and the most controversial Canadian writer of Chinese descent. Her first book, *Runaway: Diary of a Street Kid,* published in paperback in 1989, immediately became a national best-seller. Translated into German, French and Spanish, a television version of *Runaway* has also been produced by the CBC. Her first short-story collection, *Fresh Girls and Other Stories* (1993), was published simultaneously in the United States and the United Kingdom in the fall of 1994. Because of her youthful achievements, Lau was voted the most promising writer by the Canadian Author's Association in 1988 (Armstrong).

Since Lau's street experience as a prostitute and drug addict more or less constitutes the essence of her poetry and prose, the public and the media seem to be more interested in her than in her writing. While the media presents her as a reformed street kid with her diary as a witness, few members of the literary league try to nullify her tarnished reputation as an ex-prostitute by promoting her "originality and unorthodoxy as to be in a league of her own" (W P Kinsella, backcover of *In the House of Slaves*). The nationwide promotion of *Runaway* by the media and the low-key reception given to *Fresh Girls* both underline the fact that Lau is not exactly "in a league of her own." The cultural and sexual politics in the two books, which had different receptions in the media, call for a critical investigation.

Lau's prose is characterized by a single Freudian psychoanalytical drama—the Oedipal paradigm. As a result of this predominant subject matter, the family romance rules the plots of all her stories, connects the interplay of her characters, splits the subjectivity of her autobiographical narrator, and creates the typical ironic syntax of her writing. This chapter examines Lau's *Runaway* from the perspective of the mixed genre of autobiography and testimony. The CBC production of Lau's diary will also be reviewed here; its cinematography will be examined in order to unveil its hidden cultural politics. Lau's short-story collection, *Fresh Girls,* will be read for its sexual politics, which borders on erotica and soft pornography. For clarity, *Runaway* and *Fresh Girls* will be read in two different sections.

Success and Controversy of Runaway

Lau's running away from home at the age of fourteen, becoming a prostitute and a drug addict, attempting suicide and using various social and medical services, are not unusual among teenage prostitutes. According to *Prostitution in Vancouver (1973-75),* a research report based on the participation of one hundred prostitutes in Vancouver, the geographical location of the city as a stepping stone to California, and its port status and mild temperature made it possible for young prostitutes to work without having to belong to organized rings (Layton 8). Lau fits the characteristics of girls who become prostitutes in the Vancouver area. The most obvious reasons are the following: first of all, she was in the age group of high rebellion; second, she was under a lot of family pressure as the first-born daughter and third, she had a domineering mother and submissive father (Layton 17, 39, 41, 42).

Runaway personifies almost all the social circumstances of teenage runaways. Linda Rogers summarizes its value in a review for *The Vancouver Sun*: "As literature, it is flawed but promising. As a social document, it is invaluable and appalling" (Rogers H5). Commercially, *Runaway* became an instant success; Lau says: "I realize its commercial value is that it's about runaways which is a big topic these days" (Lacey C9). The media promoted Lau's diary as written testimony to the enormous social problems experienced by hundreds of high school dropouts and runaways, who are likely to become "sad and tawdry child welfare" recipients (Cuff C16).

Written mainly in the first-person narrative voice and in the form of a diary, *Runaway* combines both autobiography and testimony. Talking about testimonial writing, or "*testimonio*," John Beverly emphasizes "the intentionality of the narrator" (Beverly 94). *Runaway*, which bears witness to "the real protagonist" (Beverly 92), meaning Lau's personal life on the street from March 22, 1986 to January 20, 1988, seems to fit well into the genre of testimonial writing. Secondly, according to Beverly, the narrator in *testimonio* is supposed to be "functionally illiterate; if literate, not a professional writer"; the process of writing should be from tape-recording to transcription and finally to a professional editor's desk, so the text bears "the truth effect" of life (94-95). The process of writing *Runaway* embodies such a true-to-life process. Lau had published poetry before she ran away. During the two years while she was on the street, she carried stacks of foolscap paper around in her backpack, scribbling notes in longhand and typing them up later in an Eastside community hall (Lacey C9); the final 341-page diary was edited from the original 900-page manuscript (Lau 340). In addition to the true-to-life effect created by her process of writing, *Runaway* also contains other "paramount" aspects of *testimonio*: the narrator's "urgency to communicate" and the "struggle of survival" should be both "implicated in the act of narration itself" (Beverly 94). Lau clarifies that her published diary is "no different from all the destroyed diaries preceding it—it is a story of survival" (5). Overall, the making of *Runaway* bears the most important features of *testimonio*.

Based on the representational values of testimonial writing, media seized *Runaway* as a piece of morality literature which could be launched to teach young people, especially high school students, to stay in school. *Runaway* immediately entered the national bestsellers' list for 1989, interviews and reviews with Lau's photographs appeared in national and local newspapers and magazines. Since few Canadian writers have ever been given so much attention by the media for their first book, reviewers read Lau less for her writing than for her personal experience. Five years after the publication of Lau's diary, the publicity surrounding the launching of the CBC-TV movie of *Runaway* in 1994 was equally extensive. Some twenty days before the scheduled airing, entertainment columnist Sid Adilman of *The Toronto Star* started advertising *Diary of Evelyn Lau* in an article promoting Korean Canadian actress Sandra Oh, who played the lead in the film. In the weekends before the 1994 March break for elementary and high school students, various media heavily publicized the CBC movie of Lau's diary, which was scheduled to be aired on prime time on Sunday March 13, 1994.[1]

The uniform classification of Lau's diary as a testimonial to street life speaks obviously to the critique of didactic realism and the politics of victimization. The following are among the comments made about it in the media: "docudrama" (Quill, *The Toronto Star*);"documentary-like portrayal of the brutal lives that thousands of young runaways lead on the streets of Canadian cities" (Cuff, *The Globe and Mail*); "the frightening path of Canada's most famous runaway" (Leger, *Broadcast Week*); and "Street life: from honour student to teen hooker, *The Diary of Evelyn Lau* paints a haunting portrait of a runaway's life on the street" (Bawden, *Starweek*). While most reviewers commented on the social and moral aspects of the movie, television critic Nicholas Read of *The Vancouver Sun* pointed out the structural problems of the movie: "too much happens too quickly"; "there's never any buildup to the storms. No brooding clouds, no menacing thunder, just a constant and relentless downpour"; "the effect is like a conveyor belt of misery," "you probably won't be moved by it" (Read C1). Greg Quill of *The Toronto Star* also expressed an overall concern with the depiction in the film, which "fails as testimony to a young artist's progress from purgatory to spiritual salvation" (Quill E10). Indeed, instead of portraying a young female artist's personal and career struggle, the CBC movie simply documented the teenager's problems, especially those with her immigrant parents.

However, if the reader listens to the predominant individual voice in *Runaway*, a restrictive classification of the book as testimony writing can be problematic and suppressive. The first-person narrator in Lau's diary is not simply a testimonial narrator, "a collective subject" as per Beverly and Sommer (Beverly 96; Sommer 111). Rather, Lau's "I" speaks the voice of a strong ego wanting to be "one of the top writers in Canada" instead of just a third prize or a youth competition winner (168, 230). Lau's "I" repeatedly emphasizes her determination to "make a name for *[her]self* from *[her] writing*" (Lau 231, 247, 279; emphases mine). This determination is so strong that in one journal entry the writer replaces her own existence with her desire to be a published writer: "Evelyn isn't alive at all, it's always her writing, her writing . . . fantasies about seeing her books on shelves and people actually reading them, books that would make people think and feel" (Lau 156). Lau's expressive desire to see her writing published and gain mainstream readership speaks of individual rather than collective interest.

Lau's signature printed at the end of every poem in *You Are Not Who You Claim* illustrates her desire for authorship and individual success. The repetitive appearance of her initials in her own hand challenges the romantic and idealistic assumption made by some critics who perceive testimonial writing as an ideological opposite of mainstream autobiography. According to this critique, testimonial writing deconstructs "the individual bourgeois author (the sacred subject of autobiographical narrative)" (Kaplan 121) and translates homogeneously "a hegemonic autobiographical pose into a colonized language that does not equate identity with individuality" (Sommer 111). The first-person narrator in *Runaway* behaves differently from these theoretical postures. Rather than diminishing her subjectivity, she speaks with an undeniable individual voice searching for recognition. This individual voice transforms the otherwise colonized testimonial narrator, whose credibility relies simply on her street experience, into an independent speaking subject who demands recognized authorship.

It is debatable that in *Runaway* Lau mingles the politics of victimization with bourgeois individualism. While the former is usually embedded in testimonial writings, the latter is conventionally represented through a journey motif and is sometimes lodged in an autobiographical form. The combination of the two forms, testimony and autobiography, creates an urgent political agenda, which results in helping Lau, an emerging writer, become instantly famous. In her first journal entry immediately after her running away, Lau speaks as a self-made heroine declaring her symbolic new birth:

> I look out at the mountain, managing to convince myself that I never existed before this day, that my parents would not be expecting their teenage daughter to come home after school. I crouch on the floor and concentrate hard on my fantasy: It never happened, I was not born until today. (9)

The rest of the journals are simply acts of a live drama about "Evelyn the wronged heroine" (167).

Within this framework, the narrator constantly crosses the borders between *testimonio* and autobiography and sometimes moves even to fiction. Using the traditional journey motif, the narrator starts her journey with a quick descent from a schoolgirl to a street kid; after getting into bed with a friend named Joe and being raped by him (13) she loses her innocence and later becomes a prostitute, a drug addict and eventually a double "hooker/junkie" (155). At the turning point of her journey, before she decides to treat sex as an impersonal trade, the narrator records a callous street philosophy taught by a former male hooker: "Treat sex as a purely physical thing. That's all it is—a business exchange, a physical act for money. It's not a big invasion" (191). One can almost assume that this former male hooker is a fictional character, who is conventionally and conveniently invented by the writer to help the heroine descend quickly, before she could ascend again via the publication of her writing.

Lau's diary records the downfall of the heroine/narrator into the underworld of sex trade and drug abuse. Her moral descent illustrates what was underlined a long time ago by Simone de Beauvoir in *The Second Sex*, that "modern woman is everywhere permitted to regard her body as capital for exploitation" (153). De Beauvoir also points out a misconception that "there has always been a vague connection between prostitution and art" (630). However, only the few with superior gifts among prostitutes, whom de Beauvoir calls "creative workers," who "write poetry and prose" (631, 633), can actually "go beyond the given and make their appeal to a freedom in others for which they open the doors of the future" (631). This is probably why the public promotion of Lau's journal/journey as a reformed street kid might backfire. Instead of getting its moral message across to likely high school dropouts and runaways, it could create the wrong impression that a couple of years of street life might lead a high school dropout to a writer's career as long as one keeps a diary. Had the promotion of *Runaway* been focused on a different perspective, such as the development of a young female artist, "the wronged heroine" (163) might be able to recover from what has wronged her on the streets. After all, the few "creative workers" who have transcended the sex industry have to appropriate the collective experience and utilize their individual talents.

By exploring street politics as a victim and bourgeois individualism as a heroine, Lau transforms herself from an ex-prostitute to a writer. Other discursive strategies she employs for this identity transformation include using her true name in *Runaway* and allowing her photograph to appear on the (front) cover of most of her publications. Thus, instead of advocating for street kids, or for the cause of women in the sex industry, or using a pseudonym to protect herself as some prostitutes and ex-prostitutes have done with their publications (Delacoste 17), Lau's strategy of using her true personal identity produced effective testifiers for her own personal and career advancement. For such a personal cause, *Runaway* fuses testimony with autobiography from which the narrator achieves, unmistakably, what a bourgeois writer desires—individuality and authorship.

The politics of reading *Runaway* go beyond the debate about the literary genres of the book. Lau's depiction of the cause of her running away from home raises sensitive cultural issues. Although it is generally known that prostitution often is related to childhood abuse, especially sexual abuse by family members of the opposite sex (Alexander 15), *Runaway* testifies to a different kind of child abuse caused by the cultural gap between the immigrant parents and their Canadian-born daughter. Although expecting one's daughter to become a doctor or a lawyer may not be an outrageous demand by parents in any culture, legendary Chinese stories about ancient scholars imposing self-discipline are alien to the Canadian-born Chinese generations and more so to Western readers.[2] In the "Prologue" of *Runaway*, Lau paints her mother as a dictator who tries to impose ancient Chinese discipline on her: "rapping a ruler impatiently against her palm and forcing [her] to recite the answers to textbook questions" (Lau 2). Paradoxically, her parents are also presented as failing to support her career development even though she was on the honour roll every year and won some junior literary competitions (3-4). They forbade her any playtime and disapproved of her interest in writing and her involvement in the peace movement. In addition to dictating her daughter, Mrs Lau also abused her husband, "fighting late at night," which Lau "assumed . . . would end up hurting [her] father or making him leave the house" (1).

The parents are also attacked for their ignorance of Canadian culture and their blindness to their daughter's basic needs. Instead of buying Lau a pair of jeans and a sweatshirt, they made her wear "bright green bell-bottoms" dug out from the mother's trunk; as a result, Lau was bitterly ridiculed in school (3). To most Canadian readers, the behaviour of Lau's parents appears unreasonable and unaccountable. The only possible explanation for that could be their inappropriate Chinese cultural baggage.

By denouncing her parents as the sole cause of her running away from home, the sovereignty of the autobiographical narrator is obtained, though at the expense of her parents' subjectivity being depicted as the Other. While Lau's illustration of her parents' general lack of ability to fit into Canadian society is simplified, their failure is magnified in her presentation: her father's continuous unemployment and the tension between the parents caused by "lack of money and the need to maintain a house and a car" (3); her mother's constant screaming in the house (181); her father's unchanged silence at home (266) and his on-going lecturing about school in his letters to Lau (160). By presenting her parents as the perpetual cultural Other, the narrator makes sure the reader can see through her parents who "are so obvious, clumsy, revealing all the more starkly what they are trying to hide" (267). Later the narrator even borrows the power of her psychiatrist Dr Hightower, who compares her parents metaphorically to the permanently fixed, unchangeable sign on his car: "like the Ford sign outside his office window—no matter how much he talked to it or yelled at it, the letters would never change. 'F-O-R-D. Never, never, never!' " (160). Through a continuous process of Othering, Lau's parents are fossilized as the forever opposite of the narrator.

Following this cultural politics in Lau's *Runaway*, the CBC TV-movie is narrowly focused to construct Evelyn as a victim of her parents. With the advantage of the camera, the movie launches an on-going process of alienating the audience, or Othering the characters, in which Lau's parents are depicted as inadequate first-generation immigrants who are enveloped in a negative cultural environment. The director combines dramatic repetition with the camera's perspective to achieve a powerful alienating effect. In the two-hour movie, Lau's parents appeared six times together or singly, which seems far too frequent compared to their proportionately fewer appearances in the 341-page diary that covers two years. The film begins with Lau's mother examining fourteen year-old Evelyn on a scale after a bath. The mother's abusive behaviour is unmistakably signified initially by her repeating the same sentence, "You're fat like a pig," and hitting the daughter on the head. Because twenty-two-year-old actress Oh plays the fourteen-year-old character Evelyn, the scene is extremely disturbing. Instead of viewing a much younger child being helped by her mother after her bath, the audience observes a mother probing at her naked, full-size daughter, who is deprived of her privacy. After such a powerful beginning, the audience is immediately aware of the sexual and psychological abuse in the family.

The rest of the movie simply widens the gap between the immigrant parents and their Canadian-born daughter. While the camera always stays on Evelyn's side, especially when her parents are called in by the social workers to negotiate with their daughter to return home, the CBC movie makes it clear to the audience that Evelyn's problems are caused by her parents' lack of understanding. In the interviews, not only are the parents positioned to face the camera, their somewhat clumsy physical movements, their Chinese dialects, Mrs Lau's questionable personal hygiene, such as rubbing her son's face with her saliva, all illustrate their alien behaviour. The parents' social ineptness is contrasted to their daughter's linguistic and cultural competence, which appears to be the Canadian way: not only does Evelyn speak perfect English, she is also supported by social workers. To her immigrant parents, the social workers clearly represent the government and the law. In the face of both, they cannot possibly win their family dispute with their daughter.

Due to this powerful alienating effect, the bourgeois audience watching the CBC production of Lau's growing-up experience is successfully prevented from emotionally identifying with Lau's parents on the screen.[3] The movie has succeeded in silencing the first-generation Chinese immigrants before the mainstream CBC viewers.

A lot of the perspective shots in the movie graphically reinforce the image of the Chinese immigrants as maladjusted and isolated, a view that a mainstream audience is not likely to dispute. For example, Mrs Lau never speaks one word in English but repeats her unreasonable scolding of her daughter in Cantonese on different occasions: "You're getting fatter." Mr Lau seems more sensitive than his wife in his attitude toward his daughter, but he cannot really understand why his daughter ran away from home: "Come home, things will be different. I'll take you out. Go to movies. Eat at McDonald's." To further the death of communication in the Lau family, which already assumes a comic-tragic effect, the CBC movie-makers used their power and liberty as a mainstream medium to fabricate a linguistic barrier in the family.

The script writer and film director added a detail that is not provided in Lau's diary. They inserted an original linguistic barrier among the Laus: throughout the movie, Mrs Lau only speaks Cantonese; Mr Lau speaks Mandarin and some English, whereas Evelyn speaks English and no Chinese, although she appears to understand both Cantonese and Mandarin. To any viewer who speaks one of the two Chinese dialects and is aware of the difference between them, the result is simply ridiculous. As if inside the tower of Babel, when Mr Lau preaches in Mandarin to Evelyn about their family reputation being ruined by her notoriety as a runaway, Evelyn answers in tears in English, while Mrs Lau shows no response and says nothing. Since a foreign language can be used as a theatrical device to achieve the effect of defamiliarization, by using the Chinese dialects the CBC movie is able to isolate Lau's parents from the audience. On the one hand, the mainstream Canadian audience will not identify themselves with the abusive, unsuitable, inadequate Chinese immigrant parents, and on the other, they will see that the parents' "Chineseness" causes the unhappiness of their Canadian-born daughter. Putting Evelyn's parents on trial as the unchanged cultural Other, the CBC movie hints that the conflict in Chinese immigrant families is caused by the cultural gap between immigrant parents and their Canadian-born children, particularly by the parents' refusal to be assimilated. The cultural politics demonstrated in the CBC TV movie reinforces the prevailing racial and ethnic stereotypes of the Chinese immigrants, rendering them once again as aliens in Canadian society.

In addition to being an inadequate parent, a linguistic and cultural alien, Lau's mother is also made responsible for the psychological harassment which causes her daughter's underdeveloped sexuality. Near the end of *Runaway*, after spending two years on the street, Lau tried to deal with her psychological detachment in prostitution. Her impersonal attitude toward the sex trade could probably be related to how Chinese women were traditionally treated as sexual commodities in their own culture. In all the prose works discussedin this book so far, namely, *Tales from Gold Mountain*, *Bachelor-Man*, *Jin Guo*, *Disappearing Moon Cafe*, and *The Concubine's Children*, the writers depict Chinese cultural and ritual practices that treat women as merchandise. For example, Fong Mei and May-ying, who were sold to Gold Mountain as a paper bride and a concubine, are expected to please their buyers so they can secure status in the families. Their sexuality and reproductivity, which are the only material means they have in these activities, make their lives, in fact, not much different from that of the female sex workers on the street. This deeply-rooted, patriarchal bias against Chinese women probably made an impact on Lau's attitude toward her own sexuality and furthermore toward female prostitution. Nevertheless, in her diary, she adopts a pragmatic attitude toward her street life and psychologically she traces her resentment of female sexuality to her mother's inappropriate toilet behaviour:

> . . . my mother used to go to the bathroom without closing the door, and she often chose that opportunity to want to talk to me so that I would have to stand in the doorway and watch her urinate. As a child I had been both aroused and repulsed; I learned to associate genitals, especially female genitals, with something dirty. I still don't want to know that my vagina exists, casting it away as something horrible and ugly. (294)

Lau's final judgement that her mother's crude, unhygienic habit causes her emotional and sexual disorder not only simplifies the issue, but also finds her a solution. She wishes to have her m/Other raped on the streets for revenge: "I am flat chested and asexual. . . . my vagina . . . maybe it has never been mine, maybe it has always been my mother's—Dr Hightower and I wonder about that, if when

I am on the street, I subconsciously wish it were my mother's body the customers are defiling" (319). The raping of the m/Other helps the daughter sever the biological bond between them. In turn, it enables the daughter to gain her own sovereignty as an independent individual as well as an autobiographical narrator.

The execution of the m/Other is one of the many scenes of the family drama that permeates *Runaway* and Lau's other writings. Part of growing up, according to Freud, includes giving up a childhood sexual fixation on the parent of the opposite sex, which is developed before a child's puberty (285). What is recorded in *Runaway* seems to suggest that Lau was undergoing this stage before and after running away from home. While the narrator depicts her mother as an asexual, insensitive matriarchal dictator who should be raped on the streets, she paints her father sympathetically as a passive, meek, introverted figure. As the narrator never stops looking for the missing "man named Father" (124), her childhood sexual fixation on her father is yet to be cut.

Runaway testifies to the narrator's continuous search for "fatherly fantasy figures who are gentle, comforting, and couldn't possibly have real penises" (166). The diary lists the narrator's repeated disappointments in various relationships she has developed with white males. Right after she ran away from home, her initial desire for comfort in the arms of Joe, who "held [her] and rocked [her] like a baby," led her to his bed only to be raped (13). The narrator also plays the game of father's little girl in an imagined incestuous debauchery with Dr Graham, who seems to possess her father's strength and weakness: "How [Dr Graham] really did care. How he looked like my father, love shining through the rage" (141). Later with a john, Lau goes on to imagine herself in a sexual relationship with Dr Graham; she "continued to drink and pretend his fingers and lips were Dr Graham's. What would it be like to make love with the silver-haired man with the magnificent eyes who had sat with me across a table for over half a year?" (142) *Runaway* also records the narrator's persistent desire to obtain Dr Hightower's reserved "fatherly" love (139). The narrator speaks resentfully about her being cheated by the "little daddy" (164) who openly declares their doctor-patient relationship, "I can't bring you home with me, Evelyn. It's important that I'm not your father; I'm your psychiatrist" (145). *Runaway* is charged with

Freudian psychodrama of family romance; almost all the male-female relationships in the diary are versions of the same Oedipal game with the narrator playing the heroine/daughter, while her elder white male counterparts, who could be friends, doctors or johns, are made to play the role of the fatherly figure.

Commanded by her strong ego to win the game between the two sexes, the narrator in *Runaway* shifts back and forth between being a grownup prostitute and an innocent child. The game continues throughout Lau's journal until the last entry: "A father figure. An unsuitable, emotionally frail father figure. Larry was just a few years younger than my father" (335). In the last journal entry in *Runaway*, Lau finally manages to fuse those father and fatherly figures when playing her favourite unchanging role as father's little girl:

> Larry and Spencer, the frail and powerful sides of my father. I am seeing Spencer through the eyes of myself as a very young child, and I am distorting his strengths. *He is playing a dangerous game with me consciously or not.* I can feel once more what it was like to be lying in my bed . . . I can see my father so much bigger than me in his baggy pyjamas . . . (338; emphasis mine)

Victor Malarek, reporter of *The Globe and Mail*, who has also written about life on the streets, notes in his review of *Runaway* that "the most moving passages, although brief, describe Lau's intense love for her father" (C9). Although Malarek fails to see that Lau's fatherly figures are part of the sex games between the narrator and her clients, the on-going Oedipal drama of family romance in the diary certainly intensifies this (con)fusion. Emerging from the Oedipal drama, the conventional journey, and the personal journal *is* Lau's autobiographical narrator, whose subjectivity, instead of being completed, is split by her own narrative.

Stereotyping her parents as the cultural Other and herself as the sexual Other, Lau writes herself inevitably into a double colonization in the bourgeois discourse. Rather than feeling "integrated" (312) at the end of her journey, this double colonization—her gender identity as a sexual object for trade and her racial identity as a non-white person—creates a self-denial which splits the narrator's subjectivity. In the last fifty pages of *Runaway*, the narrator realizes that her "life was a lie" (308) symbolized by the images of the "Russian dolls":

> They are a womanly shape, wooden, with painted features. A line slices them in half. You take their two halves apart and inside is another doll, with the exact same features, only smaller. You peel them away, one by one, and there is always another one underneath—until you reach the core, the solid wooden woman, its features by now blurred. (311)

The Russian dolls signify a split between the exotic paint on the masks outside and the rather unattractive core within.

The Russian dolls resemble the narrator's personal crisis. The split subjectivity of "the ugly little girl" (308, 309, 311, 313, 319, 323) is hidden behind the narrator's daily mask, which sometimes is that of a desirable Oriental prostitute and other times of an ambitious would-be great Canadian writer. Ironically, it is only when this split subjectivity is recognized by the narrator that her personal and ethnic-minority identities are finally connected in Lau's narrative. The narrator realizes that the "ridiculed," the "beaten"-up and "hidden-away Chinese girl" is not only the Other in herself, but also the Muse of her creativity:

> Without realizing her beauty, without realizing that she in her loneliness, ugliness and despair had given birth to my writing. With drugs and the prostitution I had quickly covered her up . . . I had tried to lead a violently different life to prove that she was not real, did not exist and never had existed, but she was always there, she was myself. (308)

Though only vague and superficial, the recognition of her Chinese ethnicity seems to suggest, for the first time, that the narrator is aware of her self-imposed colonization.

The contradictory representations of Chinese ethnicity in Lau's diary—her parents' "Chineseness" is presented as an alienating factor and her own as "big pluses" (331) in the sex industry—recall historical Orientalism, a European desire for the Orient and its people to be exotic, romantic and mysterious (Said 1). In her journey to maturity, Lau has a momentary awakening, during which she sees herself play the historical stereotype of the exotic Oriental prostitute. Ironically, this awakening is offset by her persistent hope that she will meet a publisher somewhere, the sooner the better, perhaps through prostitution (310).

The sudden change of Lau's narrative voice from the persistent first-person narration to a third-person voice reflects the dilemma of the narrator and her split subjectivity. Near the end of the diary, in the journal entry of December 18, 1987, the first-person autobiographical narration is temporarily replaced by a third-person voice: "She does not know why she is not writing in the first person except that this is the way she often thinks. She likes to picture herself as a certain kind of person, a tragedy, a young intelligent girl who becomes a prostitute and a drug addict. It is suitable and dramatic" (321). As a result of this narrative shift, the writer temporarily enters the discursive territory of fiction. By doing so, she attempts to escape the double colonization effected by the fusion of the testimonial and autobiographical narrative in her diary. The third-person narrative enables the omniscient narrator to make comments on a character without being trapped in its role: "She is Eve, the original sinner, the temptress, the woman with many faces" (321). This temporary shift also allows the narrator to step out from the self-centred autobiography to examine objectively the social impact of the sex industry: "She feels used. She knows she is not alone in that. She has violated her beliefs, [that] is through her job promoting women as objects, encouraging men's violent sexual fantasies" (322). However, since the narrative shift is only as momentary as her earlier awakening, the third-person omniscient narrative cannot stabilize the form of fiction in the rest of the diary. Instead, as an interrupting force, it can only continue to split the subjectivity of the narrator.

By renouncing her parents, Lau cuts her bond with them in *Runaway*. In the prologue to the diary, Lau sees living at home as a worse experience than the combination of prostitution, drug addiction, suicide attempts and group homes all together: "All the events that took place during these two years were easier on me emotionally than living at home, which was why I have never gone back there to live" (5). The publication of *Runaway* embodies Lau's intention to seek a new family: "For a long time I thought that when I got a book published, it would be like acquiring a new family, one I wanted. This reasoning bears a remarkable resemblance to why I went on the street—to feel accepted, to find a home. Both desires are illusions" (340).

However, Lau did not find a new family in prostitution, nor did she through the publication of *Runaway*. What she did receive was massive media attention, which made her into a hot topic. Among the few mainstream writers who viewed Lau more as a person than a phenomenon was Denny Boyd, her first publisher and career adviser, before and after she ran away. Regarding himself as "her white uncle," Boyd calls Lau "a stray kitten," metaphorically. While his feelings were deeply hurt by the publication of *Runaway*, his emotional response is strong enough to indicate what Lau's parents might have felt, had they ever spoken. Boyd writes: "When *Runaway* came out, I was so furious that this cheap, exploited book would be her entry into published literature, not as a poet but as a pathetic little hooker . . . Dumb move" (B1). Boyd may not be able to understand Lau's obsessive desire to be a published writer, but in his comment, he did predict that Lau would be doubly colonized by writing about prostitution in the form of a personal diary.

The nationwide promotion of *Runaway* offended the Chinese Canadian community collectively. In an article reprinted in *Chinese Canadian Women's Forum* from an earlier publication in *The Newsletter of Chinese Canadian National Council*, Beryl Tsang, board member of the CCNC Toronto Chapter, points out that *Runaway* presents "the Chinese Canadian community in a negative light" (4). Furthermore, Tsang sees the massive promotion of *Runaway* as a national bestseller by its mainstream publisher McClelland and Stewart as a cultural war waged against the Chinese Canadian community, especially its women:

> The reason I suspect is that it perpetuates all those images about Chinese families and Chinese women and makes the reader glad that s/he is not Chinese or at least "that kind of Chinese." It presents Chinese families as authoritarian, overtly strict and unidimensional. It presents Chinese women as oppressed and powerless. It reinforces the stereotype that Chinese women are all "Suzy Wongs" in waiting. (4)

Lau's ruthless renouncing of her parents as the unchanging cultural Other helped her gain a legal separation from her family. Subsequently, she also won herself the reputation of a Vancouver writer and poet, rather than a "Chinese" Canadian writer, the racial modifier often used to introduce Canadian writers of Chinese descent.

The controversies surrounding Lau's success raise the perennial question of identity construction in Canadian society and its literature(s). As identity constructions are publicly grounded, they are limited to the linguistic tropes provided by the prevailing ideology. The contemporary Canadian ideology of multiculturalism constructs non-white Canadians as subjects of certain racial and ethnic groups in Canada. Multicultural politics provides racial minority groups, such as Chinese Canadians, with a more specific, double Canadian identity, which signifies duality, or a split, depending on how it is contextualized. The logic involved in this identity construction helps to perpetuate the concept that racial minority Canadians are "ethnic" Canadians, or "eternal immigrants" as observed by Claire Harris.

Racial identification is regarded as offensive by some non-white Canadian writers, who point out that it imposes conditions on the subjects they can treat in their writings (Hutcheon and Richmond 43, 80, 202, 232, 315). However, this identification is welcomed by others who resent the American model of the melting-pot (Hutcheon and Richmond 95, 344). Most of the first-generation Chinese Canadian writers seem to belong to the latter group, which has undertaken the historical task of writing about the collective experience to reclaim the collectively shared cultural identity. Their writings not only develop a resistant and therapeutic discourse to deal with the historical injustices imposed on the community, but also help prevent the minority culture and history from being erased by the dominant European cultures in Canadian society.

However, racialized writing is only one type of minority discourse. The subject matter chosen by racial minority writers does not have to be limited by the collective experience. While "the collective self" has been constructed as a valid version of the identity construction model in the community-based Chinese Canadian literature, there should be more than one identity model for individuals who are collectively addressed as Chinese Canadians. In this sense, Lau's diary proposes a different identity through the narrator's desire to be a mainstream writer rather than a member of the racial minority community into which she was born.

What contributes to Lau's identity ideal is more than her personal experience. In Western society the value of individualism dominates the ideal of collectivity inherited from less industrialized societies. Mainstream discourse in the West establishes individualism as a replacement for collectivity. Julia Watson and Sidonie Smith observe the negative image of collectivity in Western culture: "Western eyes see the colonized as an amorphous, generalized collectivity. The colonized 'other' disappears into an anonymous, opaque collectivity of undifferentiated bodies" (xvii). The enthusiastic reception of *Runaway* illustrates this dominant ideology. Whereas Lau's desire to become a mainstream writer can be related initially to her rebellion against her parents, it is produced directly by the predominant ideology of individualism. The instant success of *Runaway* seems to encourage more individuals to seek separated personal identities from that of the community to which they are related by birth.

Yet the role of the community remains undeniable in contemporary Canadian society. It is the communities that provide individuals with a sense of belonging. Writers need community as well. That is why Lau was very disappointed that she has received little support from the Canadian writers' community after the instant success of her diary. At the same time, since she is dismissed by the Chinese Canadian community, she has ironically "nowhere to hide from the success of *Runaway*," but to bear "the scarlet letter" "on a personal and professional level" (Dafoe C1). Nevertheless, the success of *Runaway* placed Lau in the mainstream spotlight and so gave her what a young, emerging writer needs. Lau will likely be framed and reframed as an ex-prostitute and drug addict, unless the subject matter in her future writings changes completely. Otherwise the testimonial and autobiographical tropes will probably remain the reader's preferable approach to her writings.

Fresh Girls: *A Fresh Piece for the Erotica Market*

The publication of Lau's first short-story collection, *Fresh Girls & Other Stories* (1993), moved her career from testimonial writing and autobiography to fiction. The settings of the ten stories, including a massage parlour, a fetish bar, private homes and apartments, all depict the relationships between men and women in the network of the sex industry. Written from the perspective of the female characters, who are either prostitutes or depressed women or both, most of the stories describe the characters' naïve beliefs in men, their fantasies of having an ideal love affair or marriage and, in turn, their repeated disappointments in being treated as sexual commodities.

The content of *Fresh Girls* continues the undesired connection for Lau: the link between the subject matter in her writing and her past as a prostitute. This irresistible connection between life writing and its author is not simply a naïve reader's response. Her interviewer Chris Dafoe is equally puzzled by Lau's return to prostitution as the topic of her writing: "Given her feelings, it's somewhat surprising that she has chosen similar subject material for *Fresh Girls*" (C1). In another interview, when Lau says she is utterly different from the girl who wrote *Runaway*, her interviewer points out the reader's likely response toward her: "Lau will probably continue to be associated with the teen hooker she once was, due to her new book *Fresh Girls*" (Inwood B15). Lau's own confession that "the feelings in the stories are autobiographical, but many of the scenes are not" (Dafoe C 1) and "my experience of sexuality has been, for the most part, some form of prostitution" (Inwood B15), further reinforce the unwanted connection.

Fresh Girls is but a fresh piece for the erotica market. Technically, Lau's special gratitude to "Chris Napolitano at *Playboy* for his encouragement and advice" (copyright page) seems to suggest the appropriate critical approach to *Fresh Girls*—as erotica and soft pornography. Erotica is an underdeveloped genre in Canadian literature, and so Lau, with her knowledge of the sex industry, becomes a pioneer of the field. Nickson comments on this aspect in his review: "these stories about call girls and their well-heeled customers is a departure from the genteel world of Canadian literature" (J17).

Erotica and pornography are ambivalent, yet interrelated and overlapping genres that both represent sexual relationships through art. While the word "erotica" is a sixteenth-century formation, "pornography" was coined in the nineteenth century to help further classify more illustrative sexual representations.[4] Although aesthetic differences can be traced between them, their thematic connection is indelible. While many critics try to draw differences between the two genres when studying sex in literature and art, some choose to "dispense with the distinction between pornography and erotica," because both terms are "ineffective" in describing the differences (Crabbe 45, 46). However, it is generally accepted that pornography presents "raw sex" without "a maker's style as well as a maker's name," whereas "erotica presents sexuality according to either the current artistic taste or current values or the artist's personal vision" (Faust 20, 23). This aesthetic variation, however, can make a major difference in the product. While pornography mostly exists underground, for example in the sex industry, erotica sometimes enters art galleries and literature. With good timing and a successful promotion, the makers of erotica might become artists and writers, even though the genre itself may never enter the spotlight of mainstream culture.

Among various evaluations of the social impact of erotica and pornography, Gary Day positions the relationship between pornography and society in a family romance:

> The Oedipus complex is not just a family drama but also a social one . . . This might explain why pornography flourishes only at the edge of society and why, when it appears to encroach towards the centre, it is cast out. Society, as it were, plays the father to pornography as pornography plays the son to society. (97)

Comparing the national promotion of *Runaway* with the quiet reception of *Fresh Girls*, the analogy of the Oedipal complex can be used as a working model to explain why there was such difference. If society is the domineering father, writings embedded with social causes, such as *Runaway*, are generally promoted for the moral sake of society. On the other hand, the erotica genre based on private and sexual interest is generally suppressed in society, thus the genre becomes a kind of subdued son in its relationship to society as the father. Deriving from the Oedipal complex, the male-oriented Freudian psychoanalytical model, Day's observation also helps explain why pornography and erotica are traditionally made for men's consumption.

Without changing the basic formulae, Lau's stories are not very different from the existing genres of erotica and pornography. From a male point of view, sexual relationships between male and female usually start with male sexual arousal and end with male ejaculation, and female sexual fantasy and personal feelings are suppressed. In *Fresh Girls*, this sexual politics is not only applied to stories about the sex trade, but also developed in the value system shared by most of the female characters. "The Session" can serve as an example to illustrate the male-oriented sex politics that saturates Lau's stories.

Lau uses the popular formula of romance fiction to portray her female characters as passive sexual beings. Observing this formula in her essay "Romance Fiction: Porn for Women?" Alison Assiter points out: "The man is in control, dominant; the woman gratefully, joyously accepting and submitting" (105). Lau's story, "The Session," exemplifies this formula. The story begins with a telephone call from Mary's assumed "boyfriend" who was a previous john: "After she hung up the phone, Mary went to her closet humming. Later her ex-john 'boyfriend' would be coming over, and for him she would wear lingerie and a floral perfume" (17). Here the description already corresponds to the code used in romance fiction, in which the heroine's imagination usually is associated with the objects that will arouse her ideal male lover's sexual desire to possess her (Assiter 103, 106). Although Lau inserts an episode about what Mary does for living as a female dominatrix, her own sexual fantasy of meeting her "boyfriend" remains in conformity to a romance character: "After she got home she ran to the bathroom eagerly, removed her makeup and put on a white lace teddy with a pink ribbon tied between her breasts" (25). Mary's anxiousness to meet this boyfriend and to be appreciated by him sexually outlines what de Beauvoir observes: "Of all women, [the prostitutes] are the most submissive to the male" (220). Although the boyfriend is only a ghost character in the story, lacking a personal name and a description, as long as he is male his image dominates the female character imaginatively. It is not Mary's long wait and her thirty telephone calls trying to reach this expected boyfriend but her self-pity, as noted below, that objectifies her as a sexual commodity. The conclusion of the story simply reveals that Mary is naïve and vulnerable, needing to be possessed physically: "cradling the receiver to her chest, pushing it down the lacy length of her body. Then her legs opened and she wept" (25). Mary's stereotypical characteristics are shared by other female characters in this collection, prostitutes or not; all resemble the passive heroines of romance fiction.

Erotic portraits of male sexual arousal and female submission often have taken father/daughter overtone in Lau's stories. Psychologically, these depictions continue to connect *Fresh Girls* with the Oedipal drama in *Runaway,* as well as in Lau's other writings. "Roses" describes the relationship between a middle-aged psychiatrist and a young prostitute, who tells the story in the first person. By merging their present sexual activities into the narrator's memories of her childhood, Lau resumes her favourite father/daughter motif: "At first he stretched me across his knees and began to spank me. I wiggled obediently and raised my bottom high into the air, the way my father used to like to see me do" (33). And later in a paragraph, she remembers her father's house—" [a]lways Daddy's girl, I perform according to his instruction" (35); finally the ending of the story blends past into present: "somewhere, off in the distance, my father is clapping" (36). The true and imagined father-daughter relationships mix the sexual and nonsexual situations into one ongoing Oedipal drama, through which the writer expresses what de Beauvoir calls, "the vagrant yearnings of men" (220) rather than female desire for sexual fulfilment. Furthermore the writer also offers to reinterpret male sexual arousal from the point of view of the first-person female narrator: "Slapped me human. He said my fear had turned him on. He was thirsty for the sweat that dampened my palms and willing to do anything to elicit more of that moisture so he could lick it and quench his tongue's thirst" (35). It is through the reinterpretation that the female character starts to accept the fact that their relationship is based on male sexual desire. Reading the female character's reinterpretation in the first-person voice, the reader, especially a female reader, is consciously and unconsciously participating in a sexual relationship that is based on male sexual arousal and the pain and fear of a woman.

A similar story, "Pleasures," also attends to the needs of male sexual consumption. It suggests that professional women like to be dominated sexually by violence. The story is told in a third-person omniscient voice about a "he" and a "she" who meet in the hotel lounge as total strangers. As neither of the characters is given a name, they become symbols for the two sexes rather than the two individuals. The only information provided by the third-person omniscient narrator seems to illustrate "her" emotional vulnerability as a woman and "his" ultimate dominance over her. He has only to tell her that "he had once worked as a counsellor . . . she automatically trusted people in the helping professions, saw them as full of wisdom and good intention" (40). Her naïveté and vulnerability are not only expressed in her drinking, crying and talking about the pressures of her job and her hopeless ongoing affairs with a married man in front of this stranger, but also in her letting him direct her to meet his sexual demands. Again Lau employs the technique of having the female character reinterpret her sexual encounter with the stranger: "Remembering how at the instant she knew she was incapable of movement in his restraints, she had been stunned by how safe she felt in the absolute darkness of her life given over to another" (41). The reinterpretation serves as an acceptance of male sexual imposition.

The details of their next sexual encounter eroticize the kind of male who enjoys imposing bondage on his female sex partner: he ties her down in bed; clamps leather on her wrists and her ankles; stuffs a gag into her mouth and blindfolds her. Her fear is described as a rare moment of psychological relief from her normal life. If it is not clear whose sexual desire, his or hers, is aroused here, a deliberate demonstration of her fear for the purpose of arousing him to possess her serves to clarify the ambiguity: "She thrust her hips towards the ceiling, pressing her fingers together and trying to slide them back through the cuffs. *She knew he liked to see her struggle*" (42; emphasis mine). The rest of the story describes him making love to her while she cries silently underneath the blindfold with fear and pain. The lack of communication, except that his sexual desire is met, is later described metaphorically as a thunder that fails to break through the pouring rain and lightning-filled sky (44). "Pleasures" ends with his certainty that "another night she would return. He knew" (45). This certainty, presented in a third-person statement that "women with careers and condominiums were the ones who came back" (43), objectifies the existing sexual stereotypes of both men and women: women, even professional and successful women, are sexually passive and need to be dominated; men eroticize on the basis of their physical aggression.

Lau also utilizes the linguistic code of the sex industry, which is constructed to satisfy male sexual fantasy and egotistic desires. Set in a massage parlour, an euphemism for a brothel, the title story "Fresh Girls" reveals the social order in the sex industry. Nouns such as "pantyhose," "makeup," "long hair," "high heels," "condoms," "red lights," "drug" and "fix," graphically open up the interior of the massage parlour to the reader. As the sex industry is governed by the same laws of competition, it is only natural that fresh girls, clean girls, baby girls are going to replace the worn-out girls who eat "chicken soup out of a cup" and "buy condoms for the other girls and take in a few hairy, smelly regulars wearing checked pants and bad ties" (5, 7). The I-narrator, who is no longer a fresh girl in the massage parlour, finds her business elsewhere "via certain cab drivers, tripping through the maze of gates and gardens and the exclusive apartments" with a rich old man, who not only pays her to listen to him, but also patronizes her psychologically as being his "Baby Girl" (9). The last story in this collection, "The Old Man," has a similar character, who lives in another similar cultural neighbourhood with restaurants, art galleries, picture-frame stores and bookshops (99). His sexual desire consists of seeing the I-narrator in different expensive outfits each time, naming her "Barbie," "Lolita" and "Cuddles" (100, 110). The theatrical game in bed speaks euphemistic language through which he can possess the sexual parts of her body:

> "Fine," I say, "the girls are fine."
> "They're still there, they haven't gone anywhere?"
> "They're still there, I take good care of them for you."
> The old man chuckles with pleasure. "And the lady, how is she?"
> "The lady is fine too, " . . .
>
> Incidentally, the girls are my breasts. The lady is my vagina. I am Barbie, or maybe I am Lolita. (104)

Lau's sensuous language, flavoured with dark humour but coded with male sexual desire, encourages a possessive male ego. The old man's sexual power, represented by his "impending orgasm," is expressed violently to boost his own ego: "one of these days I'll blow your head off" (109). The fact that the old man speaks in the future tense, though with a self-mocking tone, does not stop reinforcing the cliché in pornography genre, in which a male ego is directly linked to his sexual drive.

In contrast to the enlarged male ego and its overwhelming dominance, Lau's female characters often suffer a lack of self-worth and self-respect. As a result, they either accept their lack of ego as a matter of fact or suffer from a split subjectivity, which eventually leads to self-degradation or even self-destruction. Similarly to "The Session," in which Mary's hope to meet a john-becoming-boyfriend deteriorates to self-pity, in "The Apartments," "sweet Jane" is told to leave with a fifty-dollar bill in her pocket right after the expected boyfriend is sexually satisfied. The story ends with Jane's dream of getting married "becoming less and less likely with each passing night" (96), mocking the character's earlier romantic illusion:

> the man in this apartment wants her, wants her more than just the way a client wants her. Perhaps tonight will be the night he sinks to his knees and tells her that he loves her, that he can't be a client any more, he wants them to go out on real dates: movies, dinners, walks around the seawall. (92)

Many of Lau's female characters experience Jane's "bent dream" (93). The young female character in "Glass" is equally depressed because her relationship with her boyfriend Allen is based on sex rather than communication. The lack of self-worth splits her subjectivity into a "she" and an "I," virtually two characters with two narrative voices that are constantly involved in debate. The story is a poetic presuicide meditation, in which the split "I" first wants to stop, then decides to help the "she" commit suicide. The story captures the lingering moment before "she" jumps out of her apartment window: she reviews her humiliation by her boyfriend Allen, who "had said he loved her, would have married her if . . . if she wasn't so needy?" (64) Unlike Jane and Mary who can live their daily lives as prostitutes while dreaming about love and marriage, the "she" in "Glass" cannot give the "diamond" in her—presumably her worth—to anyone (61, 62, 66), not even to Allen. The story ends with two poetic paragraphs that create totally contrasting images: in his penthouse, Allen sits with his "rose-colored comforter, grateful for the silent phone."

Meanwhile, in her apartment, the self-destructive "she" is convinced by the voice of the rational "I" that they should commit suicide:

> She watches the glass swoop from the window onto the pavement below, sprawling like dancers in lewd but beautiful positions on the sidewalk. And I hold her hand and tell her that it is better this way, that I am the only one she has, the only one who can keep her safe. She nods, and the diamond glitters in a lump in her chest, intact, and I take her hand and guide her away from the music, and down a line of soft white glass. (66)

Lau's controlled poetic passage encourages the female character to follow her passive suicidal desire. The palpable poetic words that shine like diamonds in the above paragraph cannot disguise the kind of "suffering" caused by "self-pity" and "adolescent pursuit of me," as Malarek summarizes, depicted in the realistic language of *Runaway* (C9).

The only time and place in which Lau's female characters seem to suffer less from depression or self-degradation are in a fetish bar, or when acting as dominatrices. Although both situations offer the female characters an opportunity to dominate in a theatrical situation, neither provides the characters with emotional or sexual fulfilment. "Fetish Night" opens the door to an underground basement club: its walls are painted black, the bartenders are naked and all participants are dressed up in "queer" fashion for fetishism. Here sexual violence and humiliation are part of the expected theatrical game—granting torture, receiving pain, picking up a slave, or a torturer, or simply being an onlooker—all events seem to help the participants release their suppressed id through S & M role-playing. Written in a third-person omniscient narrative, a lesbian character Sabina is asked to be a dominatrix by a male worshipper. Although she seems to enjoy the game, her experience, which is not associated with her sexual orientation or personal interest, is used to reveal the hidden sexual desires of the majority of the so-called normal people, who usually wear "shirts and slacks, jeans, pantyhose and trench coats" (75). Near the end of the story, Sabina's slave gives her his telephone number and openly seeks her for future sexual needs, while Sabina gets into a cab with her girlfriend Justine, whose name reminds the reader that she is introduced earlier in the story as an equally coquettish character: "Justine scrambles closer to Sabina until she is almost sitting on her lap, the soda forgotten in her hand. Sabina curls her arm under her friend's jacket and presses her breast comfortingly" (72). During the fetish night, Justine's lesbian relationship with Sabina is replaced by the temporary theatrical bond between Sabina and the slave. Sabina's lesbian sexuality is treated as secondary to her theatrical role as a dominatrix, and Justine is totally left out of the fun until the evening is over. This depiction makes the reader question whether fetishism really provides a place for women's desire. Instead of giving female characters an opportunity to express their sexual desires openly as the male characters do in the story, "Fetish Night" is but another means to eroticize and satisfy the male libido.

Similar depiction emphasizing male sexual drive can be read in other situations in which the dominant role is played by the female characters. In "The Session," Mary services an older man who enjoys playing the role of her slave. In the narrative, the man's sick old mother, lying in bed motionlessly behind the locked door, is compared to her son's ongoing sexual drive (19). In "Mercy," the teenage prostitute seems to be Lau's only female character, who is aroused by S&M role-playing. While she acknowledges that "it is easy to become addicted to hurting you, to aching for that moment when you take off your clothes and lie on my floor" (82), her sexual arousal is ironically based on imitating the phallus in order to replace what she physically and psychologically lacks. Lau's obvious acceptance of the Freudian psychoanalytical model of penis-envy further confirms the male-oriented sexual politics in her stories. Rather than introducing a female sexual fantasy, or a different symbolic order, Lau's female character performs again to reinforce the phallic power:

> You suck the heel as you would a phallus, and I wonder what you are tasting . . . With your eyes shut and your mouth working to please the point of my shoe, you could easily be an inflatable doll or a cartoon and I am able then to withdraw my heel as carefully as a penis and rake it in pink crescents across your cheek and down your chin. (80)

Further, instead of obtaining sexual fulfilment for herself, the "torture" of him is presented as an emotional discharge of her self-hatred for lacking a phallus: "The power floods into me warm and soft and golden, dusty as pollen. I had not realized previously the extent of my emptiness that no kisses could fill, no flowers or brave words of love. The emptiness sang hollow and blue and then turned red as rage" (83). It is her self-hatred which is as strong as a murderer's drive that ironically intensifies her chance to be "equally unfulfilled" (80).

Fresh Girls depicts the sex industry as a well-established social network. The sexual exploitation of women is not confined within the massage parlour, nor is it limited to the needs of certain types of men. Lau's stories map out the web of the sex industry, in which "the public world of work [merges] into the private world of sex" (Hull 14). In "The Old Man," the writer relates prostitution with the national economy as understood by a young prostitute. Cab drivers connect prostitutes with businessmen arriving at the airport "looking to rent someone for an hour or two before a late meeting or dinner with friends" (109). The story then talks about the economic recession, which affects the sex industry as it does the national economy: "Lately the economy has been bad, business has consequently been slow, and the old man has been my one steady customer, my main squeeze, my man" (109). Discursively, the connection between the sex industry and the national economy, especially when it is perceived from the perspective of the female characters, suggests that prostitution is an acceptable labour division for women. Satisfying male sexual desire is a job for many female characters in Lau's stories.

The cover design of *Fresh Girls* makes no attempt to disguise the sexual content of the stories. First of all, "Fresh Girls" is the kind of title that signifies erotica if not pornography. The front cover of the book with Graham Law's sepia photo entitled "Nude Behind Flowers" features the nude lower part of a young female body behind some blurred flowers. This photo is itself a piece of erotica: her bare legs stretch up into an arch and stay slightly apart; her genitals, though shadowed like the flowers, are exposed. The photograph was shot perspectively to exclude the subject's face from the frame of the picture, consciously and photographically dismembering the female body, a technique widely used in hard pornography to emphasize the sexual organs. The dismemberment successfully achieves the effect of preventing the viewer from seeing the subject as a person. Instead, the viewer sees a female sexual organ waiting to be gazed upon and to be possessed. Perhaps this photograph could be viewed as artistic in a gallery setting; as the cover of Lau's short-story collection, it advertises the theme of the stories—the passive female and her sexuality as commercial property.

Other technical details in the cover design cannot be ignored because of what they signify. "Girls" is printed in light brown and much larger than the rest of the title. Graphically speaking, "Girls" is printed in "romantic" script, while the other words in the title, "FRESH" and "& OTHER STORIES," and the writer's name, all occur in small, white, straight-faced and emotion-free font. Together with Graham Law's photo, this cover design advertises sexual content and female stereotypes through the semiotic codes that are commonly shared by romance fiction, erotica and pornography.

Given the details discussed above, it seems impossible to discuss Lau's stories without having to analyze male-female relationships in sexual terms. According to Lau, the theme of her stories is power: "[p]ower and control are issues in all relationships" (Dafoe C). The interplay between power and control in sexual relationships is precisely what I have underlined in my reading. However, Lau hopes that her stories can be read differently. She speaks in an interview: "I was worried that people would construe this material as being erotic or pornographic" (Andrews D16). Assiter, who dismisses the generic boundary between pornography and erotica, proposes: "Porn, I suggest, is the representation of the eroticization of relations of power between the sexes" (103). Since Lau contextualizes the power play in sexual encounters, it would be only appropriate for the reader to pay attention to her representation of these male-female relationships in sexual situations. As examined above, both the situations and the relationships in Lau's stories are monotonously similar in all stories. They offer the reader the view that the male sex is in power and control, while the female sex is deprived of her desire and opportunity. It is impossible to read Lau's stories without paying heed to this sexual politics that saturates her narrative and syntax. In fact, the reader has constantly to decide whether to accept the patriarchal view of woman as primarily a sexual object or to resist the overwhelming sexual stereotypes of erotica and pornography that are simply reinvented in Lau's *Fresh Girls*.

Beyond Silence: Rice Paper Continues

The positive theoretical work involves a critical-discursive articulation of alternative practices and values that are embedded in the often-damaged, -fragmentary, -hampered, or -occluded works of minorities. This is not to reassert the exclusive claim of the dominant culture that objective grounds for marginalization can be read in the inadequacy or underdevelopment of "minority" work.

ABDUL R JANMOHAMED & DAVID LLOYD

The ACWW [Asian Canadian Writers' Workshop] is a collective . . . Our mandate is simple: We aim to provide a supportive and culturally sensitive environment for writers from a common Pacific Rim Asian heritage, a place for more established writers to guide emerging writers through the difficulties of the publishing field.

JIM WONG-CHU, *Rice Paper*

The Buddhist monk Hoei-shin, who embarked on his discovery voyage to *Fushang* in the year 459 AD, started the Chinese migration to the Western Hemisphere. This event may be legendary, but Gold Mountain is not a fairytale. The history of Canadian immigration is ridden with notorious anti-Chinese and anti-Asian immigration laws. In addition to being exploited as cheap labour, Chinese were targeted by racist discrimination in Canadian society and denied access to mainstream discourse and professions for one hundred years. Recent federal Canadian governments have refused to right the wrongs done historically to Chinese immigrants. One hundred and eleven years after Chinese labourers were first made to pay a head tax upon landing in British Columbia in 1884, the Chinese Canadian National Council took the case of the discriminatory Head Taxes to the Human Rights Commission of the United Nations on March 21, 1995. Although contemporary Canadian society is more tolerant, recurrence of anti-Chinese racism in Toronto and on the West Coast keeps activists reminded that the struggle for acceptance and for equality continues.

Contemporary Chinese Canadians take it as their mission to break through the historical silence. The lack of representation of their experience in Canadian Literature, in school curricula, and in other cultural spheres reinforces Chinese Canadians' feelings of inferiority and prolongs their collective invisibility and silence in contemporary society. As a response to their collective marginality in mainstream culture, Chinese Canadians wrote about the community's historical experiences. The fact that most of the first-generation Chinese Canadian writers are community activists underlines the connection between the community's history and its literature.

The establishment of community archives is pivotal for literary development. Photographic exhibitions organized by activists have helped partially to retrieve the unrecorded history. Publications such as Paul Yee's *Saltwater City*, Lee Wai-man's *Portraits of a Challenge*, and the women's memories collected in *Jin Guo* have, for the first time, established printed records of the community's past. This establishment is significant to the community, because in the records Chinese immigrants are the speaking subjects. The publication of community history marks the beginning of a historical transition from silence to voice as the minority subjects begin to voice their resistance against political and cultural hegemony in Canada's mainstream discourse.

Chinese Canadian literature is an indispensable part of the community's survival. The 1894 Chinese-English bilingual phrase book, which I have briefly discussed in Chapter Two, can be classified as an early text of nonfiction.[1] However, it is the birth of contemporary Chinese Canadian literature in English from the Chinese Canadian Writers' Workshop in the 1970s that gave voice to a collective awakening. Since then this literary movement has involved a growing number of Chinese Canadian writers who employed existing literary genres to reclaim their community's history and herstory. The birth of Chinese Canadian literature in English therefore demonstrates the possibility and process of transforming the collective historical silence into a contemporary community-based literature.

Ethnic minority experience can be represented in all existing literary genres. By using a genre division to structure the study, my discussion illustrates the vital link between lived experience and the contents of literary products rather than with different properties of the literary genres. Paul Yee's legendary stories, *Tales from Gold Mountain*; Winston Christopher Kam's play *Bachelor-Man*; Sky Lee's novel, *Disappearing Moon Cafe*; Denise Chong's family memoir, *The Concubine's Children*; Fred Wah's poetry collection, *Waiting for Saskatchewan*; and Jim Wong-Chu's volume of poems, *Chinatown Ghosts* all demonstrate their roots in the community history. This all-genre configuration confirms that silence imposed by hegemony can be transformed into a powerful resistant voice in any literary form. It also illustrates that the community-based minority literature is as capable of development as any mainstream literature.

Merging from across the generic borders are some prevailing literary tropes that further constitute the minority discourse. These tropes, such as the Gold Mountain milieu, the bone-hunting journey, and the collective self have emerged from the community's immigration history, its colloquial tradition, its collectively-shared racial experience and cultural identities. They speak the linguistic and epistemological experience of the community as a racial minority in Canada. As these literary tropes distinguish Chinese Canadian literature from mainstream Canadian literature, they indicate appropriate critical approaches to the former. Instead of universality, respect for the community is required.

The development of contemporary Chinese Canadian literature in English symbolizes a collective transition of Chinese Canadians from a position of silence to that of voice. This historical transition illustrates the ontological equality between silence and voice. The dichotomy signifies an interdependent relationship between oppositions in a field of discourse. The knowledge of equality is important to a minority or silenced subject, for its provisional status does not equal an ontological Otherness. Observing the position of being a minority, Abdul R JanMohamed and David Lloyd point out:

> "Becoming minor" is not a question of essence (as the stereotypes of minorities in dominant ideology would want us to believe) but a question of position: a subject-position that in the final analysis can be defined only in "political" terms that is, in terms of the effects of economic exploitation, political disenfran-

chisement, social manipulation, and ideological domination on the cultural formation of minority subjects and discourses. (9)

This observation confirms that silence in mainstream discourse is not equivalent to muteness or passivity but a resultant of political and economic exploitations. And literary activities conducted in the Chinese language in Chinatowns across the country have long since demystified the community's silence in mainstream culture as a reluctant silence rather than an inherent muteness or passivity.

The transformation of a historically silenced community into a speaking subject in contemporary society takes a collective endeavour. The historical transition"the epic struggles"—was launched by the first-generation writers from the Chinese Canadian Writers' Workshop in the 1970s. The two anthologies, *Inalienable Rice* published in 1979 and *Many-Mouthed Birds* published twelve years later in 1991, have proved that the anthology is a self-empowering literary form for marginalized minority communities to become speaking subjects in mainstream discourse. The anthology form helps the silenced subjects make a political statement, launch a new literature, and take up a collective agency. It also makes it consequentially easier for its contributors to publish their work elsewhere.

Articulating in English, Chinese Canadian writers are constantly engaged in dialogues with mainstream discourse. They share the same discursive strategy, which is: writing Chinese Canadian experience into mainstream discourse, reclaiming the marginalized minority experience, and redefining Chinese Canadians as agents. As the dialogue continues, the entry of minority Canadian agents into mainstream discourse will help change the composition of the existing Canadian literary canon. The genres, which are conventionally considered as neutral literary forms, will be politicized as well.

In addition to dialogues with mainstream discourse and literary tradition in Canada, contemporary Chinese Canadian literature is also a dialogue with traditional Chinese culture. Since most of the writings are set unmistakably in Chinatown with Chinese immigrants and their descendants as the speaking subjects, they impose a self-examination and a self-evaluation on Chinese cultural tradition. Winston Christopher Kam's drama *Bachelor-Man*, Paul Yee's *Tales from Gold Mountain*, Sky Lee's novel *Disappearing Moon Cafe*, Denise Chong's *The Concubine's Children*, and some of the poetry discussed in Chapter 7 all demonstrate the need to reclaim Chinese women's roles in the community. At the same time, they also express the urgency to challenge feudal Chinese cultural practices.

As a critical approach to Chinese Canadian literature, the concept of dialogue is embodied in the structure of this study. Between Chapter 1, "Rereading Chinese Canadian History," and all the following chapters, an initial dialogue occurs between the community history and its literature. Chapter 2 and Chapter 3 establish the essential dialogues between the creative writings and the critical approaches. Chapters 4, 5, 6, and 7 each contain an internal dialogue with one specific genre, and altogether they embrace the collective voice of contemporary Chinese Canadians as a minority discourse. These chapters jointly constitute a dialogue with Chapter 8, in which Evelyn Lau's diary and short stories depict a different subject matter and hence a very different identity construction model that departs from the community resources. Therefore, instead of individual writers grouped together by their ethnic identity, the concept of dialogue presents Chinese Canadian literature as a minority literature in negotiation with mainstream history, culture, and literature. In that, Chinese Canadian literature has displayed characteristics of a strong branch of Canadian literature.

Today the Chinese Canadian Writers' Workshop has become the Asian Canadian Writers' Workshop. Since the "Writing Thru' Race" Conference held in the summer of 1994, the Asian Canadian Writers' Workshop has expanded to include seventy members from coast to coast. A newsletter named *Rice Paper* was established and is published three times a year by its members. Jim Wong-Chu, who wrote "A Brief History of the ACWW [Asian Canadian Writers' Workshop]" for the first issue of *Rice Paper,* emphasizes that "[t]he ACWW is a collective" (1). *Rice Paper* continues where *Inalienable Rice* initially started, as a forum for the Workshop, where members can discuss their writings, art work, music and theatrical performances.

"A thousand-*li* journey starts from beneath the feet." This well-known Chinese proverb describes the current stage of Chinese Canadian literature. Ahead and beyond the stage of breaking through the hundred-year silence endured by the community, a much longer journey is awaiting the contemporary and future generations of writers.

December 1996

Notes

Introduction

1. From *Chinese in Canada: 125 Years of Continuous Community*, published by the Chinese National Council: "Although the Chinese came to the shores of Canada long before 1858, it is generally agreed that 1983 marks the 125th anniversary of continuous Chinese community in this country."

2. *Report of the Royal Commission on Chinese Immigration*. Ottawa: 1885; *Report of the Royal Commission on Oriental Immigration, or Report of the Commission Appointed to Inquire into the Subjects of Chinese and Japanese Immigration into the Province of British Columbia*. Ottawa: printed by S E Dawson, 1902; *Report of the Royal Commission Appointed to Inquire into the Methods By Which Oriental Labourers Have Been Induced to Come to Canada*. Ottawa: Government Printing Bureau, 1908.

1. Rereading Chinese Canadian History and the Need to Access Mainstream Discourse

1. M Deguignes, "Mémoires de l'Académie des Inscriptions et Belles Lettres," vol xxviii, 1761. Preface to Charles G Leland, *Fushang or The Discovery of America by Chinese Buddhist Priests in the Fifth Century*. v. The modern translation of the Buddhist monk's name in *ping yin* (phonetic Mandarin) is "Hui-shen".

2. References to the Nootka settlement can be found in the following books, with slight variations only: Li Donghai, *Jianada Huaqiao Shi* or *History of the Overseas Chinese in Canada*, 60; Stan Steiner, *Fushan: The Chinese Who Built America*, 154; Anthony B Chan, *Gold Mountain: The Chinese in the New World*, 33; Lee Wai-man, *Portraits of a Challenge: An Illustrated History of the Chinese Canadians*, 17. For pictures of historical artifacts, see Lee Wai-man, 22-23.

3. Based on a random sampling among the Chinese in Vancouver in 1884-85, 23% came from Taishan; between 1885 and 1903, 45% entering Vancouver came from the same county. The phenomenon that so many prime-age males left the same county resulted from local disasters. Between 1851 and 1908 Taishan was hit by fourteen floods, seven typhoons, four

earthquakes, two droughts, four plague outbreaks and five famines (Paul Yee 10). In addition to these local disasters, a local war between clans in 1856-64 caused 20,000 to 30,000 deaths (Peter Li 15).

4. Between 1848 and 1852, about 25,000 Chinese emigrated from the south and southeast regions of China to work along the Sacramento River in California. In 1958, a second Gold Mountain was discovered in the Fraser Valley, British Columbia, which attracted many Chinese from California and later from China. By 1883, among 2000 gold miners in British Columbia, 1500 were Chinese (Paul Yee 12).

5. Canada House of Commons, *Debates*, 12 May 1882, 1477, 1287.

6. Canada House of Commons, *Debates*, 1947, vol III, 2644-46.

2. The Transformation from Silence to Voice and Other Discursive Strategies

1. See Hayden White, *Tropics of Discourse: Essay in Cultural Criticism* (94–95, 104). According to White, language provides four principal modes of figurative representation: metaphor, metonymy, synecdoche and irony.

2. I have used the term "the collective self" previously in my "The Collective Self: A Narrative Paradigm in Sky Lee's *Disappearing Moon Cafe*," in *Cross Addressing: Discourse on the Border*, ed. John C Hawley and S J Abony (Albany, NY:SUNY Press, 1996), 234–57.

3. According to *The Big Aiiieeeee: An Anthology of Chinese American and Japanese American Literature*, the phrase book was originally published in 1875, revised two years later by Wong Sam and his assistants, and republished and distributed by Wells Fargo free of charge in more than two hundred towns with Chinese American populations. (92)

According to Paul Yee, the book was distributed by Thomson Stationery Company in Vancouver in 1897 and was republished in 1910 (*Saltwater City* 35).

In the preface, written in Chinese, author 李祥晋 (Li Xiangjin in phonetic Mandarin, though it is unlikely the name was either spelt or pronounced this way since he used a phonetic representation based on the Taishan dialect in the phrase book) dates the book in the nineteenth year of the Emperor Guang Xu of the Qing Dynasty. As Guang Xu's reign lasted from 1875 to 1908, it would seem that according to Li Xiangjin the phrase book was written in 1894.

It is possible that there were several versions of the phrase book. I have a version distributed by Thomson Stationery in Vancouver. Its publication was registered "according to Act of Parliament of Canada" in 1897 and then "according to Act of Congress" in 1903 as stated on the title page.

4. See Amy Ling, "Pioneers and Paradigms: The Eaton Sisters" in *Between the Worlds*; Xiao-huang Yin, "Between the East and West: Sui Sin Far—The

First Chinese-American Woman Writer"; "Sui Sin Far" in *The Big Aiiieeeee!*; and James Doyle, "Sui Sin Far and Onoto Watanna: Two Early Chinese-Canadian Authors."

5. In her master's thesis, Anita Jennifer Wong examines the relationship between the dominant ideology and the representations of Chinese Canadians in a number of works by white Canadian authors.

The list includes: Hilda Glynn-Ward's *The Writing on the Wall* (1921); Edna Lysle Fewster's *Lengthening Shadows* (1957); Ethel Wilson's *The Innocent Traveller* (1949), *Swamp Angel* (1954) and others; W O Mitchell's *Who Has Seen the Wind?* (1947); Michael J Culler's *Goodnight Sammy Wong* (1982); Margaret Lawrence's *The Stone Angel* (1964); Gabrielle Roy's "Where Will You Go, Sam Lee Wong?" collected in *Garden in the Wind* (1977); and Lee Maracle's "Yin Chin" collected in *The Sojourner's Truth and Other Stories.*

6. "Deterritorialization" and"reterritorialization" are two related concepts used to analyze postcolonial and postemigration literatures. These terms indicate the discursive transition in the Chinese Canadian community from a collective displacement caused by migration and racism to the birth of a community literature written in the official language that enforced the silencing. See Gilles Deleuze and Felix Guattari 17–18; Barbara Godard 131–32.

7. See *The Empire Writes Back.* (38):

"The crucial function of language as a medium of power demands that post-colonial writing define itself be seizing the language of the centre and re-placing it in a discourse fully adapted to the colonized place. There are two distinct processes by which it does this.

Abrogation is a refusal of the categories of the imperial culture, its aesthetic, its illusory standard of normative or "correct" usage, and its assumption of a traditional and fixed meaning "inscribed" in the words. It is a vital moment in the de-colonizing of the language . . .

Appropriation is the process by which the language is taken and made to "bear the burden" of one's own cultural experience . . ."

3. *Anthologizing the Collective: The Epic Struggles to Establish Chinese Canadian Literature in English*

1. Because of the focus of this study, the discussion of *Inalienable Rice* will not include the Japanese Canadian writers found there.

2. One of the best examples is *The New Oxford Book of Canadian Verse*, edited by Margaret Atwood; in the introduction, she says directly that she positions herself and her anthology in the A J M Smith tradition, except for the bilingual component. (xxvii)

3. Eagleton observes:

It is important to note that the character of an *LMP* [literary mode of production] is a significant constituent of the literary product itself. We are not merely concerned here with the sociological outworks of the test; we are concerned rather with how the text comes to be what it is because of the specific determinations of its mode of production. If *LMPs* are historically extrinsic to particular texts, they are equally internal to them: the literary text bears the impress of its historical mode of production as surely as any product secretes in its form and materials . . . [t]he character of an *LMP* is an internal constituent rather than merely an extrinsic limit of the character of the text. (*Criticism and Ideology*)

4. From the Declaration of Independence: "We hold these truths to be self-evident that all men are created equal, that they are endowed by their Creator certain unalienable Rights, that among these are Life, Liberty, and the Pursuit of Happiness" (quoted in Morison 223).

4. *Mythologizing the Collective History and Reclaiming "Chinamen":* Tales from Gold Mountain

1. From Earle Birney's well-known "Can.Lit": "it's only by our lack of ghosts / we're haunted" (Birney 116). The line became popular in Canadian literary criticism in the 1960s and 1970s. For example, Eli W Mandel's article "A Lack of Ghosts and Poetry" (Mandel 65).

2. Historically when Canadian politicians used anti-Chinese racism to recruit supporters, they emphasized the Chinese idiosyncracies as signs of racial inferiority. Some examples are given in Chapter 1, e.g. Sir John A Macdonald's speech in Parliament.

5. Bachelor-Man: *"A Silence Crying Out to be Broken"*

1. As *mimesis,* or imitation, or representation, figures so largely in Aristotle's *Poetics* and in Plato's Book III and Book X of *The Republic,* it is a principle in classical literary criticism. See T S Dorsch 11.

2. In his comparison of epic with tragedy in *Poetics,* Aristotle notes the "difference in their length: tragedy tries as far as possible to keep within a single revolution of the sun, or only slightly to exceed it, whereas the epic observes no limits in time or action" (Dorsch 38).

6. *The Collective Self: A Narrative Paradigm and Self Expression in Three Prose Works*

1. According to the Chinese-English Dictionary, *lanxin-goufei* means 1. rapacious as a wolf and savage as a cur; cruel and unscrupulous; brutal and cold-blooded; 2. ungrateful (Jinrun Wu 407).

2. At the beginning of his essay, Graham Huggan says that "racial resent-

ment" against Chinese immigrants in Canadian history "demonize[d]" the latter as "an irreducible, threatening 'other' " (Huggan 34).

The focus of his paper, however, leaves this sociohistorical context simply to illustrate how the Romance genre dominates *Disappearing Moon Cafe* and Marilyn Bowering's *To All Appearances a Lady* (1989). A few quotations from Sky Lee's novel are used narrowly to show how Lee follows the Romance genre almost self-consciously.

Later in his essay, picking up the event of incest in Lee's novel and ignoring all the social and cultural circumstances, Huggan shows how "contamination" in Romance novel works in Lee's (Huggan 39).

3. For the historical formation of the concept of "the sojourner generation" and "the sojourner mentality," see Paul C P Siu and Jin Tan.

7. Dialogue: A Discursive Strategy in Chinese Canadian Poetry

1. *Haiku*: A form of Japanese poetry that states in three lines of five, seven, and five syllables a clear picture designed to arouse a distinct emotion and suggest a specific spiritual insight. (Holman 247)

8. From Testimony to Erotica: The Split Subject and Oedipal Drama in Evelyn Lau's Prose

1. The *Globe and Mail* and the *Toronto Star* published articles by their television critics to promote the CBC movie of *Diary of Evelyn Lau*; full-page reviews were also published in their TV Guides. *Starweek* gave the film a prominent position on its front cover. The *Vancouver Sun* published two reviews.

2. One well-known legend is about a scholar who ties his long hair to a rafter and works around the clock before the national examination. If he dozes, the weight of his body will pull him from the rafter, thus waking him up. (*Dictionary of Literary Quotations 445).*

3. I see the dramatic effect achieved in the CBC movie, preventing the audience from emotionally identifying with Lau's parents, as similar to the "alienation effect" in Brechtian theatre. See Willet 23, 31.

4. According to *The Compact Edition of the Oxford English Dictionary*, "erotic" means 1. sexual love; 2) of or pertaining to the passion of love, concerned with or treating love. "Pornography" means an obscene writing or pictorial representation. Both terms were used to discuss presentations of sexual love. (891, 2242)

Notes

Beyond Silence: Rice Paper Continues

1. I am indebted to Jim Wong-Chu for this original idea in a telephone conversation in May 1995. The phrase book is not alphabetically arranged, the topics are thematically compiled according to the needs of the labourers; to classify it as a dictionary would therefore be a misreading of its historical function. As nonfiction and as a historical document of the racial and social relationships between Chinese labourers and European immigrants, the phrase book presents vivid and realistic historical accounts.

Bibliography

Adilman, Sid. "The story of Oh: Poet, Prostitute, TV personality." *The Toronto Star* 20 Feb. 1994: E10.

Andrews, Marke. "Breaking the Code of Silence." *Vancouver Sun* 19 May 1990: D17.

———. "Evelyn Lau confronts the writing life." *Vancouver Sun* 2 Oct. 1993: D16.

Armstrong, John. "Young writer in from the cold." *Vancouver Sun* 16 Oct. 1989.

Ashcroft, Bill, Gareth Griffiths and Helen Tiffin. *The Empire Writes Back: Theory and practice in post-colonial literatures.* London, New York: Routledge, 1989.

Asian Canadian Writers' Workshop. *Rice Paper: The Newsletter of the Asian Canadian Writers' Workshop.* Number 1 (1994); Number 2 (1995).

Assiter, Alison. "Romance Fiction: Porn for Women?" *Perspectives on Pornography: Sexuality in Film and Literature.* Ed. Gary Day and Clive Bloom. New York: St Martin's, 1988. 101–109.

Atwood, Margaret, ed. *The New Oxford Book of Canadian Verse in English.* Toronto: Oxford UP, 1982.

———. "Cannibal Lecture: How could a culture so apparently boring as ours have embraced the flesh-devouring Wendigo?" *Saturday Night* Nov. 1995: 81–90.

Austin, Gayal. *Feminist Theories for Dramatic Criticism.* Ann Arbor: U of Michigan P,1990.

Balan, Jars. Introduction. *Identifications: Ethnicity and the Writer in Canada.* Ed. Balan. Edmonton: Canadian Institute of Ukrainian Studies, U of Alberta, 1982.

Barthes, Roland. *Mythologies.* Trans. Annette Lavers. London: Paladin Grafton Books,1973.

Baughman, Ernest W. Introduction. *Type and Motif-Index of the Folktales of England and North America.* Bloomington, Indiana: Indiana U P, 1966. vi–xx.

Baureiss, Gunter. "Chinese Immigration, Chinese Stereotypes, and Chinese Labour." Canadian Ethnic Studies XIX.3 (1987): 15–34.

Bawden, Jim. "Street Life: From honor student to teen hooker, The Diary of Evelyn Lau paints a haunting portrait of a runaway's life on the street." *Starweek Magazine.* 12 March 1994: 4.

Beverly, John. "The Margin at the Centre: On *Testimonio* (Testimonial Narrative)." *De/Colonizing the Subject: The Politics of Gender in Women's Autobiogra-*

phy. Ed. Sidonie Smith and Julia Watson. Minneapolis: U of Minnessota P, 1992. 91–114.

Birney, Earle. "Can. Lit." *The New Oxford Book of Canadian Verse in English*. Ed. Margaret Atwood. Toronto: Oxford U P, 1982. 116.

Bowering, George, ed. "Introduction: the Poems of Fred Wah." *Selected Poems: Loki Is Buried at Smoky Creek*. Vancouver: Talonbooks, 1980. 9–22.

Boyd, Denny. "Bleak side dominates mind of brilliant child writer/fugitive." Vancouver Sun 21 July 1988: B3.

———. "An avuncular suggestion to Evelyn Lau: let go of woe, you have far to go." Vancouver Sun 16 March 1994: B1.

Bryden, Diana Fitzgerald. "Lau novel offers glimpse into alienation." *The Globe and Mail*. 9 September 1995: C21.

Campbell, Joseph and Bill Moyers. *The Power of Myth*. London: Doubleday, 1988.

Canada. *Report of the Royal Commission on Chinese Immigration*. Ottawa: printed by Order of the Commission, 1885.

———. *Report of the Royal Commission on Oriental Immigration, or Report of the Commission Appointed to Inquire into the Subjects of Chinese and Japanese Immigration into the Province of British Columbia*. Ottawa: printed by S E Dawson, 1902.

———. *Report of the Royal Commission Appointed to Inquire into the Methods by which Oriental Labourers have been Induced to Come to Canada*. Ottawa: Government Printing Bureau, 1908.

———. House of Commons. Debates (Macdonald) 12 May 1882.

Chan, Anthony B. *Gold Mountain: The Chinese in the New World*. Vancouver: New Star Books, 1983.

Chan, Jeffery Paul, et al., eds. *The Big Aiiieeeee! An Anthology of Chinese American and Japanese American Literature*. New York: A Meridian Book, 1991.

Chan, Marty. *Mom, Dad, I'm Living with a White Girl*. Dir. Sally Han. Perf. Mark Gee, Li Fen Gee, Paul Lee, etc. Theatre Passe Muraille and Cahoots Theatre. March 16-April 9, 1995.

Chao, Lien. "The Collective Self: A Narrative Paradigm in Sky Lee's *Disappearing Moon Cafe*." *Cross-Addressing: Discourse on the Border*. Albany: SUNY, 1996. 239-57.

Chin, Frank, et al., eds. *Aiiieeeee! An Anthology of Asian-American Writers*. Washington DC: Howard University Press, 1974.

Chinese Canadian National Council. *Chinese in Canada: 125 Years of Continuous Community*. Toronto: Chinese Canadian National Council, 1983.

The Chinese Times. Dec. 1915. Asian Studies Archives in the University of British Columbia.

Chong, Denise. *The Concubine's Children: Portrait of a Family Divided*. Toronto:Viking, 1994.

———. "Amy Tan goes to the heart of a family matter." *The Globe and Mail* 21 October 1995, Review of Books: C27.

Choy, Wayson. *The Jade Peony*. Vancouver/Toronto: Douglas & McIntyre, 1995.

Chu, Garrick, et al., eds. *Inalienable Rice: A Chinese & Japanese Canadian Anthology*. Vancouver: Intermedia Press, 1979.

———. Introduction. *Inalienable Rice*. viii-ix.

The Compact Edition of the Oxford English Dictionary. Oxford: Oxford U P, 1971.

Crabbe, Anthony. "Feature-length Sex Films." In *Perspectives on Pornography: Sexuality in Film and Literature*. Ed. Gary Day and Clive Bloom. 44–66.

Cuff, John Haslett. "Talk about pathetic clichés, talk about dismal reality." *The Globe and Mail* 12 March 1994, Arts+: C16.

Culler, Michael J. *Goodnight Sammy Wong*. Calgary: Westlands, 1982.

Dafoe, Chris. "Nowhere to hide from the success of Runaway." *The Globe and Mail* 14 Oct. 1993: C.

Dauenhauer, Bernard P. *Silence: The Phenomenon and Its Ontological Significance*. Bloomington: Indiana U P, 1980.

Day, Gary. "Looking at Women: Notes toward a Theory of Porn." In *Perspectives on Pornography: Sexuality in Film and Literature*. Ed. Gary Day and Clive Bloom. 83-100.

de Beauvoir, Simone. *The Second Sex*. 1953. New York: Vintage Books, 1974.

Delacoste, Frédérique and Priscilla Alexander, eds. *Sex Work: Writings by Women in the Sex Industry*. 1987. London: Virago, 1988.

Deleuze, Gilles, and Felix Guattari. "What Is a Minor Literature?" *Kafka: Towards a Minor Literature*. Ed. Deleuze and Guattari. Trans. Dana Polan. Minneapolis: U of Minnesota P, 1986.

Derrida, Jacques. *Writing and Difference*. Trans. Alan Bass. Chicago: U of Chicago P, 1978.

Dorsch, T S. Introduction. *Classical Literary Criticism*. Baltimore: Penguin, 1965. 7-27.

Doyle, James. "Sui Sin Far and Onoto Watanna: Two Early Chinese-Canadian Authors." *Canadian Literature* 140 (1994): 50-58.

Eagleton, Terry. *Criticism and Ideology: A Study in Marxist Literary Theory*. 1976. London: Verso, 1986.

———. *Literary Theory: An Introduction*. Oxford: Basil Blackwell, 1983.

Easthope, Antony. *Poetry as Discourse*. London and New York: Methuen, 1983.

Engkent, Garry. "Why My Mother Can't Speak English." *Many-Mouthed Birds*. Ed. Lee and Wong-Chu 9-16.

Fewster, Edna Lysle. *Lengthening Shadows*. New York: Pageant Press, 1957.

Foucault, Michel. *The Archaeology of Knowledge*. 1969. Transl. A M Sheridan Smith. London: Tavistock Publications, 1972.

———. "The Order of Discourse." *Untying the Text: A Post-Structuralist Reader*. Ed. Robert Young. 1981. London and New York: Routledge & Kegan Paul, 1987.

Fowke, Edith. *Folklore of Canada*. Toronto: McClelland and Stewart, 1976.

Fredman, Stephen. *Poet's Prose: The Crisis in American Verse*. London: Cambridge UP,1983.

Freud, Sigmund. *A General Introduction to Psychoanalysis*. Trans. Joan Riviere. New York: Washington Square Press, 1966.

Fung, Richard. "Multiculturalism Reconsidered." *Yellow Peril*. Ed. Paul Wong. 17–19.

Glynn-Ward, Hilda. *The Writing on the Wall*. 1921. Toronto: University of Toronto, 1974.

Godard, Barbara. Comments. *A/Part: Papers from the 1984 Ottawa Conference on Language, Culture and Literary Identity in Canada / La langue, la culture et l'identité littéraire au Canada*. Ed. J M Bumsted. *Canadian Literature*. Supp. 1. May 1987. 130–37.

———. "Between Repetition and Rehearsal: Conditions of (Women's) Theatre in Canada in a Space of Reproduction." *Theatre Research In Canada /Recherches Théatrales au Canada*. Vol. 13 No. 1/2. Spring/Fall (1992). 18–33.

Gunn, Sean. "And Then Something Went." *Inalienable Rice*. Eds. Chu et al. 56–67. Rpt. in *Many-Mouthed Birds*. Eds. Lee and Wong-Chu. 28-31.

———. "Assimilation." *Inalienable Rice* 44.

———. "Orientation #1." *Inalienable Rice* 38.

Harlow, Barbara. *Resistance Literature*. New York: Methuen, 1987.

Harris, Claire. "Poets in Limbo." *A Mazing Space: Writing Canadian Women Writing*. Ed. Shirley Neuman and Smaro Kamboureli. Edmonton: Longspoon /NeWest Presses, 1986. 115–125.

Hepburn, Allan. "Eighteen years in the writing and worth the wait: *The Jade Peony* by Wayson Choy." *Financial Post* 2 Dec. 1995: 25.

Holman, C Hugh. *A Handbook to Literature*. New York: The Odyssey Press, 1972.

Huggan, Graham. "The Latitudes of Romance: Representations of Chinese Canada in Bowering's *To All Appearances A Lady* and Lee's *Disappearing Moon Cafe*." *Canadian literature* 140 (1994): 34-48.

Hull, Jillian. "*Fresh Girls and Other Stories*: a Review." *Georgia Straight* 19–26 Nov. 1993: 14.

Hutcheon, Linda. *The Canadian Postmodern: A Study of Contemporary English-Canadian Fiction*. Toronto: Oxford UP, 1988.

———, and Marion Richmond, eds. Other Solitudes: Canadian Multicultural Fictions. Toronto: Oxford UP, 1990.

Inwood, Damian. "Evelyn Lau: Wishes the past would go away." *The Province* 3 Oct. 1993: B15.

Ismail, Jam. "From *Sacred Texts*." *Many-Mouthed Birds*. Ed. Lee and Wong-Chu. 124–135.

JanMohamed, Abdul R, and David Lloyd. "Introduction: Towards a Theory of Minority Discourse: What Is to Be Done?" *The Nature and Context of Minority Discourse*. Ed. JanMohamed and Lloyd. New York: Oxford UP, 1990. 1–16.

Kam, Winston Christopher. *Bachelor-Man*. Dir. Peter Hinton. Perf. Jane Luke, Terry Barclay, etc. Theatre Passe Muraille, Toronto. 12 Nov. 1987 and ran through the month. Text adopted for this study is the author's fourth draft, 1985, copyright belongs to the author.

———. "Mabel's Hockey Game." *Many-Mouthed Birds*. Ed. Lee and Wong-Chu. 136–59.

Kaplan, Caren. "Resisting Autobiography: Out-Law Genres and Transnational Feminist Subjects." In *De/Colonizing the Subject*. Ed. Sidonie Smith and Julia Watson. 115–138.

Kelman, Suanne. "Exquisite novel provides child's vision of alien world: Wayson Choy's first offering is worth the 18 years of labour he put into it." *Globe and Mail* 2 Dec. 1995: E13.

Knight, Alan R. "Growing Hegemonies: Preparing the Ground for Official Anthologies of Canadian Poetry." *Prefaces and Literary Manifestoes /Préfaces et manifestes littéraires*. Ed. E D Blodgett and A G Purdy with S Tötösy de Zepetnek. Edmonton: U of Alberta, Research Inst. for Comparative Literature, 1990. 146–157.

Kwa, Lydia. *The Colours of Heroines*. Toronto: Women's Press, 1994.

Lacey, Liam. "'I was caught between two cultures': Paul Yee explores the history of the Chinese in Canada's 'Saltwater City'." *The Globe and Mail* 9 Dec. 1988: C11.

———. "Evelyn Lau's experiences on the street tend to set her apart from other writers." *The Globe and Mail* 30 Nov. 1989: C9.

Lacroix, Jean-Michel. *Anatomie de la Presse Ethnique au Canada*. Bordeaux: Presses UP de Bordeaux, 1988. 87–111.

Lai, Larissa. *When Fox Is A Thousand*. Vancouver: Press Gang Publishers, 1995.

Laiwan. "Ubiquitous China." *Yellow Peril*. Ed. Paul Wong. 40.

———. "The Imperialism of Syntax." *Many-Mouthed Birds*. Eds. Lee and Wong-Chu. 57–58.

Lau, Evelyn. *Runaway: Diary of a Street Kid*. Toronto: Harper Collins, 1989.

———. *You Are Not Who You Claim*. Victoria: Porcpic Books, 1990.

———. *Oedipal Dreams*. 1992. Toronto: Coach House Press, 1994.

———. *Fresh Girls & Other Stories*. Toronto: HarperCollins, 1993.

———. *In the House of Slaves*. Toronto: Coach House Press, 1994.

———. *Other Women*. New York: Random House, 1995.

Laurence, Margaret. *The Stone Angel*. 1964. Toronto: McClelland and Stewart, 1968.

Layton, Monique. *Prostitution In Vancouver (1973-75)—Official and Unofficial Reports*. A Report to the BC Police Commission Submitted in September 1975.

Vancouver: Department of Sociology & Anthropology of University of British Columbia.

Leach, Maria, Jerome Fried eds. *Standard Dictionary of Folklore, Mythology and Legend*. 1949. New York: Funk & Wagnalls, 1972.

Lee, Bennett. "Early Casualties, or How to Lose Out to the History Books: The Chinese in British Columbia." *Inalienable Rice*. Eds. Chu et al. 3–7.

———. Introduction. *Many-Mouthed Birds*. Eds. Lee and Wong-Chu. 1–8.

Lee, Sky. *Disappearing Moon Cafe*. Vancouver/Toronto: Douglas & McIntyre, 1990.

———. *Bellydancer Stories*. Vancouver: Press Gang Publishers, 1994.

Lee, Wai-man. *Portraits of a Challenge: An Illustrated History of the Chinese Canadians*. Toronto: Council of Chinese Canadians in Ontario, 1984.

Leger, Louise. *"How Lau Can She Go?" Broadcast Week* 12 March 1994: 10, 12.

Leland, Charles G. Preface. *Fushang: Or, The Discovery of America by Chinese Buddhist Priests in the Fifth Century*. New ed. London: Curzon, 1973.

Leung, Lily. *"Lonely in the Gold Mountain." Dialogue* Dec. 1987: 13. The article is Collected by Theatre Passe Muraille Archives and kept in the Archival Collections, University of Guelph Library.

Lévi-Strauss, Claude. *The Savage Mind*. 1962. Chicago: U of Chicago P; London: George Weidenfeld and Nicolson, 1966.

———. *The Elementary Structures of Kinship*. Revised ed. by John Richard von Sturmer and Rodney Needham. Transl. by James Harle Bell from French. Boston: Beacon Press, 1969.

Li, Donghai. *Jianada Huaqiao Shi* 加拿大華僑史 or *History of the Overseas Chinese in Canada. Taibei:Haidian, 1967.*

Li, Peter S. The Chinese in Canada. Toronto: Oxford UP, 1988.

Li, Xiangjin 李祥晋. Preface. *Chinese and English Phrase Book and Dictionary*. Vancouver: Thomson Stationery, n.d.

Liang Shan-po yu Chu Ying-t'ai. Ed. I Pan Hsin. Shanghai: Shanghai *wen i ch'u pan she, 1979.*

Lim, Sing. *West Coast Chinese Boy*. Montreal: Tundra Books, 1979.

Ling, Amy. "Pioneers and Paradigms: The Eaton Sisters." *Between Worlds: Women Writers of Chinese Ancestry*. New York: Pergamon, 1990.

Liu, Yuzun, Lucie Cheng Hirata, and Zheng Dehua. "Overseas Chinese, the Xinning Railroad and Taishan Country." *Journal of Sun Yat-sen University* 4 (1980): 24-47.

Lo, Chung-To. *Canada: Jia Na Da Di Fang Zhi*; 加拿大地方誌 Toronto: Relief Map Service, 1987.

Lupul, Manoly R. "Networking, Discrimination and Multiculturalism as a Social Philosophy." *Canadian Ethnic Studies* 2 (1989): 1–12.

Mandel, Eli. "A Lack of Ghosts: Canadian Poets and Poetry." *Humanities Association Bulletin 16 Spring (1965). 59–67.*

Many-Mouthed Birds: Contemporary Writing by Chinese Canadians. Ed. Bennett Lee and Jim Wong-Chu. Vancouver/Toronto: Douglas & McIntyre; Seattle: U of Washington P, 1991.

Maracle, Lee. "Yin Chin." *The Sojourner's Truth and Other Stories*. Vancouver: Press Gang, 1990.

Mitchell, W O. *Who Has Seen the Wind?* Toronto: Macmillan, 1947.

Moore, John. "Lau lards on the literary lip gloss." *Vancouver Sun* 23 May 1994: D18.

Morison, Samuel Eliot. *The Oxford History of the American People*. New York: Oxford UP, 1965.

Mukherjee, Arun. *Towards an Aesthetic of Opposition: Essays on Literature Criticism & Cultural Imperialism*. Stratford, Ont.: Williams-Wallace Publishers, 1988.

———. *Oppositional Aesthetics*. Toronto: TSAR, 1994.

New, W H. "Inside Gold Mountain." *East Asian Canadian Connections. Canadian Literature* 140 (1994): 4–7.

Ng, Lucy. "From 'The Sullen Shapes of Poems'." *Many-Mouthed Birds*. Eds. Lee and Wong-Chu. 160–168.

Nickson, Keith. "The dark side of desire." *The Toronto Star* 16 Oct. 1993: J17.

Phillips, Alan. "The Criminal Society that Dominates the Chinese in Canada." *Maclean's* 7 April 1962: 11, 40–48.

Porter, John. *The Vertical Mosaic: An Analysis of Social Class and Power in Canada*. Toronto: U of Toronto P, 1965.

Pratt, E J. *Towards the last spike: a verse-panorama of the struggle to build the first Canadian transcontinental from the time of the proposed terms of union with British Columbia, 1870, to the hammering of the last spike in the Eagle Pass, 1885*. Toronto: Macmillan, 1952.

Quan. Betty. Mother Tongue. Victoria, BC.: Scirocco Drama, 1996.

Quill, Greg. "Sex-and-drugs docudrama outshone by the real thing." *The Toronto Star* 13 March 1994: E10.

Read, Nicholas. "Conveyor belt clip costs diary its depth." *Vancouver Sun* 10 March 1994: C1.

Rogers, Linda. "Fire and Fury from a Precocious Poet." *Vancouver Sun* 14 Oct. 1989:H5.

Romell, Karen. "Open Sky: For more than a century the Canadian Chinese experience has been hidden from the literary world . . . But Sky Lee's novel, *Disappearing Moon Cafe*, changes all of that." *Step Magazine* July/August (1990): 56–59.

Roy, Gabrielle. "Where Will You Go, Sam Lee Wong?" *Garden in the Wind*. Trans. Alan Brown. Toronto: McClelland and Stewart, 1975. 51–104.

Rubin, Gayle. "The Traffic in Women: Notes on the 'Political Economy' of Sex."

Toward Anthropology of Women. Ed. Rayna Reiter. New York: Monthly Review Press, 1975. 157–210.

Said, Edward W. *Orientalism*. 1978. New York: Vintage, 1979.

———. *Culture and Imperialism*. New York: Alfred A. Knopf, 1993.

Scott, F R. "All the Spikes But the Last." *The Collected Poems of F R Scott*. Toronto: McClelland and Stewart, 1981. 194.

Siu, Paul C. P. "The Sojourner." *American Journal of Sociology* 58 (1953): 34–44.

Smith, A J M., ed. *The Book of Canadian Poetry*. Toronto: Gage, 1943.

Sommer, Doris. " 'Not Just a Personal Story': Women's *Testimonios* and the Plural Self." *Life /Lines: Theorizing Women's Autobiography*. Eds. Bella Brodzki and Celeste Schenck. Ithaca, NY: Cornell U P, 1988.

Sontag, Susan. "The Aesthetics of Silence." *Styles of Radical Will*. New York: A Delta Book, 1970. 3–34.

Steiner, Stan. *Fushan: The Chinese Who Built America*. New York: Harper and Row, 1979.

Stevens, Barry, et al. *The Diary of Evelyn Lau*. Dir. Sturla Gunnarsson. Cinematographer Tony Westman. With Sandra Oh at al. CBC-TV Movie aired at 9:00 p.m. Prime Time, Channel 5, Sunday, March 13, 1994.

Stoffman, Judy. "Atwood, Choy split award." *The Toronto Star* 24 April 1996: E4.

Tan, Jin. "Chinese Labour and the Reconstituted Social Order of British Columbia." *Special Issue. Canadian Ethnic Studies* 3 (1987): 68–88.

Thompson, Stith. Introduction. *Motif-Index of Folk-Literature*. Vol. One. Bloomington, Indiana: Indiana U P, 1955. 9–27.

Tsang, Beryl. "Book Review: *Runaway*." *Chinese Canadian Women's Forum*. Newsletter of the Women's Issues Committee of the Chinese Canadian National Council. Summer 1990: 3–4. Rpt. from the Newsletter of Chinese Canadian National Council Toronto Chapter.

Vassanji, M G, ed. *A Meeting of Streams: South Asian Canadian Literature*. Toronto: TSAR, 1985.

Vaughn, Jack A. *Drama A to Z: A Handbook*. New York: Frederick Ungar Publishing Co., 1980.

Wah, Fred. *Waiting For Saskatchewan*. Winnipeg: Turnstone Press, 1985.

———. *Seasons Greetings from the Diamond Grill*. *Canadian Literature* 140 (1994): 8-11.

———. *Diamond Grill*. Edmonton: NeWest, 1996.

Walker, Susan. "A different kind of writing: Evelyn Lau has come a long way to a reading at Harbourfront." *The Toronto Star*. 12 September 1995: E4.

Watson, Julia and Sidonie Smith, eds. "Introduction: De/Colonization and the Politics of Discourse in Women's Autobiographical Practices." *De/Colonizing the Subject: The Politics of Gender in Women's Autobiography*. xiii-xxxi.

White, Hayden. *Tropics of Discourse: Essays in Cultural Criticism*. Baltimore and London: The Johns Hopkins UP, 1978.

Wickberg, Edgar, ed., et al. *From China to Canada: A History of the Chinese Communities in Canada*. Toronto: McClelland and Stewart in association with the Multiculturalism Directorate, and Department of State, 1982.

Willett, John, trans. *Brecht on Theatre: The Development of an Aesthetic*. London: Methuen & Co., 1964.

Wilson, Ethel. *The Innocent Traveller*. 1949. Toronto: McClelland and Stewart, 1990.

———. *Swamp Angel*. 1954. Toronto: McClelland and Stewart, 1988.

The Women's Book Committee. Chinese Canadian National Council. *Jin Guo: Voices of Chinese Canadian Women*. Toronto: Women's Press, 1992.

Wong, Anita Jennifer. "Chinese-Canadian in Canadian Literature: changing images, emerging voices." MA thesis. Carleton U, 1992.

Wong, Cynthia. *Reading Asian American Literature*. Princeton, NJ: Princeton U P, 1993.

Wong, Paul ed. *Yellow Peril: Reconsidered*. Vancouver: On Edge/On the Cutting Edge Productions Society, 1990.

Wong-Chu, Jim. *Chinatown Ghosts*. Vancouver: Pulp Press, 1986.

———. "Old Chinese Cemetery (Kamloops 1977/July)." *Inalienable Rice*. Eds. Chu et al. 8.

———. "How Feel I do?" *Many-Mouthed Birds*. Eds. Lee and Wong-Chu. 17.

———. "A Brief History of the ACWW." *Rice Paper: The Newsletter of the Asian Canadian Writer's Workshop*. Vol. 1. No. 1 (1994): 1-2. Woodcock, George. "Poetry." *Literary History of Canada: Canadian Literature in English*. Vol. Three. Ed. Carl F Klinck. 1965. Toronto: U of Toronto P, 1976. 284-317.

———. Introduction. *Canadian Poetry: Volume Two*. Ed. Jack David and Robert Lecker. Toronto: General Publishing and ECW P, 1982. 13-31.

Wu, Chengen (1500-1582). *Journey to the West*. Beijing: Foreign Languages Press, 1982.

Wu, Cheng-Tsu. Ed and intro. *"Chinks!": A Documentary History of Anti-Chinese Prejudice in America*. New York: The World Publishing, 1972.

Wu, Jinrun et al. *A Chinese-English Dictionary*. Beijing: Commerce P, 1982.

Yates, J. Michael, ed. *Volvox: Poetry from the Unofficial Languages of Canada . . . in English Translation*. Victoria: Sono Nis, 1971.

Yee, Donald. "Pender Guy: Are You Listening?" *Inalienable Rice*. Eds. Chu et al. 65–67.

Yee, Paul. "The Grass Dragon." *Inalienable Rice*. Eds. Chu et al. 39-40.

———. "Last Word II." *Inalienable Rice*. Eds. Chu et al. 32. Rpt. in *Many-Mouthed Birds*. Eds. Lee and Wong-Chu. 180.

———. *Saltwater City: An Illustrated History of the Chinese in Vancouver*. Vancouver: Douglas; Seattle: University of Washington P, 1988.

———. *Tales from Gold Mountain: Stories of the Chinese in the New World*. Paintings by Simon Ng. Vancouver: Douglas, 1989.

———. *Ghost Train.* Paintings by Harvey Chan. Vancouver: A Groundwood Book /Douglas & McIntyre, 1996.

Yhap, Beverly. Review. *Fuse.* Winter (1987/88): 45. The article is Collected by Theatre Passe Muraille Archives and kept in the Archival Collections, University of Guelph Library.

Yin, Xiao-Huang. "Between the East and West: Sui Sin Far—the First Chinese-American Woman Writer." *Arizona Quarterly* 47. 4 (1991): 49-84.

Yu, Shi, Wong Guanhan and Xu Chengzhi. *Dictionary of Literary Quotations.* Shanghai: Ci Shu P, 1983.